The Fundraising Feasibility Study

It's Not about the Money

MARTIN L. NOVOM, CFRE

EDITOR

John Wiley & Sons, Inc.

Library of Congress Cataloging-in-Publication Data:

ISBN: 978-0-470-12074-3 (cloth)

Printed in the United States of America

10 9 8 7 6 5 4 3 2 1

Alexis de
TOCQUEVILLE
INSTITUTE
Guiding Volunteer Leaders

Martin L. Novom, CFRE
Principal

Alexis de Tocqueville Institute

I dedicate this book to my mother and father.

They each had a separate gem of wisdom to offer me.

My mother, Doris, said that good things come in small packages.

My father, Ben, said I should always stand tall.

The AFP Fund Development Series

The AFP Fund Development Series is intended to provide fund development professionals and volunteers, including board members (and others interested in the nonprofit sector), with top-quality publications that help advance philanthropy as voluntary action for the public good. Our goal is to provide practical, timely guidance and information on fundraising, charitable giving, and related subjects. The Association of Fundraising Professionals (AFP) and Wiley each bring to this innovative collaboration unique and important resources that result in a whole greater than the sum of its parts. For information on other books in the series, please visit:

http://www.afpnet.org

THE ASSOCIATION OF FUNDRAISING PROFESSIONALS

The Association of Fundraising Professionals (AFP) represents 28,000 members in more than 185 chapters throughout the United States, Canada, Mexico, and China working to advance philanthropy through advocacy, research, education, and certification programs. The association fosters development and growth of fundraising professionals and promotes high ethical standards in the fundraising profession. For more information or to join the world's largest association of fundraising professionals, visit www.afpnet.org.

2006-2007 AFP PUBLISHING ADVISORY COMMITTEE

Samuel N. Gough, CFRE, Chair
Principal, The AFRAM Group

Nina P. Berkheiser, CFRE
Principal Consultant, Your Nonprofit Advisor

Linda L. Chew, CFRE
Associate Director, Alta Bates Summit Foundation

D. C. Dreger, ACFRE
Senior Campaign Director, Custom Development Solutions (CDS)

Audrey P. Kintzi, ACFRE
Chief Advancement Officer, Girl Scout Council St. Croix Valley

Robert Mueller, CFRE
Vice President, Hospice Foundation of Louisville

Maria Elena Noriega
Director, Noriega Malo & Associates

Leslie E. Weir, MA, ACFRE
Director of Gift Planning, Health Sciences Centre Foundation

Sharon R. Will, CFRE
Director of Development, South Wind Hospice

John Wiley & Sons:

Susan McDermott
Senior Editor (Professional / Trade Division), John Wiley & Sons

AFP Staff:

Jan Alfieri
Manager, New Product Development

Walter Sczudlo
Executive Vice President & General Counsel

Contents

CHAPTER 12 Seeking Help—The Benefits and Burdens of Working with a Consultant   **129**
Simone P. Joyaux, ACFRE

CHAPTER 13 Taking It Home—Applying What You Learned   **145**
Martin L. Novom, CFRE

About the Editor

Martin L. Novom, CFRE

Martin describes himself as "a student of the mysteries of gift money."

His years of work with nonprofit organizations in charitable giving, volunteering, and volunteer leadership gave rise to this book. He is the principal of the Alexis de Tocqueville Institute, whose slogan is "guiding volunteer leaders."

Martin has 20 years experience as a professional philanthropic fundraiser as staff, adviser, coach, and adult educator. He has held a variety of senior development staff positions (Lukas Foundation, New Hampshire Public Radio, Monadnock Community Hospital, National Arborist Foundation). He began advising nonprofits in 1992 when recruited by the Rudolf Steiner Foundation to bring his experience in philanthropic programs to their advisory services for Waldorf schools. Extensive and frequent travel all over the United States and Canada helped him develop what he calls his "diagnostic antennae."

Leaving the foundation in 1995, he began private practice and later formed the Institute to advise nonprofit organizations of all types. Martin became certified fundraiser, CFRE (Certified Fund Raising Executive), in 1992 and has maintained very active involvement in the training and education of nonprofit professionals and volunteer leaders. He currently advises a wide range of nonprofits around the United States and Canada. Through the Institute he presents an annual multi-institution workshop series, each year on a new subject, especially for Waldorf schools. To date, more than 80 Waldorf schools and close to 700 staff and volunteer leaders have participated in one of his workshops. For nonprofit professionals of all kinds, he teaches at Continuing Education in Fund Raising–New Hampshire (CONFR), New England Association for Healthcare Philanthropy, the Governor's Conference on Volunteerism and AFP of Northern New England (AFP-NNE). He is the cofounder and core faculty for AFP-NNE's unique intensive educational seminar, The Academy. He regularly teaches as part of the CFRE Review Course. Martin is a graduate of the AFP International's Faculty Training Academy, one of 90 graduates among AFP's 27,000+ members. Martin is the president of the board of directors of AFP of Northern New England. He attended high school in Tokyo, Japan, and is a graduate of California State University at Northridge. After advising and teaching, Martin's passion is downhill skiing.

Martin can be reached by email or at his website:

mn@adtinstitute.org
www.adtinstitute.org

About the Authors

William L. Carlton, ACFRE (WLCarlton@aol.com, www.fundraising.org) is chairman of Carlton & Co., a national major gifts consulting firm specializing in the construction and renovation of facilities and allied endowments. Mr. Carlton is one of 81 individuals who hold the ACFRE credential and is Chairman of the Certification Board. He also serves on the national boards of AFP and the Giving Institute, a collection of leading consulting firms in America. Bill is a Trustee of Westminster College and Senior Warden of St. Peter's Episcopal Church in Osterville, MA where he resides with his wife, Adrienne. Mr. Carlton is a graduate of Westminster College (PA), Princeton Theological Seminary, and the Social Enterprise Program of the Harvard Business School.

Betty Ann Copley Harris, FAHP (bach@copleyharris.com, www.copleyharris.com) is the founder and president of Copley Harris Company, Inc., a full-service fundraising consulting firm serving nonprofit organizations in the Northeast since 1987. Her firm's team of senior philanthropy consultants direct capital campaigns, feasibility studies, development audits, board retreats, planned giving programs, and executive searches for major health care, academic, cultural/historic, and social service organizations. A fellow in the Association for Healthcare Philanthropy since 1984, she has contributed to the professional advancement of fundraising executives serving on the CFRE accreditation board and the AFP fellow's board of examiners. She previously directed philanthropy programs at Salem Hospital in Salem, Massachusetts, and Catherine McAuley Medical Center in Ann Arbor, Michigan. A mentor to development professionals for 30 years, Betty Ann is a frequent faculty and seminar leader for regional and national fundraising conferences for the Association for Healthcare Philanthropy, Women in Development, and Association of Fundraising Professionals. She is a graduate of Colby Sawyer College, New London, New Hampshire.

Simone P. Joyaux, ACFRE (www.simonejoyaux.com) is recognized internationally in the philanthropic sector. An expert in fund development, board and organizational development, and strategic planning, Simone is the author of *Strategic Fund Development: Building Profitable Relationships that Last*. Simone presents all over the world and is a faculty member in the master's program in philanthropy and development at Saint Mary's University, Minnesota. Simone serves regularly on boards, is the founder and chair of the Women's Fund of Rhode Island, and is the former chair of CFRE International. She is the recipient of the 2003 Rhode Island Outstanding Philanthropic Citizen Award and the 1987 Fundraising Executive of the Year Award for Rhode Island.

Linda Lysakowski, ACFRE (cvlinda@cox.net, www.cvfundraising.com) is president and CEO of Capital Venture. She is one of 81 professionals worldwide to hold the Advanced Certified Fund Raising Executive designation. She has managed capital campaigns, conducted planning studies, helped dozens of nonprofit organizations achieve their development goals, and trained more than 8,000 professionals in all aspects of development. Linda received the Outstanding Fundraising Executive award from both the Eastern Pennsylvania and the Las Vegas chapters of AFP and was recognized internationally with the first Barbara Marion Award for Outstanding Service to AFP. She is a graduate of AFP's Faculty Training Academy and serves on the board of the AFP Foundation for Philanthropy, chairing the Strategic Initiatives Committee, to raise funds for strategic initiatives of the Association including Diversity, Youth in Philanthropy, Research, and Education.

J. A. (Tony) Myers, CFRE, MA, LLB (tmyers@ucalgary.ca) is the adviser to the president (Strategic Initiatives) at the University of Calgary. Tony helped establish three charitable foundations in Canada and participated in the largest fundraising campaign in Alberta. He continues to speak at conferences in the United States, Australia, and Europe. He is an active participant in the Association of Fundraising Professionals; a member of AFP's International Research Council; a member of AFP Calgary Chapter; and a former member of the AFP Canada Council. He taught at Saint Mary's University of Minnesota from 2003–2005, is a board member of a capacity-building nongovernmental organization (NGO) CentrePoint, and has consulted with many NGOs. Tony brings enthusiasm, passion, and commitment to all that he does. He has a law degree, a master's degree and is currently working on his PhD in philanthropy and development.

Elliott S. Oshry, CFRE (eoshry@viscern.com, www.ketchum.viscern.com) is executive vice president of Ketchum, an international fundraising consulting firm established in 1919. Mr. Oshry is responsible for the most sophisticated in-house training program in the profession, for Ketchum's client-service focus, and for counsel with some of Ketchum's most prestigious clients. Mr. Oshry is recognized for his significant contribution to the field of not-for-profit counseling, strategic development planning, and volunteer leadership development. He is a member of the board of the Western Pennsylvania Chapter of Association of Fundraising Professionals (AFP) and has earned Certified Fund Raising Executive (CFRE) status with AFP. He is a frequent speaker at regional and international conferences for professional organizations within the fund-raising arena. Prior to joining Ketchum in 1974, Mr. Oshry had a successful career in corporate public relations and newspaper publishing. He is an active volunteer with nonprofit agencies in Pittsburgh, where he resides.

Anne Peyton, CPF, CFRE, of Yellow Brick Road Consulting™, facilitates strategic planning processes, works with boards on leadership and governance, and with staff on quality management tools and systems thinking. Appreciative Inquiry is the foundation of most of her planning work, integrating logic models and strategy mapping as man-agement tools. Anne also specializes in fundraising: development assessment and planning, stewardship and donor relations, annual funds, major gifts, corporate and foundation relations, and capital/endowment campaigns. She has a BA in sociology, an MS in library science, an MS in organization and management, is a Certified Fund Raising Executive (CFRE) with the Association of Fundraising Professionals and is a Certified Professional Facilitator (CPF) with the International Association of Facilitators. Anne's Web site is www.yellowbrickroadconsulting.com. She's a senior associate with www.demontasso-ciates.com and a charter partner with www.aiconsulting.org and www.positivechange-core.org.

Eugene Scanlan, CFRE, PhD (eascan@aol.com, www.escanlancompany.com) is president of eScanlan Company, a nonprofit management consulting firm. Prior to founding his firm, he spent 18 years as vice president and senior vice president of the Alford Group, Inc. He has also served as a foundation program officer and fiscal man-ager at a major grant-making foundation, and in senior development positions at a national environmental organization and with a major think tank. He holds academic appoint-ments at several universities, including the University of Maryland University College; Elliott School of International Affairs, George Washington University; and as a member of the advisory council for the George Mason University Nonprofit Management Pro-gram. He chaired AFP's Research Council, served on the committee for the Profes-sional Advancement Division, and served three terms as a board member of AFP's D.C. chapter. He is a published author and a frequent presenter. He holds a BA degree in psychology, a MEd in counseling, and a PhD in higher education/student personnel work (Loyola University of Chicago).

S. Sanae Tokumura, APR, ACFRE (solidconcepts@hawaii.rr.com) is fundraising and public relations consultant, founder, and president of the Honolulu firm Solid

Concepts, Inc. An active advocate for responsible fundraising and public relations practice, she is known for completing challenging multimillion capital campaigns in small
communities throughout Hawaii. She serves on the Association of Fundraising Professionals Foundation for Philanthropy board and the Association of Fundraising
Professionals board, and is chair of the Advanced Certified Fund Raising Executive
Professional Certification board. She is also nationally accredited (APR) in the practice of public relations through the Public Relations Society of America. Tokumura
holds BA degrees in journalism and communication from the University of Hawaii at
Manoa.

Preface

What Was Once Undisclosed

This book offers us in the nonprofit world our first in-depth exploration of an important but once closely held process: the fundraising feasibility study. When I began looking into this topic as a possible subject for a book, I was surprised at how little in-depth information I was actually able to locate. I continued looking far and wide, inquired with my circle of fundraising colleagues, and researched the libraries of both the Association of Fundraising Professionals and the Association for Healthcare Philanthropy. From the beginning, I assumed that someone must have written a book or put together a manual on the subject. Not so. I did find lots of articles, pamphlets and even a chapter in a book. But, I couldn't find anything more extensive. How could that be? As I continued gathering material for a possible bibliography, I continued to expect I would eventually find something substantial. It never happened.

It seems hard to believe, with the level of sophistication we have achieved and the extent to which we utilize the fundraising feasibility study for campaign preparation, that this is the first book on the subject. I am both excited to be responsible for making it happen and more than a little chagrined that it has taken us, as fundraising professionals, this long. It's about time, don't you think?

A Range of Donors, a Range of Authors

As I was preparing the early versions of the outline for this book, I had planned on incorporating two or three other professionals as contributing authors. After all, I reasoned, I don't have all the answers and certainly don't consider myself the penultimate expert on the topic. Instead, I see myself as a serious student of fundraising feasibility studies. So, it seemed only natural to incorporate a few others in the writing task. This reflected my recognition that there is more than one way to do a feasibility study.

I began with two professionals I have known for a number of years, Bill Carlton and Simone Joyaux. Not only are they senior people in our profession, but they have made it a part of their professional life to encourage newer professionals. They were quite enthusiastic in my early conversations with them, and they each asked me some tough and probing questions. As I pondered their questions, I began to understand that there were even more nuances than I had thought in the way different consultants do feasibility studies. In order to do justice to this wide variety, and to the many different kinds of nonprofit organizations there are, I needed to make my vision of the book as wide as possible. I chose, therefore, to include an even greater number of voices in the book. It was only in the final stages of working with this great team of professionals that another layer of understanding made itself known to me. I believe these many voices give our book its real power and strength.

Here is what I discovered. As I continued to work with the authors, refining the chapters and selecting samples for the appendix, I found woven into the background of the book's design of many voices an authentic reflection of the very topic itself. I recognized that the feasibility study process unites a variety of voices in the organization, a group much larger than was interviewed. So, too, does this book. I wish that you could join with all ten of us authors and meet in a single room. You would experience, as I do, not only the depth and quality of insight of these professionals, but also you would hear the echo of a range of voices, much larger than just the ten of us, just as we do in the fundraising feasibility study process.

In a Place of Honor

I cannot pass up the opportunity to point out the arena in which I gained both my enthusiasm for the feasibility study and my passion for its use as a tool for organizational self-knowledge. I am not sure I could have understood the full measure of what the fundraising feasibility study can be if I had not had a deep and wonderful involvement with Waldorf schools, both as clients and as a source of participants for my educational workshops. Having worked extensively with Waldorf schools in almost every part of the United States and Canada, I am very appreciative of the general atmosphere alive in them that encourages staff, faculty, and volunteer leaders in individual growth and self-knowledge. I know that Waldorf schools do not have a monopoly on this characteristic, but I have not experienced it as often or as deeply in other nonprofit settings. I am extremely grateful for all that I have learned about feasibility studies and human relationships within that setting.

An Opportunity for Greater Dialogue

I imagine it is natural that I am already witnessing expressions of relief from consultants and others. "Finally," they seem to be saying, "we are really talking about feasibility studies."

It will be very interesting to watch the extent to which this book starts a wider dialogue. Certainly, there is no going back to a time when full disclosure of the tools, the techniques and the methods of conducting the fundraising feasibility study was not available or not talked about. Those days are over.

It is my hope that a new level of openness, signified by this book, will lead to a growing chorus of discussion, in print and in our educational forums. I believe that open dialogue on this important subject can, like the rising tide, raise all boats. For those of us already passionate about the feasibility study, it can encourage us to dig deeper in our work, reach farther in our applications, and stretch our capacities with experimentation. For those of us who already respect the process but were ignorant of the inner workings, I hope it brings us greater understanding and increased appreciation. For those of us for whom it had been a previously undiscovered tool, it is my hope it brings us renewed energy and commitment to develop and improve our beloved nonprofit organizations.

If you have questions, concerns, or observations about this book or about this topic that you would like to share with me, I welcome such inquiries. Please e-mail me.

Your colleague,
MARTIN L. NOVOM, CFRE
Principal
Alexis de Tocqueville Institute
mn@adtinstitute.org

CHAPTER 1

Stepping Up to the Challenge— Philanthropic Program Effectiveness

MARTIN L. NOVOM, CFRE
ALEXIS DE TOCQUEVILLE INSTITUTE

IMPORTANT TRENDS

If we are honest with ourselves, those of us for whom the nonprofit sector houses our work, harnesses our passion, or hopefully both, then we not only care about our activities but we may take long "walks" through the terrain of nonprofit life in an attempt to make sense of it all. Since you are reading this, I will assume you too take the long view of our sector and pay attention to the trends. Watching for trends can help us make sense of the flurry of daily activity. In the Preface I spoke briefly about some observations. Now I want to focus on some more recent trends. What are some of the trends that have captured our attention in recent times? There are four I wish to focus on.

An Increase in Requests for Charitable Contributions

There is both hard and anecdotal evidence that the number of nonprofit organizations has been increasing at a steady rate. I say hard and anecdotal because I am not convinced that all the activity is being captured on paper accurately. One cannot read the philanthropic trade publications, go to a conference, or speak to nonprofit trustees or staff without hearing about this trend. The size of the nonprofit sector is growing and growing.

The rationale for this increase is certainly worth pursuing at some length but would, I believe, take us too far a field of our subject. At the very least we can say that there are continuing pressures on our federal and state governments to shrink their budgets in order to lower the tax burden for the general public. Less federal and state funding leaves ever larger numbers of social programs turning to private funding for operational support. We have also seen the emergence and growth of fundraising activity from entities that in the past were fully supported by tax dollars. The most frequently cited seems to be public education, especially primary and secondary public schools.

Despite what has been described as the bursting of the dot-com bubble, there has been a noticeable rise in the attention paid by high-profile and successful dot-com entrepreneurs to the nonprofit sector. Admittedly, much has been made of their arrival in the nonprofit arena, especially of those seeking more innovative ways to utilize their financial support. Nevertheless, I maintain that the size and frequency of their involvement also adds to the increased congestion.

Another factor contributing to this perception of the increasing volume of philanthropic support requests has been the rapid and widespread increase in the use of the Internet for fundraising activities.

Simone Joyaux, ACFRE, who contributed our Chapter 12, "Seeking Help—The Benefits and Burdens of Working with a Consultant," likes to say that we don't have increased competition, we have increased congestion. She brings us an important perspective.

Intensification of Public Scrutiny on the Nonprofit Sector

For most of our daily news coverage, bad news seems to get more airplay than good news, and the nonprofit sector seems to be no exception. The greed and excess of some nonprofit executives have played loudly in print and electronic news. Equally apparent as "signs of the times" have been a number of highly publicized lapses of appropriate nonprofit governance by some well-known, and not-so-well-known, boards of trustees. That so many of us can recall at least one incident is evidence of the intensification of this scrutiny.

Correspondingly, these lapses in individual and collective oversight have caused our elected representatives to consider and even to pass stronger legislative measures. The same is true of our public servants, the attorneys general of the various states. They have been quite active in considering, and implementing, stronger and more cooperative measures to bring uniform oversight to the nonprofit sector. All of this attention, much of it happening in the public eye, has been a source of considerable public discourse. Therefore, it is not surprising that one can say, without too much fear of strident argument, that our nonprofit sector has experienced a general decline in the level of public trust.

Greater Attention by Donors on Improving Fundraising Effectiveness

If you have taken time to listen to the donors to your organization or to discuss with your colleagues the state of philanthropic program effectiveness, a common theme is the widespread desire for us to do a better job with our fundraising. As prospective donors, we all comment on the deluge of solicitations we receive, many of which appear to be of poor quality or to lack any originality. I am still surprised at the frequency of telephone solicitations I receive from local police and fire fraternal organizations, which are generally conducted by companies that give back only a fraction of the revenue to these organizations.

Fortunately, more and more nonprofit organizations are being more strategic with constituencies and targeting with greater focus their solicitation efforts. Those of us who are staff members know how hard we work to stretch the value of our paid and unpaid resources so that we can make every philanthropic program as effective as possible. However, I contend that a significant percentage of donors continue to believe that most organizations still have vast room for improvement. In many cases, I dare say they are right.

Increased Emphasis on Improving the Quality of Relationships with Donors

This is an area the philanthropic professionals, fundraisers employed by nonprofits and outside consultants, have been focusing on with considerable intensity in recent years. Even an informal review of regional and national fundraising conferences shows how much this direction is being stressed. It is now almost an industry "mantra" that relationship building is an essential element in making our programs more effective. Another way to view this is to point out that more and more of our nonprofit organizations, especially our smaller and midsize ones, are professionalizing their efforts in raising charitable revenue. With the professional approach comes a much greater emphasis on relationship building.

At the same time, I frequently hear a complaint from donors about the frequency of solicitations from organizations that they currently give to. The common complaint is that as soon as they make a gift, say by telephone or by mail, they get another solicitation. Those of us in the field know that other mantra, "the best donor prospect is a current donor." Regardless of the knowledge that each gift should be followed by one or more interactions before we ask again, it appears that here, too, there is room for improvement in the sector overall.

How Nonprofit Organizations Are Responding to These Trends

Increasing Philanthropic Program Budgets

One of the ways that experienced philanthropic professionals have been successful in improving philanthropic programs has been in demonstrating the leverage effect of a properly funded budget. As a result, we are seeing more instances of adequate staffing and sufficient resources to do the job. We have applied some of the approaches our counterparts in the commercial sector use to justify increasing operating budgets. Attaining an increase in revenue often requires an increase in investment. Budgets in our nonprofit organizations appear to have become more realistic. While few philanthropic professionals are telling their families and friends about their "commercial-sized" salaries and benefit packages, finance committees are more likely than in past years to understand the leverage power of an investment in the philanthropy department budget.

Renewed Emphasis on Ethics and Ethical Behavior

A good starting place for this point is the Association of Fundraising Professionals Code of Ethical Principles and Standards of Professional Practice. (See a copy in Appendix N.) Developed and revised over a period of years, this document represents a long-term effort to focus the attention of philanthropic professionals on what is and is not acceptable behavior.

The proliferation in the number of programs on philanthropy and nonprofit management, both degree and nondegree bearing, is testament to the growing awareness of the value of professionalism in our nonprofit sector. Many of these programs have a course on ethics.

Greater Focus on Strategic Thinking in Philanthropic Programs

Increasing attention is being paid by philanthropic professionals to the understanding and effective use of the "life cycle" of donors. We are working smarter by linking up our donors with programs designed to meet their personal needs and interests at each stage of their involvement with our organization. More and more nonprofits are engaging in relationship-based major gift programs such as "moves management."

Recent data and studies have allowed us, as philanthropic professionals, and as clear-thinking volunteer leaders, to intensify our efforts by examining the assumptions we make on how donors make decisions. The work of professionals like Judith Nichols and her book, *Pinpointing Affluence in the 21st Century* (Chicago: Bonus Books, 2001), has allowed us to understand more about the motivations of different generations of donors.

Increasing Sophistication of Trustees and Staff

Traveling around the country teaching and advising, I have noticed over the last decade that trustees have become more sophisticated and more interested in increasing their grasp of the concepts of nonprofit governance. I find this reflected in the increase in the number of books now available on nonprofit governance. Trustees know that things are not as simple as they once were, and, as a result, they know they have to be more knowledgeable so that they can be more effective.

The activity of fundraising, conducted as it is by tens of thousands of full- and part-time staff and consultants, is being viewed more and more by those inside and outside the nonprofit sector as professional work. The certification of fundraisers, once done by AFP, is now conducted by a separate certification organization, CFRE International, and as of this writing has brought to 4,184 the number of certified fundraisers in the United States, Canada, Australia, New Zealand, and the United Kingdom.

AFP introduced an even higher level of certification, Advanced Certified Fund Raising Professional, ACFRE, and there are now 75 of them as of August 2006. Both of these groups continue to grow.

Is This Enough?

The responses enumerated above are positive and encouraging. But are they enough? We know that the congestion referred to above is not just for dollars. Nonprofits are also competing for volunteers, and especially for volunteer leaders. It is clear that all forms of philanthropic participation (charitable dollars, volunteer time, and volunteer leadership) flow to those organizations that create and maintain philanthropic programs that are:

- Highly intentional
- Keenly strategic
- Well timed
- Very distinctive
- Donor centered
- Volunteer driven

What else do we need to be doing to ensure that our nonprofit organizations are attracting the necessary funding, volunteers and volunteer leaders?

Paying Attention to Risk

Of all the types of philanthropic programs in which a nonprofit organization can engage, the capital campaign often carries the greatest risk for the organization. It usually has the highest community visibility of all the philanthropic programs for a nonprofit. It can also be that the very urgency that is needed as a necessary ingredient in the case for giving can also cause a nonprofit organization to hurry through the vital precampaign planning.

This highlights how important it is for an organization considering a capital campaign to:

- Plan carefully
- Move deliberately
- Act in consensus

Minimizing Risk and Maximizing Effectiveness

For all the reasons given above, nonprofit leaders, both paid and unpaid, must make sure that the philanthropic programs of their organization are well designed and effectively carried out. Because a capital campaign requires even greater involvement from internal and external constituencies, the cost of failure runs high.

Like any enterprise, the leaders must arrange their activities so as to minimize the risks. Because excess timidity in the conduct of a capital campaign can actually be counterproductive, the board and the top staff must make sure that the plans for the campaign are well considered and soundly tested. For these reasons we offer this book, and in it we take great care to fully explain the importance and value of the fundraising feasibility study and the process to conduct it.

In the remaining 12 chapters the assembled authors explore with us everything you have ever wanted to know about this greatly appreciated, but sometimes misunderstood diagnostic tool—the fundraising feasibility study. Our contributing writers lay out in great detail how to understand, why to utilize, and when to employ a fundraising feasibility study to ensure successful capital campaign planning.

To assist in your use of this book we have assembled a collection of sample documents (Appendices A–M). We have also compiled a rather extensive bibliography for future study and, if you are so inclined, additional research.

As the lead author and editor, I welcome your comments and questions. I also accept responsibility for any errors or omissions. Should you wish to communicate or correspond with me, I will do my best to respond to your comment or query in a timely fashion.

CHAPTER 2

Looking in the Mirror—What Is a Precampaign Planning Study?

Elliott S. Oshry, CFRE

Introduction

There is considerable ambiguity within the profession regarding the purposes, structure, format, and implementation of a precampaign study. In fact, even the name of this exercise changes from agency to agency, from sector to sector. This chapter will establish the value of the study, delineate deliverables, provide options for structure, and offer an overview of the components of the study, clearing the way for a more detailed view of these issues in subsequent chapters.

Planning or Feasibility?

A major-gift capital or endowment campaign will test every seam within the nonprofit agency that is about to engage in this activity. Because the campaign has high visibility and is often volunteer driven, the success of the campaign has a direct impact on the credibility and self-image of key volunteers, as well as on the agency's future fundraising capacity. For these reasons and others, a precampaign study is generally a wise investment.

The term *feasibility study* originated when the process was designed to determine the literal feasibility of the campaign and to test and validate a dollar objective. As nonprofit fundraising has matured, feasibility is rarely the question. The most negative study today might indicate that the agency is not yet ready for a goal of the tested magnitude or for a campaign to fund particular projects in which the constituency is not engaged. The process, therefore, is a *planning* exercise designed to develop the comprehensive campaign plan, to broker the case among key constituents, to raise the sights of prospective donors, and to accelerate the pre-ask cultivation process.

A precampaign planning study is focused on the very top of the agency's philanthropic market. Everyone who is interviewed in such a study should be a realistic prospect for one of the top 10 gifts in the proposed campaign (relevance and capacity, not inclination) and/or a candidate for a high-level leadership role in the campaign. Exceptions for individuals who have intimate knowledge of the agency or the market should be few and considered carefully.

Benefits of a Well-Crafted Study

The study is often the first opportunity to "presell" the need to selected key constituents. How that need is articulated, by whom, and in what context will often impact the constituents' reaction. Personalized and tailored to the person being interviewed, the marketing impact of the study is dramatic.

While there may be a well-managed database from which to work, campaigns are constructed around in-depth, empirical research and vital anecdotal research. The study generates invaluable data upon which to plan. The anecdotal research gathered during the study is often available from no other source.

Objectivity is the cornerstone of the study. It provides a balance with the passionate and emotional perspectives of those closest to the project. Because the success or failure of the campaign has such long-range implications to the future of the agency, an objective analysis of the likelihood for success makes the study worthy of investment.

Gifts required to meet the proposed goal are often the largest gifts in the agency's history. A firsthand indication of intended support from prospective donors establishes the baseline from which to plan. Gifts secured during the actual campaign are almost always higher than those indicated during the study, but accurate projections are possible only when firsthand responses are secured during the study. As noted below, study participants are asked not only about their own level of support, but about support that might be secured from others.

Access to volunteer leadership of the highest caliber will determine the success of the campaign more than any other factor. The study identifies those leaders without whom the campaign cannot succeed and gathers the data from which an enlistment strategy can be developed. Leadership candidates see their suggestions and opinions reflected in the study report and begin to feel ownership of the subsequent plan. It is only when the first-choice leadership candidates are actually interviewed that the study begins to have true value.

The study minimizes risk to the agency and to its leaders by testing assumptions before there is a public announcement. It is incumbent upon nonprofit management to protect the image of the agency and the personal credibility of its leaders. The study is a unique tool to accomplish these objectives.

The study is a public relations resource. By the time the study has been completed, a significant sample of the constituency's most influential leaders have been informed, educated, and engaged in the vision of the agency.

A precampaign study is constructed around personal interviews, generally conducted by an objective third party to ensure the confidentiality of the interview. The interview should be a far-reaching and in-depth process and is built around two key documents: a case for support and a gift table.

Case for Support

As noted in Chapter 8, a compelling and credible case for support is based on a current or recent strategic plan that reflects the vision of the agency's leadership: How will this agency best service the community five years from now, and what resources are needed to achieve that vision?

The case is not a wish list; it is a credible articulation of a plan to address needs within a well-defined constituent group. The central question to be addressed in the case is: What is *central to our mission* that we do not do now, or do not do as well as we should, that we could do with additional private-sector resources. The case must define the problem, identify the solution, provide a budget for that solution, and link private-sector philanthropy to that budget.

Among the most common risks in case development is to underestimate costs and then have to go back to the market for additional funds after the goal has been reached. Credibility is essential.

Crisis fundraising does not work. Needs must be urgent and real, but the threat of "going out of business unless we reach this goal" tends to repel donors. Oral Roberts's statement that God had threatened to "call him home" if he did not reach their campaign goal is an example of urgency gone awry.

Elements of a sound case might include:

- History of agency (track record of service)
- Summary of services or programs (what makes us unique)
- The need (the community's need, not the agency's need)
- The plan (solution)
- The campaign
- Anticipated project costs
- A vision of the agency once the campaign has reached its goal

Gift Table

Based on an adequate database of successful campaigns for similar agencies and for similar dollar goals, a gift table (standards of giving) should be developed to reflect the number and size of gifts that must be approximated in the proposed campaign. A road map provided by those who have gone before, the gift table is tested through the study's confidential interviews.

Among the objectives of the study are to determine where on the gift table the study participant's gift is likely to be and to identify other sources for the top gifts on the chart. The following samples reflect the "standards" around which gift tables are constructed: a top investment in the range of 15 to 20 percent of goal; the top 10 gifts in the range of 50 to 55 percent. As noted on these two samples, the gift table can be a simple chart or a graphic illustration (see Exhibits 2.1 and 2.2).

QUALITY CONTROL

As will be noted in Chapter 6, the validity of a study is in direct proportion to the quality of the interview sample. With suggestions from board members, program officers, and development staff, a participant list in the range of 40 to 60 interviews should be drafted. The sample may be larger for a national campaign or for a larger-membership agency.

EXHIBIT 2.1   SAMPLE GIFT TABLE CHART

SAMPLE

Gift Table	Guidelines	
Objective: $10,000,000	Top Investment	15–20% of Objective
	Top 10 Investments	50–55% of Objective
	Next 100–150 Investments	40–45% of Objective

No.	Amount	Total	Cumulative Total	% of Objective
1	$2,000,000	$2,000,000	$2,000,000	20.0%
1	$1,000,000	$1,000,000	$3,000,000	
2	$500,000	$1,000,000	$4,000,000	
3	$250,000	$750,000	$4,750,000	
3	$150,000	$450,000	$5,200,000	52.0%
10	$100,000	$1,000,000	$6,200,000	
12	$75,000	$900,000	$7,100,000	
15	$50,000	$750,000	$7,850,000	
20	$25,000	$500,000	$8,350,000	
30	$15,000	$450,000	$8,800,000	
40	$10,000	$400,000	$9,200,000	
50	$5,000	$250,000	$9,450,000	94.5%
Many	Below $5,000	$550,000	$10,000,000	100.0%

EXHIBIT 2.2   SAMPLE GIFT TABLE GRAPHIC ILLUSTRATION

This chart represents the numbers and levels of gifts needed to achieve our objective of $10,000,000.

Shaded blocks represent pledges that now total $_____.

When all the blocks are shaded, the goal will be met.

Your completed solicitations will help fill the few remaining blocks and ensure success!

SAMPLE

Standards of Giving for $10,000,000

$	2,000,000	1									
$	1,000,000	1									
$	500,000	2	1								
$	250,000	3	2	1							
$	150,000	3	2	1							
$	100,000	10	9	8	7	6	5	4	3	2	1
$	75,000	12	11	10	9	8	7	6	5	4	3
		2	1								
$	50,000	15	14	13	12	11	10	9	8	7	6
		5	4	3	2	1					
$	25,000	20	19	18	17	16	15	14	13	12	11
		10	9	8	7	6	5	4	3	2	1
$	15,000	30	29	28	27	26	25	24	23	22	21
		20	19	18	17	16	15	14	13	12	11
		10	9	8	7	6	5	4	3	2	1
$	10,000	40	39	38	37	36	35	34	33	32	31
		30	29	28	27	26	25	24	23	22	21
		20	19	18	17	16	15	14	13	12	11
		10	9	8	7	6	5	4	3	2	1

(continues)

EXHIBIT 2.2   SAMPLE GIFT TABLE ILLUSTRATION (CONTINUED)

SAMPLE

$ 5,000	50	49	48	47	46	45	44	43	42	41
	40	39	38	37	36	35	34	33	32	31
	30	29	28	27	26	25	24	23	22	21
	20	19	18	17	16	15	14	13	12	11
	10	9	8	7	6	5	4	3	2	1

A mix of 45 to 50 personal interviews, coupled with a direct-response instrument, will create a valid sample even for large-constituent agencies. Each study interview participant should be a bona fide prospect for a top 10 gift, a candidate for campaign leadership, or a person of unique and intimate knowledge of the agency and/or community.

The composition of the sample might include:

- 100 percent of the board if the board has fewer than 15 members.
- Maximum of 40 percent of the board if board membership is 15 or more.
- 30 to 35 top-level prospects (may overlap with other categories).
- 15 to 20 candidates for leadership in the campaign (may also overlap with other categories).

EDUCATIONAL ORGANIZATIONS

The academic and administrative communities of an educational institution cannot be omitted from a study, but must be represented in proportionate numbers. Parents and alumni must also be represented. For example:

- No more than 10 percent (5) faculty/staff (president, deans, development officers, department heads, etc.).
- Minimum of 20 percent (10) parents (if independent school).
- Minimum of 40 percent (20) alumni (may overlap with other categories).

HEALTH CARE ORGANIZATIONS

In a study for a health care organization, the study must include data from physicians and administrators as well. For example:

- No more than 10 percent (5) staff (chief executive officer [CEO], chief financial officer [CFO], development staff, department heads, etc.).

- Minimum of 20 percent (10) physicians, including the chief of staff or medical department heads (may also be board members)

AREAS OF INQUIRY

While considerable data on wide-ranging issues is gathered during the study, the principal areas of analysis include:

- *Public image of agency.* How do prospective donors and leaders view the value of the agency to the community and to specific constituent groups? Are the agency and its leaders well respected in the community?

- *Understanding of the need.* Is the community's need that the agency proposes to address evident to prospective donors and leaders? Is there some urgency associated with that community need?

- *Opinion of the plan to meet the need.* Is the agency's plan to address these needs credible and practical? Is the budget credible? Is the timing immediate? Is the plan competitive with other projects being considered within the community?

- *Appraisal of the project (priority rating).* Among the study participants' many volunteer and philanthropic interests, will this project be a high priority for the next several years? If it is not yet at the top of the priority list, what is? What can this agency do to elevate the priority assigned to its project?

- *Appropriateness of a campaign.* Are there other sources of funds available for this project or is a private-sector campaign the most appropriate source of funding? Has government funding or debt been considered, or is the campaign one component of a larger financial package?

- *Receptivity to a capital campaign.* Is the community likely to embrace the campaign? If not, what can be done to modify that response? Is it a matter of goal, case, or timing?

- *Attainability of the goal.* Is the proposed goal and each of the gift levels within that goal, within the agency's reach at this time and for this project? Have other agencies in the region or sector been successful at this level of support? If this goal is seen as beyond reach, with what goal would the market be more comfortable?

- *Willingness to give: personal and corporate gifts.* Is the study participant likely to make a personal, corporate, or foundation investment in the proposed campaign, and at what approximate level?

- *Willingness to volunteer/accept a leadership role.* If asked by the right person or team, will this study participant serve within the campaign organization? Is there a particular position in the campaign structure that this participant would like to fill? To whom can this participant not say "no"? The study must test the competency of leadership within the reach of the agency.

- *Fundraising strength of the board.* Does the board have the networking capacity and fundraising clout to spearhead this effort? Should the chair come from the board? Can the board reach out to others of clout? Is the leadership competency of the board adequate for the task?
- *Economic outlook for the region.* Is the "economic morale" of the community positive?
- *Proposed timing of the campaign.* Are there other private-sector initiatives that will compete with the proposed campaign?
- *Conditions to proceed.* Under what specific conditions would the participant suggest that the campaign move forward?

OBJECTIVES AND DELIVERABLES

The planning study process interjects time-tested principles into a highly methodical format that minimizes the risk associated with goal setting and preparing for a capital campaign. The information gathered during the planning study will provide a comprehensive assessment of the philanthropic potential that is detailed in the final report and includes:

- A description of the process used to conduct the study and formulate recommendations.
- An explanation of the purpose of each question asked of interview participants.
- A statistical report of participants' responses by constituency category.
- A narrative analysis of each finding.
- A report of strengths that can enhance the opportunity for success.
- A report of challenges that should be addressed.
- Recommendations for the next steps in achieving the recommended campaign goal.
- A gift table demonstrating the gifts necessary for achieving the tested goal.
- A gift table demonstrating the gifts necessary for achieving the recommended goal.
- Suggested top donors and campaign leaders (confidential data presented to key leadership).

Note: If the *only* outcome of the study is identification of the best possible leadership and the data from which sound enlistment strategies can be developed, the study has been a valuable investment.

PROCESS

A precampaign study has a natural sequence and process:

1. It originates with a strategic plan. The concept of testing capacity before a plan is developed is not effective and is risky.

2. A consultant should be retained to guide the process and to ensure the objectivity and the confidentiality of the interview process.

3. It is embraced by the CEO and board. If board members are not passionate about the project, others will sense their hesitation.

4. It is linked to a credible budget to be funded, wholly or in part, through philanthropy.

5. Internal influence. Leaders must be presold before the study goes to the community. Faculty, physicians, and others within the agency can be effective ambassadors if they are engaged early, or can be serious impediments if they believe they have been taken for granted.

6. Board members must participate in identifying the study sample so the board owns the results of the study. A board member is often needed to open the door to a prospective study participant.

7. Prospective study participants must be invited to participate by a person of clout (i.e., the CEO or board chair).

8. Confidential interviews are conducted by a consultant.

9. The study report should be previewed to the CEO, chief development officer, and chair of the development committee before it is shared with the board. If an ad hoc committee has been formed to guide the planning study process, a preview of the study may also be provided to this committee.

10. Study results should be presented to the board in a workshop or retreat dedicated to the study so the agency receives maximum benefit from the process.

11. Board members must be prepared to act with dispatch, whether they like the study results or not. A revised budget, plan, or pace may be the result of a study.

12. An executive summary of the study should be shared with each person who was invited to be interviewed, whether they agreed to be interviewed or not.

TIMING

By the time a precampaign study has been added to the agenda of the development office, it is often too late. For the study to have real impact, adequate study preparation is needed as well as time after the study to effectively implement the recommendations that result. Depending on the agency's readiness for a study, the process can take between 14 and 20 weeks.

Much of this prep time is dedicated to development of the case. The study serves as a catalyst for the agency to articulate its mission and vision, often for the first time. Key stakeholders, such as program staff, administration, consumers, and trustees, may be involved in the process of case development.

A second major block of time is needed to secure appointments with the right people. Once an introductory letter has been mailed, two weeks is needed to initiate phone calls (and to play telephone tag) to secure interview dates. Because these are often very busy people, the date that is confirmed is likely to be two to four weeks after the call.

Starting too late and filling the interview schedule with participants who do not meet the donor capacity or leadership qualities of the study will dilute the validity of the study (see Exhibit 2.3).

The person responsible for setting interview appointments must be senior level, have a solid understanding of the relative importance of each participant, know the geography of the community, and have the flexibility to remain at his or her desk for a week of telephoning. If interview candidates cannot reach the development office to schedule an appointment without extensive callbacks, they will lose interest in the process (see Exhibit 2.4).

WHEN TO DO A STUDY

A precampaign study is a solid investment, in most cases, when a campaign is being planned. There are no real downsides to a study, and the time and expense generally pay clear dividends. A study should *always* be considered when:

- There is any question about the community's acceptance of the project.
- There has been any major board or CEO transition.
- It is a "first" campaign for the agency.
- It has been 10 years or more since the last campaign.
- The annual fund has been stagnant.
- There is no clear and accessible first-choice for campaign chair.
- The lead gift is not clearly identified.

EXHIBIT 2.3   INTERVIEW SCHEDULE

Phase I (6–8 weeks)	Phase II (3–4 weeks)	Phase III (4–6 weeks)	Phase IV (2 weeks)
• Case preparation	• Conduct interviews	• Analyze findings	• Board retreat or workshop to digest report
• Interview list development	• Add interview names suggested by others	• Test assumptions	
• Board/staff orientation		• Report development	
• Schedule interviews			

EXHIBIT 2.4   MASTER LOG

Activity									Week Number									
Preparation of Case for Support	1	2	3	4	5	6	7	8	9	10	11	12	13	14	15	16	17	18
Materials from agency	■																	
Research case	■	■	■															
Draft case for support				■	■	■												
Final case for support (approval)							■											

Interview Process	1	2	3	4	5	6	7	8	9	10	11	12	13	14	15	16	17	18
Letters to board members	■																	
Select prospective candidates				■	■													
Mail interview requests							■											
Schedule interviews							■	■										
Conduct interviews									■	■	■	■						

Report and Recommendations	1	2	3	4	5	6	7	8	9	10	11	12	13	14	15	16	17	18
Compile and calculate responses													■					
Analysis of data														■	■			
Preparation of report																■	■	
Final report presentation																		■

In contrast, a study may not be a useful tool when:

- The agency has had seamless, back-to-back campaigns.
- The campaign is mandated by an accrediting body.
- The project is mandated by code or other external enforcement bodies.
- The chair has been enlisted.
- The lead gift has been secured.

SUMMARY

The study process is an intensive exercise through which plans for a major-gift campaign are tested and vetted. The study is a public relations opportunity through which the organization draws its best friends closer and through which new relationships are established. The study becomes the vehicle through which ownership of strategic plans are shared among those without whom the campaign is not likely to succeed. For a study to be of maximal value, executive leadership must be engaged and adequate time must be allocated. A study cannot be delegated to midlevel staff or completed overnight. Undertaking a planning study presupposes the willingness of the board and CEO to consider the opinions of the test sample and to accommodate those opinions in the final analysis.

CHAPTER 3

Standing at the Threshold—It Takes More Than a Feasibility Study to Get Ready for a Capital Campaign

BETTY ANN COPLEY HARRIS, FAHP

INTRODUCTION

The rationale for conducting a feasibility study is presented in this chapter along with the desired outcomes you should expect from the study process—beyond the written report of findings and recommendations. There are many benefits gained from conducting a feasibility study, but there can also be potential pitfalls. In certain situations, a feasibility study may not prove beneficial and could potentially do more harm than good. Understanding the conditions that will lead to a good feasibility study outcome will help determine if, when, and how a feasibility study should be undertaken for your organization. The overarching goal of every feasibility study should be to enhance your organization's readiness for success prior to embarking on a successful campaign.

Over the past 20 years, I have been invited to meet with hundreds of nonprofit chief executive officers (CEOs) and board leaders looking to hire a campaign consultant to conduct a feasibility study on their behalf. Before attending the first meeting to discuss my firm's approach to directing a feasibility study, I conduct research about the organization, have conversations with the development director to learn about the projects to be funded by the campaign, and inquire about the caliber of board leadership and fundraising staff involved with the organization. In the course of the first meeting with leadership, more often than not, I learn that while an organization thinks it is ready to embark on a capital campaign and wants the feasibility study to tell them how much they can raise, I am the bearer of bad news, recommending the need for more work to better prepare the organization before undertaking the feasibility study. If there is one thing these past 20 years of service to hundreds of nonprofits has taught me, it is that a feasibility study is best undertaken when the organization is ready to move quickly from the completion of the study right into the start of the first phase of its campaign.

Unfortunately, many organizations do not maximize the potential benefits and impact that can be garnered from the feasibility study process. And even more unfortunate is the fact that some consulting firms do not caution an organization's leaders that conditions are not right before undertaking the feasibility study. Think about it. You are about to invest anywhere from $15,000 to $40,000 or more in a consulting firm who is expected to do everything in their power to ensure a successful feasibility study and help you prepare for a campaign to raise the millions of dollars needed to fund that special capital or endowment project. What good does it do to have a consultant go out into your community of donors and meet one on one with your most influential philanthropic leaders if they aren't likely to have good things to say? Do you really want a feasibility study report that concludes you are not ready for a capital campaign? Not likely. You want a feasibility study to further enhance your organization's readiness for the campaign. Therefore, it is important to know what it takes to be ready to undertake a capital campaign.

Why does your organization need to be ready to move into the campaign shortly following the completion of your feasibility study? Because the feasibility study is the start of the campaign, it puts your organization and your project on the giving agenda of key donors in the community and it lights a fire of excitement under prospective donors. Prospective donors whose advice you are seeking through the study interviews should be flattered to be interviewed for a feasibility study, and the right interviewer asking the right questions will subtly encourage the prospect to begin thinking about her or his gift. This is not to be confused with a solicitation, but is a significant cultivation opportunity that leaves the donor feeling very enthusiastic about your organization. You do not want to lose the momentum and anticipation garnered from the one-on-one meetings with your most precious donor constituents by waiting six months to a year before you start your campaign. Rather, you want all the elements required for a successful campaign to be lined up to the extent possible before you do your feasibility study.

Are You Ready to Undertake a Capital Campaign?

One of the most enlightening comments I have ever heard from a hospital trustee was the woman who responded to a question I asked while leading a board retreat. The question was: "What is the most important role of a board member relative to fundraising?" Her answer was simply: "I think it is our job as trustees to make sure that our hospital could move into a capital campaign tomorrow—if we needed to." Her insightful reply was no doubt the result of having previously served in the leadership of other capital campaigns. She knew from her experience that if board leaders were diligent about their roles of helping to build an influential board of trustees; helping to grow a generous community of influential donors; helping cultivate and solicit increasing levels of support from a growing base of annual fund donors; and actively fulfilling their roles as advocates and stewards by continuously introducing new friends to the hospital, they would indeed be doing everything in their power to ensure its readiness to someday undertake a very successful capital campaign.

Why Conduct a Study?

The most important reason for conducting a feasibility study is tied to the inherent risks of embarking on a campaign where the potential for success is not assured. A failed campaign leaves a dark cloud over a nonprofit organization's reputation for decades and can severely damage its potential for future fundraising success. A failed campaign creates an overwhelming sense of frustration and disappointment for volunteers and staff leaders who believe deeply in the mission and want only the best for the organization. Campaigns simply cannot afford to fail.

Two Years before Starting a Campaign

In the best of all worlds, I like to see that an organization has been taking steps to get ready for two years before it needs to launch its capital campaign. This 24-month window gives an organization ample time to prepare for a campaign. Two years before a campaign begins is the time to examine the organization's strategic plan to validate the priorities around which the campaign agenda will be developed. It is also the time to review your prospect and donor pool to identify and research those who will be your best donors and campaign leaders. You can also further strengthen your annual giving program to continue building the base of donor support, since it is the rare gift in a campaign that comes from people who are not already giving to your annual fund. And two years before you begin your campaign is the time to start hosting information/cultivation receptions (I like to call them vision parties) to tell your organization's story to as many people of influence as you can bring together to hear it.

One Year before the Campaign

One year before launching your campaign is when you should begin interviewing potential campaign consultants whom you might hire to conduct your feasibility study. The process of interviewing fundraising consultants to conduct your study is a wonderful opportunity to better educate your board leaders and executives about what it takes to run a successful campaign. When you have three or four consulting firms coming in to make presentations for one hour, talking about how they do their work in feasibility and campaign projects, this is four hours of free education for your best fundraising leaders. You can bet you want them to benefit from this free advice.

It is also the time to begin writing your preliminary case for support—the prospectus that describes the organization and its campaign vision and plan.

It is also the time to consider how much you think your organization could raise in a capital campaign. I like to see this process undertaken by creating a few sample gift charts (i.e., $5 million, $7.5 million, or $10 million) and begin plugging in the names of donors you believe have the potential to give at the highest levels required on that table of gifts. If the top-level gift in a campaign is typically 5 to 10 percent of the overall goal, who are the people that could commit at the $1 million lead gift level in your $10 million campaign? If you are working through the names and the gift levels for at least a year before the feasibility study gets under way, you have a good chance of ensuring that you have identified the ideal prospects to participate in your feasibility study from among your many thousands of donors.

Meanwhile, as the months are passing by, keep digging up new prospect sources, building new relationships, and nurturing your long-time loyal donors so that they are ready to hear from you again when the campaign feasibility study is ready to get under way.

Six Months before the Campaign

Six months before your campaign begins is when you should be undertaking the feasibility study, which in itself takes two to three months to complete. In these final six months you will conduct the study, receive the study results, and make recommendations to the board based on the study findings. If the report declares that you are well positioned to proceed with a campaign, you then need to seek unanimous board approval for plans to move into the campaign. You also want to retain your campaign consultant (hopefully, the same firm that did your feasibility study). And now it is time to recruit your campaign leadership. With the help of your campaign consultant and endorsement from your eager team of campaign leaders, the campaign strategy, plan, timetable, and budget can now be prepared.

Form a Precampaign Planning Committee

I usually recommend that our clients form a precampaign planning committee comprised of five or six board leaders, physicians, or deans or other staff whom you would really like to serve among the campaign leadership. By inviting them to participate in this early planning process, you are getting their buy-in long before the campaign gets under way. If they have been part of building the planning and strategy, they are likely to be more invested and willing to participate as a campaign leader later on. The precampaign planning committee can be charged with confirming the projects to be included in the campaign and help make the decision on hiring your fundraising consultant for the study and campaign; they can also be extremely helpful identifying the prospects and leaders to be interviewed in the feasibility study. This committee should also be the first group to review the results of the feasibility study once it is completed as a sure way for building consensus before taking it to the entire board of trustees. You should hope that the precampaign planning committee would be the group who endorses the plan to launch a campaign before you call for a vote of the entire board. If you have done all these things during the two years preceding your campaign, you should now be ready to undertake your feasibility study—with the best chances for a successful study report indicating that you are ready to move into the first phase of your campaign.

You Know You're Ready When . . .

There are three absolute elements of readiness or prerequisites to planning a campaign including: a compelling case/cause that will attract support; a donor constituency that is ready to support a campaign; and, most importantly, leadership commitment right from the start. You will know that your organization is ready to embark on a capital campaign when:

- Your organization is prominently recognized and valued in the community.
- Your needs are well planned and presented in a compelling case for support.
- Your feasibility study is completed, reporting favorable results of fundraising potential and leadership support.
- Your donor constituency is well informed, interested, and involved in your organization.
- The board and administration are committed to a successful campaign.
- You have sufficient staff and budget resources to lead the campaign over 18 to 24 months.
- You have identified, qualified, rated, and screened a strong field of major-gift prospects.
- You have the ability to recruit strong volunteer leaders to chair important divisions of your campaign.
- You have allowed adequate time to plan and conduct the campaign.

What You Want from Your Feasibility Study

Ideally, you want a final study that:

- Confirms and validates your assumptions about what people think of your organization.

- Identifies who the best leaders for your campaign are likely to be and learns that these individuals are willing to take on key leadership positions in the campaign.
- Confirms who the top 20 donors are and what their indications of support are likely to be.
- Confirms that the preliminary campaign goals you have proposed can in fact be achieved.

You also want the study to confirm that study participants:

- Think highly of your organization's executive leadership.
- Are impressed by the people of influence already serving on your board.
- Agree that your campaign addresses very important needs that will greatly improve your organization's ability to better fulfill its mission.
- Think highly of the staff who delivers the programs and services provided by your organization (i.e., the clinicians and nurses in a hospital, the faculty and staff in an academic institution, the scientists in a research organization, the program officers and counselors in a social service organization, etc.).
- Are willing to put your organization high on the list of their many charitable interests over the next three to five years.
- Are giving highly favorable indications of their ability and inclination to make five-, six-, and seven-figure gifts to support your campaign.

ELEMENTS OF CAMPAIGN SUCCESS

When you begin thinking seriously about conducting a capital campaign of any size, it is crucial to plan your campaign based on the results of a successful feasibility study. A professionally managed study will allow your organization to further cultivate your top donors while determining an attainable campaign goal and defining to what degree the essential elements of success are assured as you plan for your campaign. These "time-tested" elements of campaign success include:

1. Consensus and urgency of the need:
   - Unanimous agreement by the board on the projects and plans to be funded by the campaign.
   - Campaign priorities must be deemed as valid and important to potential donors and prospective campaign leaders.
   - Determination and commitment by board leaders to contribute to and work for the success of the campaign.
   - Recognition of the capital campaign as an institutional priority and willingness of staff and board members to commit the necessary time and energy.

2. Leadership, adequate sources of support, and giving potential:

   - Identifiable sources for the leadership gifts required to achieve the campaign goal.

   - Enthusiastic endorsements from those who will be expected to provide a major portion of the funds to be raised.

   - Ability to enlist volunteer campaign leaders who possess personal and/or corporate giving potential to assure pace setting investments.

   - Sufficient prospects to secure the top 10 campaign gifts (accounting for approximately 45 to 50 percent of goal); the next 100 to 125 gifts (to provide an additional 40 percent of goal); leaving only 10 to 15 percent of goal to come from the general community and other gift sources.

3. Campaign plan, campaign staff, and budget resources:

   - A well-planned and organized campaign plan that outlines strategies for bringing the project, the constituency, and the leadership together in an organized effort to achieve the campaign goal.

   - Qualified professional direction and adequate staff support to manage and direct the campaign's volunteers and leaders.

   - Sufficient campaign budget providing the financial resources needed to fund and implement the campaign plan.

To ensure a successful capital campaign, you need the feasibility study (also called the precampaign planning study) to determine your position against these requisite measures of success. The study should provide a thorough assessment of your readiness to undertake the campaign, the amount that might be raised, and the time and resources that will be required to raise the funds. Through the feasibility study, you research, analyze, and evaluate fundamental factors present (or capable of development) that might influence a successful capital campaign.

BENEFITS OF A FEASIBILITY STUDY

Gaining Internal Consensus

Because the feasibility study interview process takes your campaign vision and plan to the public, you must first ensure that there is strong internal consensus on the case for giving. The feasibility study tests the validity of the projects around which the campaign is centered. It helps determine whether your community understands the importance of the proposed projects, whether it is for capital improvements, endowment growth, or other special projects. Because the study presents the case for giving to people outside the organization, there must first be absolute agreement inside about the proposed plans and the need for a campaign to fund the plans. Once your organization has successfully achieved consensus and support about the project development components for the campaign from those on the inside, you are in a better position to test the community's support by conducting the feasibility study. The study is going to tell you what key donors think of the case for giving. It gives you a measure of how "donor centered" your campaign appeal is and provides clues as to how well the projects and priorities match the interests and priorities of key donors whose support will be critical to the campaign's success.

Board Members Begin Thinking of Their Own Commitments

The feasibility study brings the reason for a campaign into focus for both internal and external constituents. It allows volunteer and staff leaders to seriously evaluate their own commitment to a campaign and enables the organization to start getting its house in order from an operations perspective. Included in this phase is a careful internal evaluation of infrastructure and staffing needs, discussion of whether or not full-time resident or nonresident campaign counsel is needed, and an honest appraisal as to whether the organization is ready for such a major undertaking.

The Urgency of the Case for Support Is Validated

The feasibility study questions seek to find what donors think about the projects around which the campaign is built. The study should take a measurement of the degree of understanding and agreement that exists for the needs and priorities presented in the case for support. The study will tell you how your case for fundraising is viewed by leaders and donors. The community should endorse the proposed plan based on a sound understanding of your mission and need for the proposed projects.

Top 10 Prospects Are Qualified

Are the top 10 donors to the campaign clearly identifiable? The feasibility study forces you to focus on the leadership prospects and determine the likelihood of their investment in your campaign. Leadership or "lead" gifts given early in a capital campaign by top prospects have a catalytic effect, setting the benchmark for every single other gift throughout the life of a campaign. The difference between a lead gift of $500,000 or $1 million for a $5 million campaign can be remarkable because with the smaller lead gift you'll need many more donors to achieve the goal. Thorough research and evaluation of major gift prospects will help determine the chart of gifts that is right for each campaign and the right gift-level amounts at the top of the pyramid. But bear in mind, whatever its dollar value, the first gift and the few that follow will set the sights of all subsequent campaign donors. Working smarter, not harder, is the way to go.

Cultivation Value

The cultivation value of a feasibility study is immense. Prospective donors are flattered to be interviewed for feasibility studies, and the right interviewer asking the right questions will subtly encourage the prospect to begin thinking about her or his gift. The study can be the "excuse" you need to have an opportunity to get to potential donors who otherwise might not have a reason to get involved and learn about your organization.

Donors Are Asked for Advice

The study provides you with an opportunity to seek the advice of philanthropic leaders in the community. The essence of the feasibility study is asking potential donors to provide a measurement of their acceptance of the plan for your capital project. The community should be in a position to support the proposed capital campaign, which includes being receptive to the idea of having a capital campaign for the projects that are proposed in the case.

Most people appreciate being valued for their views and opinions. I once heard some sage advice about soliciting donors that speaks to the importance of asking donors what they think. The saying goes: *"If you want advice, first ask me for money. But, if you want my money, first ask for my advice."*

The Fundraising Acumen of Leaders and Staff Is Tested

The feasibility study process tests the fundraising acumen of senior management, board leaders, and other leadership sources. You want your feasibility study to provide an assessment of your board's ability to raise funds. Ensuring that those who will be involved in all steps of a campaign have had proper training and that each and every personal face-to-face solicitation is rehearsed and tailor-made will be the keys to success. Staff and board members who are well-informed about major-gift fundraising are often pleasantly surprised to learn that asking for a gift of $100,000 or $1 million does not involve that much more work than asking for $10,000. While the stakes are higher, the same essential steps—prospect identification, research, cultivation, solicitation, and follow-up—must be carefully followed. Your board members must be willing to solicit gifts from major donors. The number one reason most campaigns fail is that people were not asked to give to the campaign.

Development Office Readiness Is Assessed

The feasibility study assesses the readiness of the development office to manage a campaign. It provides an assessment of the staff and volunteer capacity to mount a campaign successfully. Assuming the donors are there, you still require a dependable infrastructure to solicit contributions, conduct cultivation activities, record and report pertinent campaign pledge data, and provide effective stewardship to those who are investing generously in your campaign. Through interviews with executive leaders and key board members, the study can affirm whether or not the organization is prepared to make the appropriate investment of resources to support the campaign organization. By educating your leadership that it takes anywhere from 3 to 15 percent of a goal to properly fund a campaign will help ensure that the organization is prepared to make the proper investment.

Your Image in the Community Is Confirmed

The feasibility study provides critical clues for how to position the organization in the community—its image and reputation and how others see you are affirmed—giving you important clues as to how to fix those things that are not in good stead. The feasibility study offers an opportunity to determine how your organization is viewed in the eyes of prospective donors and other important players. The community should have a favorable opinion of your organization. If they don't, you should get important clues from the study about how to effectively reshape your marketing strategy to better position your organization for fundraising success. If understanding of community perceptions of the organization is insufficient, you are surely not ready to undertake a capital campaign. The feasibility study provides a measurement of the degree of importance your organization has in the community.

When study participants view the list of your board leaders, are they impressed? Do they recognize the names of your board members, and do they consider them to be influential leaders in the community? If you don't have a strong board of trustees, other influential philanthropic leaders from the community will be less inclined to support your organization at levels that match their capability. People give to people—and more likely, they give to people whom they know.

The "Feasibility" of Your Campaign Goal Is Tested

How much money realistically can be raised? Focusing on major gifts is the hallmark for capital campaign success and beyond for every nonprofit organization. More than 75% of the funds raised in any campaign will come from pledges of $25,000 or more. Studies of philanthropic trends document that contributions from individuals make up the majority of charitable gifts, and individual major gifts in a capital campaign can account for as much as 90% of the dollars raised from as few as 5% of all campaign donors. Because of the early momentum, excitement and confidence that a truly awesome lead gift can generate, striving for generous campaign leadership gifts at the highest possible amount in the top of the gift chart are principles that should not be compromised. Focusing on the small pool of individuals who have both the capacity and interest in the organization's mission is the only way to achieve campaign success. The feasibility study must provide important clues to confirm that you have the right sources of support lined up for your campaign.

Opinions are sought through the study as to the availability of large, midrange, and lower-level gifts needed for your campaign to be a success. In this section of the study, you are assessing the potential to attain your *hoped-for* campaign goal. Study participants are asked: *"Who, in your opinion, could provide support at the highest levels for this campaign?"* Study participants are asked to provide the names and potential giving levels of other prospect sources for the campaign.

The Best Sources for Campaign Leadership Are Confirmed

Do you already know who is willing to step up to the plate and lead your campaign? What volunteer leadership is available to head the campaign? If potential campaign leadership is not immediately evident, you need the feasibility study to effectively identify and persuade one or two community leaders that this is the opportunity for them to lead. The study asks interviewees about their willingness to get involved working as a volunteer leader in the campaign. The feasibility study should tell you whether quality leaders are available to help in the campaign—and what the likelihood of their willingness to step up is. Study participants are also asked to suggest the names of others who might serve in the campaign leadership.

I have used the feasibility study as an opportunity to confirm the right fit of a proposed campaign leader and have (on more than one occasion) advised against recruiting the individual an organization had in mind as its campaign chair. After interviewing an individual who had already been asked to serve as a campaign chair and graciously accepted, I learned that while he had considerable wealth, he had no prior involvement with any nonprofit organization, nor had he ever made a significant gift to any charity, much less having had any solicitation or volunteer leadership experience. Needless to say, we found a way out of that premature recruitment and successfully engaged this donor in the campaign in a position other than chairman.

Likewise, I have used the study interview to bring the favored candidate for campaign chair closer to saying yes before he or she is officially asked by an organization's leaders. There is immense influence in being able to say to a potential chairman, "Everyone I've met with in this study believes you are the only one who can effectively lead this campaign, and we are hoping you will say yes when asked." Key leaders from the community must be willing to commit to the capital campaign both through the giving of their time and their financial resources.

Timing for Your Campaign Is Indicated

The feasibility study should provide important clues about the ideal timing for the campaign. By asking questions such as, "When should the campaign begin, and how long should it last?" "What other charities are already out there or who else may be entering into campaigns that may conflict with our plans?" will garner the answers needed through the study to answer this question.

Other Important Discoveries

There are any number of other important findings that can come from a feasibility study that will have a very significant impact on your planning for a campaign. Examples might include the need for a labor issue to be resolved before starting a campaign, the need for heightened visibility of the CEO or executive director, the need to merge with a larger organization, and so on.

Benefits Beyond the Dollars Raised

A successful feasibility study sets the stage for a capital campaign, which yields benefits to the organization long after the campaign has ended. Aside from helping to gather the funds necessary for time-limited "bricks and mortar" projects, successful capital campaigns can have a transformative effect on the fundraising culture of nonprofit organizations. Many nonprofits find that their first capital campaign is the force that finally brings the definition, commitment, and organization to support an ongoing major-gift program. Too often, overcoming inertia or an organization's history of relying on the "safe," smaller-scale approaches (e.g., special events, direct mail, annual fund) can be real obstacles to implementing a major-gift program. A capital campaign focused on major gifts provides everyone—senior management, board leadership, and loyal donors—with their own personal experience and firsthand proof that seeking large gifts is not only possible for your organization, but in many cases hugely exhilarating.

Second, a capital campaign creates an organization-wide sense of unity where all factors of an institution's constituency—staff, board leaders, volunteers—are all working together toward a common goal. The successful achievement of campaign goals creates a tremendous sense of pride and accomplishment both inside and outside the organization. Employees are honored to be part of an organization that the community is so willing to support with their generosity.

Third, when an entire community rallies behind an organization's capital campaign, you have built a wide circle of friends and champions in the community who will likely support you in the future—in both good times and bad.

Finally, recognition of the importance of philanthropy as a resource to support the mission and growth of the organization is strengthened in organizations that have conducted successful capital campaigns. The success of a capital campaign is a springboard for the continuing growth of a strong fundraising program, with new donors and increasing contributions coming your way for years to come.

WHEN A FEASIBILITY STUDY IS UNNECESSARY

There are certain circumstances that would not warrant the investment in a feasibility study before launching a campaign, although they are few. Not having enough time to conduct the study should not be one of them. Perhaps the goal for your campaign project is too small and you have been successful in identifying some early lead gift sources. Perhaps you already have a strong team of volunteers ready to lead your campaign, and you already know that the campaign projects will be readily embraced by your donors. Or perhaps your organization undertook a study within the past two years and it would be harmful to go out and ask many of those same prospects what they think two years later. In these instances, I recommend instead that a precampaign planning process be instituted where the advice of top prospects is sought in a less formal way. Perhaps you invite key donors in to meet with the president to discuss the *refreshed* plans for a campaign. You can also hold cultivation receptions where you discuss the vision and plan for the campaign with individuals whose advice was sought earlier. When circumstances are such that you are not undertaking a feasibility study in advance of a capital campaign, do not overlook the importance of asking for advice before you ask for money.

CHAPTER 4

Development Assessment— Ready! Aim! Fire!

ANNE PEYTON, CFP, CFRE

Ready! Aim! Fire! Is an excellent metaphor for:

- Strengthen your development program to full capacity (Ready!).

- Conduct a precampaign planning study that helps you plan for a successful campaign (Aim!).

- Start a campaign (Fire!).

Relying on a planning study—the Aim!—as a tool to fix your fundraising needs—the Ready!—can be a costly process in both time and money. This chapter focuses on a development assessment as a right-size tool for the right need at the right time to address an organization's long-term success in fundraising.

Many nonprofit organizations have campaigns looming on their horizons—some sooner than later—with leaders eager to raise funds to address needs. Frequently, the urgency toward a campaign narrows your vision—creates a tunnel vision—toward a planning study as the *one and only* next step, no matter where your organization is in its life cycle, in its fundraising strength, in its board development, in its strategic planning. Planning studies are often marketed as the one-stop-shopping solution, responding to your organization's sense of urgency and affirming your assumption that strengthening your fundraising program will become swept up in the momentum of campaign planning. To a certain extent, this perception has tremendous appeal: a campaign is often seen as the impetus to upgrade fundraising software, hire new staff, or to start a planning giving program—to catalyze growth.

The difficulty arises when planning study recommendations are likely to take months to implement. Strengthening the board's fundraising muscle, installing and using effective and efficient software, bringing the staff up to full strength—these may be key factors in attracting influential community leaders to your campaign team or in strengthening your relationships with your top donors. If your fundraising program is short of a full deck, volunteers and donors may defer a decision to support you until you can demonstrate that you're truly a winning team that they want to join. The message of "we're trying" is not as attractive as "we're ready."

Planning studies have limited shelf lives that consultants tend not to talk about with potential clients. In surveying colleagues for this chapter, combined with my own experiences, about a quarter to half of the organizations that ask for a precampaign study (they *think* they're ready) are not really ready to launch a campaign within 6 months. My closest colleagues agree that a planning study has a shelf life of no more than 12 months.

Organizations with less fundraising history and strength, with less philanthropy in their cultures, are more volatile and thus the data has a shorter life span. Organizations with long-term relationships with donors and leaders have built a stronger presence among their constituents, their precampaign planning study data reflect that strength, and the information has a longer shelf life.

Why such a short shelf life? How can the interview data get old? Community leaders who were excited to champion your cause a year ago during a study may have become swept up in other campaigns. Some of your top donors may have become convinced that they can have a greater impact in other organizations' futures. A planning study does not put a hold on anyone's time or energy—you have not reserved anyone's commitment to your future campaign. If another organization has built a stronger relationship with your top donor who supports both organizations, you may end up in second place if you have a number of recommendations to implement that cause you to be late to the campaign start line. Once volunteers and donors make a commitment to you, you can usually count on their allegiance. You have to ask your volunteers and donors; the study is *not* a solicitation for time and/or money.

There are other factors that age the information in a planning study; for example, the chief executive takes "an opportunity of a lifetime," the stock market crashes, the United States gets involved in a war, hurricanes and tsunamis wreak havoc all over the world. Any one of these factors can create a speed bump and delay the start of a campaign. The 9/11 attacks stopped every campaign in its tracks. There may be both internal and external factors; you can control most of the internal ones. My advice: Don't buy a planning study until you know you'll be ready to use it. There will always be factors you can't control, but pay attention to your intuition. If you know in your heart-of-hearts that you need to strengthen your fundraising program, address that first, then conduct a precampaign planning study when your fundraising is tuned up and fit for the complexity and rigor of a campaign.

Planning studies are essential to illuminate your way to and through a campaign. They simply have shelf lives that can be overlooked in the organization's eagerness to get going and the consultant's desire to satisfy a customer.

A development assessment may be the perfect tool in your toolbox *before* you pay for a precampaign planning study. You can spend from $25,000 to over $50,000 for a planning study that's valid for up to 12 months. If the study contains recommendations that require more than 12 months of organizational planning, staffing, and/or board building, the campaign-related information may have become out of date or stale by the time you want to start your campaign. A development assessment for $5,000 to $15,000 may be a right-sized process to address your fundraising infrastructure, and then you are in a prime position to consider a planning study—the right tool at the right time.

You can do a lot of the development assessment yourself to hone your knowledge and sharpen your expertise, then ask a fundraising consultant to help you finish the work and implement changes.

ROCKET SCIENCE AND MAGIC BULLETS

Two essential factors in rocket science are knowing where you want to go—your goal —and having enough thrust to get there—the strength of your engine. It's the same in fundraising—knowing where you want your fundraising to go and strengthening your program to get you there. The day-to-day tasks involved in receipting and acknowledging gifts, maintaining your data base, planning and executing your annual appeal, personalized stewardship with your top donors, foundation research and grant seeking, developing your board's confidence and competence in thanking and asking, using a development plan to guide your year-long efforts, and so on—these programs need to be in good working order *before* you spend money on a precampaign study. More often than not, a board member or chief executive will envision a campaign as a magic bullet —an answer to all your organization's fundraising needs, driving everyone on a fast track, eager to be heroes.

Campaigns are major efforts—rockets, if you will—that require a sustainable fundraising foundation just as NASA has a well-tuned infrastructure and operations in place before launch. Campaigns can provide the impetus to begin any number of projects: planned giving with a legacy society to recognize donors, new database software and information management practices, establishing gift and endowment policies. Rushing toward a campaign with the hope that these fundamentals will become swept up in the momentum of a campaign is like jumping into the deep end of a swimming pool before lessons. Don't let the illusion of a campaign as a magic bullet become the silver bullet that burns out your staff and volunteers and embarrasses your donors in public.

"We Want to Start a Campaign..."

Eager (for whatever reasons) to start a campaign, an organization may distribute a request for proposals (RFP) for a precampaign planning study. Consultants responding to that RFP usually conduct some fundraising basic fact finding:

- How much money does the organization raise annually?
- How efficient is the annual giving program?
- How deep is the pool of top donors?
- Is there a major-gift program? A stewardship program and donor recognition? A planned giving program?
- How effective is the database, software, and information management?
- Are gift acceptance policies and procedures in writing?
- Does every board member give financial support each year?
- Do board members embrace fundraising as part of their responsibilities?
- Is the board fully committed to soliciting funds?
- Do the staff and board have strong fundraising experience?
- Is the fundraising program fully staffed?
- Do the staff and board, as individuals or as a working team, have campaign experience?
- Has the organization conducted a successful campaign before?
- What's the driving force behind *this* campaign?

If the answers to these kinds of questions are slippery, the consultant can identify a number of elements in the organization's day-to-day fundraising that need to be strengthened, even before he or she steps into the facility or interviews a single staff or board member. Basic fundraising programs need to be running smoothly and efficiently before you add the scope and complexity of a campaign.

If the consultant combines organizational development expertise with development and fundraising, a deeper examination of broader issues can open the conversation into a governance assessment:

- Are members of the board influential and well known in the community?
- How well do the chief executive and board members articulate their outcomes?
- Is there an effective strategic plan in place, with estimated costs and a dashboard?
- Does the board regularly assess the CEO's performance and organizational results, as measured against the plan?
- Does the board regularly conduct its own performance review and improve its efficiency and accountability?

- How effective is the board's committee structure and function?
- Does the board utilize a governance committee?

Any fundraising consultant should ask you these kinds of questions in preparing a proposal to address your needs. Let's stay with this conversation between the organization and the consultant for a while—we'll explore more about actual assessments later in this chapter.

Speak Truth in Love to Power

With the fact finding complete, the consultant may be in a quandary about how to respond to the RFP: how to satisfy your asking for a planning study on the one hand— you're the customer—and on the other hand, how to illustrate that you may be less ready for a campaign than you would like to believe. Some organizations may disregard one consultant's expert observations and hire another one who will deliver the product they think they need. I have interviewed with organizations not ready for campaigns that have ended up contracting with another consultant for a planning study; my initial disappointment is compounded months later when I check back and they're right where I thought they might be—strengthening the board, installing software, coming up to full staff, and they've spent a lot of money for a study that has become out of date.

All of us rely on the profession to ensure the highest level of integrity and honesty. Here is an ethical choice point for both the organization and the consultant: for the organization, being truthful with itself about its infrastructure, and for the consultant, speaking truth to power. My colleagues tell me that each year they conduct more planning studies than development assessments. I wonder if that ratio would be reversed if organizations appreciated how a development assessment can help them in long-term fundraising growth.

Someone may suggest that a development assessment suggested by one consultant is only a means to more income, a "double dipping" of fees, if you will: a first contract for a development assessment and a second contract for a precampaign planning study. That response may be a red herring to distract attention away from fundamental fundraising needs in a rush to get on with a campaign.

Later in this chapter, we will explore how much of a development assessment may or may not be included within a planning study.

What's in a Development Assessment?

A development assessment is an analysis of the organization's fundraising programs with recommendations for strengthening all aspects of those programs and adding new activities when appropriate. It can be an independent, stand-alone process, or it can be part of a precampaign planning study.

Betty Ann Copley Harris, another author of this book, gives a brief description of a development assessment (she calls it an audit) on her Web site, www.copleyharris.com.

> A development audit generates an overview of your organization's fundraising program—its strengths, weaknesses, and potential. Each audit is based on careful scrutiny of all revenue sources, fundraising expenses, operating systems, and staffing, as well as benchmarking data from similar organizations. Interviews with key volunteers and supporters help clarify how others perceive your organization and gauge the potential for greater support. The audit report analyzes the data and findings and presents recommendations for immediate action.

An assessment examines the broad organizational context: vision, values, mission, and how well the leadership and staff can articulate the organization's impact on the public good; annual and long-range planning; staff and board leadership; marketing and communications; how development relates to the overall health and vitality of the organization; operations, policies, and practices; and a culture of philanthropy. A second layer of examination brings the internal, practical fundraising activities into sharper focus: development planning, development marketing and communications, staff leadership and expertise, budget and resources, stewardship and recognition, gift and pledge processing, software and information management, and a host of other details. The development assessment focuses primarily on the internal aspects of a fundraising program; a precampaign planning study focuses primarily on the external world as the marketplace. Each kind of study includes some aspects of both internal and external worlds, while each has its specific primary focus.

AUDIT OR ASSESSMENT?

Either term works. Some fundraising professionals borrow the *audit* label from financial audits; others prefer the term *assessment* to avoid confusion. I prefer *assessment* because that's what it is. It's similar to the kind of confusion with the label *feasibility*. Some organizations contract for a feasibility study to examine the business plan in relation to the marketplace, with more attention to operating funds than to fundraising, asking the question, "If we build it, will they use it?" A planning study asks, "Will they buy it?" No one is the expert in which term is "right," so decide how you want to use which terms and be consistent in your organization.

METHODOLOGY

A consultant will examine development-related documents: policies, written practice manuals, annual and donor reports, internal and external communications, annual appeal letters, measured progress toward the development plan, and so on. Analysis will include interviews with development staff and board, selected other staff, past board members, and key stakeholders and donors. The interviews are based on a protocol of questions designed for each organization as well as covering a standard range of programs and processes. When a development assessment expands into governance issues, a broader net is cast: by-laws, agendas and board minutes, retreat documentation, board self-assessments and improvements, board decisions and group process, regularity of the chief executive's performance review, board goals in relation to the organization's plan, measured progress toward the strategic plan, utilization of a governance committee, succession planning for the chief executive and board, and so on. Recommendations usually include an observation and then suggested steps to improve efficiency, effectiveness, and accountability, for both the organization and the board.

I encourage a development officer to begin a development assessment with tools and checklists that are outlined later in this chapter, then bring in a consultant's expertise and perspective to add to what you know, creating a partnership to work together to bring the development program forward.

RECOMMENDATIONS

The following are examples of observations and recommendations from a development and governance assessment of a small organization in 2006, requested by the executive director (ED). The organization serves region-wide customers with a budget below $500,000. The ED anticipates the organization's need for a capital campaign in several years and sees a development assessment as a way to strengthen fundraising, build relationships with donors, restructure staff responsibilities, and to create a culture of philanthropy among the leadership. The assessment took 10 service days and was the equivalent of $10,000 of service. The report was 31 pages long and contained 44 recommendations, spread over a three-year timeline.

1. *Observation:* Staffing: Over the next three years, the board and staff are considering shifting (name [the ED]) to become a full-time fundraiser, building on his natural talents with people and strengthening his fundraising skills with training and coaching, and to relinquish his chief executive role at the end of three years to the current assistant director. Given the extensive history of intergenerational volunteer involvement and politics, promoting (name) to become the ED would place her in a provocative position with long-term volunteers in leadership roles.

   Recommendation: I suggest that (ED's name) continue as executive director with a focus on fundraising, as 75 percent of his job description, and that he continue to be the chief executive. Promoting (name [assistant director]) to become the operations director with a focus on day-to-day operations is an excellent utilization of her talents and expertise. Reporting to (ED's name) gives her a buffer between her responsibilities and her extended relationships among lifelong volunteers and members of the board of directors.

2. *Observation:* Governance: The membership and work of the board of directors embraces much of the working needs of the physical facility, resulting in current operations' taking precedence over governance and future needs. Many members actively avoid fundraising, preferring to lend their time and talent toward operations and facilities.

Note: The nonprofit sector frequently mixes volunteerism with governance, and many nonprofits have dissolved advisory councils due to lack of work rather than lack of focus. If we have a number of members who actively volunteer in the organization, the board agenda can overflow with operations needs and leave little or no time for governance and forward thinking. This phenomenon became clear to me in working with a health clinic where most of the board members were health care providers in the clinic, and operational issues demanded immediate attention and overshadowed governance responsibilities.

Recommendation: Consider separating the governance function from the volunteer function by creating an operations council that would focus on operations and advise the operations director and the ED. Select and ask specific members of the board to transfer their membership to this new council. Redefine the board of directors' responsibilities to focus on governance, strategic thinking, and long-range planning, working with the ED in a classic board-executive relationship. The council would have influence in decisions focused on day-to-day operations with the concurrence of the operations and executive directors; the board would have governance decision-making authority.

"YOU CAN START THE PROCESS"— RESOURCES TO HELP YOU

As Yellow Brick Road Consulting, I use the metaphor of Dorothy's helping her fellow travelers to realize they have inner strengths they thought had to come from the outside. My best suggestion is to begin a development assessment yourself. This chapter has included a number of good questions to address to start you on your way.

There are many resources for you to figure out what to include in your assessment. There is no "one size fits all." The size and scope of your organization and development effort, the amount of time and money you can dedicate to the process—any number of factors can lead you in one direction or another. I suggest you start where you are. Figure out what you know and what you don't know, then focus a consultant's services to supplement your expertise.

Explore a number of Internet Web sites for tool kits and surveys. Realizing that Internet sites change over time, I limit my suggestions to a few and give you pathways to more. Searching Web sites requires patience and noodling around among buttons and bullets for services, resources, library, popular topics, articles or publications, and so on.

Let's start with a systematic search for fundraising firms in order to explore their Web sites for free assessments, checklists, and toolboxes. Large fundraising firms that are members of the American Association of Fund Raising Counsel are listed on www.aafrc.org, with links to their Web sites. There's a "smaller firm" version of AAFRC that is the Association of Philanthropic Counsel (APC), www.apcinc.org, with links to member firms (and Web sites) under the "Need a Consultant?" button on their home page. I've found that the Web sites of smaller firms to be more user friendly—they tend to be more generous, offering more free surveys and toolkits than the larger firms that focus more on marketing.

The Association of Fundraising Professionals (AFP) Web site, afpnet.org, lists its members (and Web sites) and has a resource center with an online catalog on lots of fundraising topics. If you are a member of AFP, the service is free; there's a fee for non-members. In searching the catalog for "development assessments," I found Betty Ann Copley Harris's article, "Rx for Healthy Development: the Development Audit and Board Retreat" in the *Association for Healthcare Philanthropy Journal,* spring 1998, a "two-prong approach to give your program the shot of adrenaline it needs." She is an author in this book, and the *AHP Journal* can be found in any hospital development office. The AFP resource center has a library with helpful resource staff who can put together packages of information for you that they have on file, free if you are a member.

The Association for Healthcare Philanthropy Web site has a resource information center with "thousands of publications" on common topics in health care philanthropy. Both the AFP and AHP Web sites focus on member services more than information to the general public, so they may be less helpful to you if you are not a member.

Let's start where *we* are and look at the Web sites of several authors in this book. Simone Joyaux's Web site, www.simonejoyaux.com, has buttons across the top of her home page; the "Resources" button takes you to her "Free Library" page with a list for Fund Development, Board Development, and Miscellaneous. There is a wealth of resources here, including materials developed from her presentations at conferences. "Fund Development" leads you to an extensive list of documents and checklists, one of which is a "Sample Development Audit." This listing opens directly to "Sample Questions for a Development Audit," a self-scoring survey of over 80 questions that embraces best practices and covers the organization's purpose, planning, leadership, by-laws, marketing and communications, a culture of philanthropy, and so on, and a more specific focus on development roles and responsibilities, operations and practices, and development planning. This checklist is also published in her book, *Strategic Fund Development, Building Profitable Relationships That Last,* 2nd ed. (Gaithersburg, Md.: Aspen, 2001). Explore the remaining resources—she is extraordinarily generous. Keep in mind that she updates her Web site regularly, and buttons and labels may be rearranged over time.

Lynda Lysakowski's Capital Venture Web site home page, www.cvfundraising.com, has a "Popular Topics" button for various topics that you can download to your desktop.

One of the "Popular Topics" is "Mini Evaluation Document," which downloads as "AuditFrmEvl.doc" and opens as "Evaluating Your Development Program." This self-scoring survey of over 60 questions takes you through organizational vision, board leadership, staff skills and expertise, policies and procedures, information management, donor stewardship, and so on, and your self-score indicates that your program may be excellent, may need improvement, or you might consider a total restructure—all in the privacy of your office.

As well as being an independent consultant, I am a senior associate with Demont and Associates and work with wonderful colleagues on specific projects. Our Web site, www.demontassociates.com, has a button on the home page for a quick survey, "Are You Ready to launch a campaign?" that helps you assess 12 broad areas critical for campaign success; the development operation sections lead you through best practices. The Demont home page has a top row of buttons, one of which is "Fund-Raising Tools," which leads you to a "Basic Infrastructure Checklist" that covers organizational and development questions. Another button, "What is your fund-raising IQ?" offers you over 35 questions that help you develop a broad understanding of fundraising with facts and statistics to sharpen your knowledge of philanthropy.

There are more Internet resources than you have time for, so find a survey or checklist that outlines questions you want to ask. Use it to reaffirm what you know and to reaffirm what you want to know—to sort out what's working well and what can be strengthened. Remember that each Web site is subject to change—what's available at the time of this writing may be changed or replaced in several years. More firms may offer similar user-friendly checklists. These suggestions give you search techniques to get to useful sites.

Likewise, there are more published sources than you have time for, so I refer you to one excellent source: Andrea Kihlstedt's *Capital Campaigns Strategies that Work,* 2nd ed. (Sudbury, N.M.: Jones and Bartlett, 2005). This book focuses on capital campaigns, so the donor and organizational checklists aim toward the infrastructure needed for successful campaigns. The section "Development Office Readiness" is an excellent checklist to assess the strengths and weaknesses of your program, whether or not you're getting ready for a campaign (see Exhibit 4.1).

The companion section, "Preparing the Development Office," provides a checklist for you to develop written procedures in gift processing, gift acknowledgment, gift accounting, donor information and tracking, volunteer information, and computer and information technology.

"WHAT'S IN IT FOR ME? SO WHAT?"

Never a prophet in your own land, you can use a development assessment to strengthen and affirm your development planning, especially if you've prepared well and are ready with a focused approach to what you need from a consultant. An assessment can help the chief executive to hire a first-time, full-time development professional, enhance

---

EXHIBIT 4.1   DEVELOPMENT READINESS CHECKLIST

Administration	Volunteers
Development Program	Donor Relations
Staffing and Leadership	Culture
Prospect Research	Annual Giving
Information Systems	Major Giving
Gift Accounting, Acknowledgement	Corporate, Foundation Relations
Communications, Public Relations	Endowment and Planned Giving

---

software for better database management, build the board's fundraising skills—everything in the broad array of topics we've already covered in this chapter. As a consultant, I know that I've provided extraordinary service when, years later, I hear from an executive director or development officer that they still refer to their development assessment that had long-term, philosophical, and practical recommendations. A frequent recommendation focuses on building a culture of philanthropy in the organization—helping the staff, board, and volunteers transform themselves from a position of "Do I have to ask for money? It feels like I have to hold out a tin cup!" to a strength-based culture of philanthropy where "the glass is half-full and we are filling it to overflowing."

An assessment can be well over 30 pages of observations and analysis, dozens of recommendations aimed at every aspect of fundraising, and a suggested timeline of activities. The staff and board will need to determine when they can add specific implementation steps to their schedules and who may be appropriate to coach and train staff and volunteers, and a timeline can keep everyone on track.

Assessments may have two or three years' worth of culture change and initiatives, especially when governance is involved. Sometimes what starts as a development assessment expands into a governance assessment—when a lot of the fact-finding answers slide down the slippery slope of "Who's watching the store?" The depth of study and length of time to implement changes gives you a keener sense of why a precampaign planning study may contain over a year's worth of recommendations to strengthen fundraising. Meanwhile, the information you paid for in the rest of the precampaign planning study becomes out of date

A GOVERNANCE ASSESSMENT?

If you were to draw a Venn diagram of "development" and "governance," you would see the overlap between the two. They have common and independent functions (see Exhibit 4.2).

EXHIBIT 4.2   VENN DIAGRAM OF DEVELOPMENT
AND GOVERNANCE

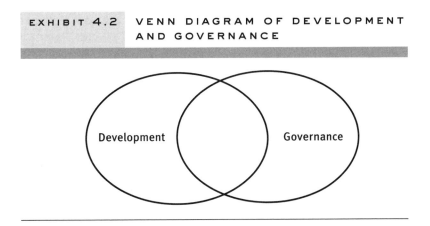

The opening paragraphs of this chapter referred to a consultant's initial fact-finding conversations with an organization. The narrow focus that looks at fundraising can expand to include issues of governance and leadership when people comment on the board's lack of involvement, board members' observations that fundraising is staff work, there is no succession planning, the balance of power between the chief executive and the board seems more like a struggle than a dance, and so on.

Governance seems to be well tuned when an organization is clear about its values, vision, and mission, and can articulate how it changes people's lives (using Peter Drucker's guidelines on mission statements) or how it makes the world a better place (Andrea Kihlstedt's emphasis on why donors give). Its strategic plan contains cost estimates and yearly updates with significant dashboard measurements. Resources are fully supportive of programs and responsive to new opportunities, and 100 percent participation—both giving and getting—is in the board's culture as well as in their job descriptions.

There are Web-based resources for governance just as there are for development. On Simone Joyaux's Web site, www.simonejoyaux.com, the "Resources" button links to her free library, and the Board Development section has surveys, self-assessments, and best practices to assess your board's effectiveness and accountability. Likewise, the www.-demontassociates.com Web site "Fund-Raising Tools" button brings you to a "Basic Infrastructure Checklist" that includes governance and organization-wide areas of planning, financial management, transparency and accountability, evaluation, and the like.

The Corporate Fund, a partner with the New Hampshire Charitable Foundation, has a free board self-assessment at www.thecorporatefund.org, complete with instructions on administering the survey that covers 12 basic areas of board responsibilities and an extensive list of resources. It's an excellent first step for a board that has never conducted a self-assessment, and you can adapt and add questions to address your board's unique needs.

An extensive Web site is www.managementhelp.org, the library page of the Help for Nonprofits Web site of Dr. Carter McNamara, Authenticity Consulting LLC. Click on

"Boards of Directors," then the "Free Complete Toolkit for Boards," and scroll down to "Evaluating the Board." There is a wealth of resources on this Web site: some are more up-to-date than others.

There are more Web sites and publications on development and governance than you can imagine. My goal in this chapter is to give you an overview and next steps in order to highlight development assessments as a right-sized tool for strengthening your fundraising program. One word to the wise: Find a champion among your board, likely the governance committee, to steward the use of any checklist or survey so that the board takes action with the information. It's easy to conduct an annual survey and put it on the shelf and conduct board business as "same old, same old." Develop the political will to make changes.

DEVELOPMENT ASSESSMENT AND/OR PRECAMPAIGN PLANNING STUDY?

As an independent process, a development assessment has one purpose: to strengthen your fundraising program. Its focus is more internal than external, examining the workings of development policies and practices. It addresses issues of volunteer leadership and donor support, and it examines the board's and key stakeholders' relationships with the organization. Overall, its primary focus is the development program.

Questions focus on philosophical as well as operational levels, and implementing the recommendations may take months or years. A development assessment—the Ready! —has a shelf life that is inherently much longer than a precampaign planning study.

A precampaign planning study's primary focus is the organization's preparation for a campaign—the Aim! The study identifies factors leading to campaign success in four key areas:

1. Resources to conduct the campaign
2. Leadership to make it happen
3. A compelling and urgent case
4. Donors and prospects

While the development program is a constant resource central to both types of study, think of a target as one single bull's-eye or as one bull's-eye divided into four (Exhibit 4.3).

While this graphic may appear to be simplistic, it demonstrates the levels of focus of the two different processes. In a development assessment, the focus is wholly on development; in a planning study, development is only one part of the whole. Either kind of study can result in a report of 50 pages or more; the sense of scale and attention to detail are different.

From a practical point of view, folding a development assessment into a precampaign planning study may result in less of a focus on development issues than on the more

EXHIBIT 4.3   DEVELOPMENT BULL'S EYE

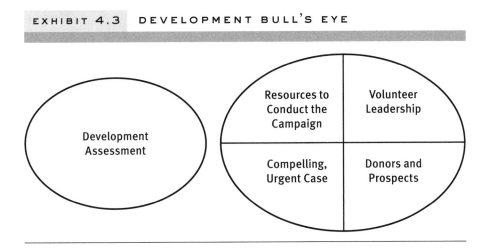

immediate elements of campaign success. Recommendations may draw attention to areas of development operations to be strengthened, possibly with more of an overview and with less practical steps. The real focus and attention of a planning study is campaign success.

A planning study's shelf life is inherently shorter, up to 12 months, even though your campaign may extend for several years. A study contains *the best information at the time*. It's more of a snapshot than a video. A development assessment is focused on the long term and thus not time limited by the focus on campaign preparation.

If you want to blend a strong development assessment into a precampaign planning study, be sure that your RFP clearly outlines a development assessment and a possible expansion into governance issues. Your conversations with consultants will be more responsive to your needs and more productive, and the consultants' proposals will give you more choices about what and how you want to invest in your future. When you are clear about what the focus of each process is and its potential benefits, you demonstrate your expertise—you affirm what you know—and acknowledge what answers you seek with your consultant. Before you contract with a consultant for a precampaign planning study, ask for honest advice about your readiness and ask to see reports from previous clients who also asked for significant attention to development issues so that you can appreciate the consultant's attention to development in both processes.

"WHEW, THAT'S A LOT TO THINK ABOUT"

Yes, and you'll be the better off for asking good questions and having good choices to make. Often, a development assessment results from an initial conversation that starts with, "We're thinking about a campaign in the next few months. . . ." Fact-finding leads to more specific development and possibly governance issues, and a consultant on the outside, looking in, can see the forest for the trees. Sometimes the best advice can be to just slow down and do it right.

These two, simple questions are my litmus-test questions to help you broaden your vision to sharpen your focus:

1. Can you readily describe the one to three most important needs that your organization agrees are the top priorities from your strategic plan? Answering "yes" to this question implies that your organization has gone through a priority-setting process, that everyone is on the same page, and that everyone can articulate how these priorities will make the world a better place.

2. Can you readily identify your top 30+ donors, with complete, lifetime giving records; individuals, families, foundations, and/or business owners who regularly receive top-level stewardship? Do they have the interest, wealth, and generosity to give 60 percent of the financial goal for your top priorities? Answering "yes" to these questions implies that you have good information in your database, efficient software to utilize the information, a personalized stewardship program that connects you with your top donors, and that your top donors are on the same page as your organization's leadership and readily support your outcomes.

If you can answer both of these broad questions in the affirmative, you may be as ready as you need to be to contract for a precampaign planning study. If you fudge a bit on either, I suggest you consider a development assessment first, and start with an online or print resource to help you ask the tough questions.

In 2002, the Bush Foundation in St. Paul, Minnesota, commissioned a study of the impacts of capital campaigns on their human services grantee organizations. *Building Stronger Organizations* is a publication available through www.bushfoundation.org. Many of the campaigns involved buildings and facilities, and when problems occurred, the second most frequently reported problem was fundraising, after construction problems. From a perspective of seeing the forest for the trees, obstacles to success included lack of rigorous planning, overly ambitious plans, failure to consider the long-term impact of a facility, ignoring feasibility studies, and lack of input from staff, board, clients, and community members. Those obstacles span the gamut of project management, budget forecasting, development effectiveness, organizational planning, and governance issues.

Again, the purpose of this chapter is to highlight the value and use of a development assessment while the rest of the book gives you a full picture of precampaign planning. You can appreciate that a development assessment and a precampaign planning study are different tools to answer different questions in an organization's life cycle and fundraising maturity. The more you know, the better you can negotiate for what you need. The right tool for the right job may mean that you focus on strengthening your development program *before* you pay for an expensive planning study.

CHAPTER 5

Ensuring Successful Outcomes— Assignment of the Tasks

LINDA LYSAKOWSKI, ACFRE

So far, this book has discussed the why, when, and how of a feasibility/planning study, but who conducts the study? Who should be involved, who should be interviewed?

Occasionally, an organization will attempt to conduct its own study, which is not recommended. It is rather like an organization trying to do its own financial audit or an employee doing his or her own performance evaluation. Obtaining objective input is critical. For this reason, it is recommended that outside counsel be engaged to conduct the study. However, there are various people within the staff and volunteers of the organization that must be involved in one way or another. This chapter discusses the role of the consultant and the role of the staff and volunteers of the organization.

THE CONSULTANT

Choosing a consultant to do the feasibility/planning study is an important step. There will be discussion in a later chapter about working with consultants, but the selection process for finding the right consultant is such a critical step that it bears mention now. It is important that there is a feeling of comfort and trust between the organization's leadership and the consultant. The consultant selected should be one with experience in conducting studies and one who has a good knowledge of accepted campaign principles and study processes. While it is not critical that the consultant has experience with organizations just like the one engaging him or her for the study, it is important that the consultant be willing to become immersed in the organization and that he or she understands and supports its mission. Once the steering committee or the board has selected the right consultant, what should the organization expect from the consultant?

In most cases, the consultant will do an internal assessment before assessing the public's willingness to support the campaign. If a full-blown audit has not already been done, the organization should work with the consultant to examine its internal readiness for a campaign. Some of the things consultants typically evaluate are:

- Staffing of the development office.
- The board's history of support and strength of the board.
- Technology for the development office, especially donor software systems.
- Annual fund history.
- Communications with donors and prospective donors, such as Web site, brochures, and the annual report.
- The reasonability of the organization's plans and expectations of the campaign.
- The chief executive officer's (CEO's) willingness to devote his or her time to the campaign.
- The financial stability of the organization.

In addition to the internal assessment, the consultant is usually responsible for developing a preliminary case for support for the campaign. It is important to have the plans as final as possible and to provide the consultant with all the necessary information he or she will need to prepare the case—for example, architectural plans; specifications of the land and the current facilities; the mission, history, and vision; a complete list of the board of directors and key staff people; and details of programs that will be provided in the new facility. In the case of an endowment campaign, the facility information is not relevant, but there should be a well-thought-out plan for spending the endowment income, and the consultant will need this information to incorporate into the case. In cases where the organization has already written a case for support, the consultant's role may be to review and edit the case's statement, to suggest possible changes or additions to the case, and to recommend how to present the case.

The consultant should also assist the organization in developing a list of people to be interviewed. At the very least, the consultant should supply a list of general areas of people suggested to be interviewed. If the consultant is local, he or she may also have suggestions for individuals or companies to be interviewed based on his or her knowledge of the community. The consultant also guides the discussion of selecting the final list of prospective interviewees and ranking those that definitely should be interviewed, should be interviewed, and could be interviewed, usually using an A, B, or C ranking. The consultant prepares letters of introduction, which the organization usually mails to prospective interviewees on the organization's letterhead. Often, consultants also provide confirmation letters to send out after the person agrees to an interview and thank-you letters to be sent to interviewees after the interview. Many consultants prepare a viewbook or a summary of the preliminary case statement, which they use when conducting interviews. The consultant also prepares a list of questions that will be asked during the interviews and reviews these questions with the steering committee (whose role will be discussed later in this chapter).

Consultants prefer scheduling interviews differently, but the organization needs to understand up front whose responsibility this will be. Many consultants prefer that someone within the organization schedule the interviews for several reasons—prospective interviewees are likely to be more familiar with the organization than they are the consultant and will respond better to a call from the organization. Also, if the consultant is not local, he or she may not be familiar with the geographic area, which may make it difficult to judge timing between interviews. However, some consultants prefer to schedule their own interviews. Who is responsible for scheduling interviews should be outlined in the contract with the consultant. If the organization is scheduling the interviews, the consultant provides his or her available dates and times with which the interview scheduler will work.

Once interviews are scheduled, a confirmation letter and the preliminary case for support are mailed to interviewees so they can review this information before the consultant arrives. The consultant should always conduct the interviews one on one, and staff people do not accompany the consultant on interviews. This is critical to getting needed information from the interviewee, and the interviewee must feel certain that the information he or she shares will be held in the strictest confidence. In addition to the confidentiality issue, consultants are better prepared to conduct interviews because they are experienced in the interview process and know not only what questions to ask and how to ask them, but also how to interpret answers. Some firms provide two or more consultants to conduct interviews; others may have all the interviews done by one consultant. Both of these options are acceptable, but the organization should meet with all the consultants who will be involved to assure that they are comfortable with these persons presenting their case to interviewees and that each interviewer is well versed in the organization and its case.

The consultant is responsible for producing a written report for the board of directors and the executive leadership of the organization. The format of the report, the method of presentation of the report and the number of copies of the report should be spelled out in the contract with the consultant so there are no misunderstandings about what to expect.

THE STEERING COMMITTEE

The steering committee generally consists of a small, select group of people and it is usually this committee that determines a study is needed. This group often plays a key role in selecting the consultant who will do the study. The steering committee usually includes the chief executive officer of the organization, the chief development officer, and the facilities director if there is one in the organization, the chief financial officer, the chair of the board and/or the chair of the development committee, and one or two key volunteers. If there is already someone in place who will be serving as chair of the capital campaign, this person or persons should be included on the steering committee. This committee's work begins early on in the process, and generally the steering committee remains active throughout the study process and the entire campaign.

The steering committee has several key roles:

- Guiding the building project itself (if this campaign will be for bricks and mortar).
- Determining if a development audit is required.
- Selecting counsel for the feasibility/planning study.
- Working with counsel and staff to approve the preliminary case for support.
- Developing a list of potential interviewees.
- Planning the presentation of the study report to the board.
- Encouraging the board's full participation in the campaign.
- Working with counsel and staff to plan the early stages of the campaign and selecting the campaign cabinet.

The act of guiding the building project involves selecting and working with an architect, a project manager, and/or a construction firm. This committee generally selects the companies that will be involved in designing and building the facility, determines the final design, and approves the budget. All of these steps are important to the study process, because it will be vital to have preliminary plans to present to the interviewees as well as accurate project costs. Architectural drawings and plans will help counsel prepare the preliminary case statement that includes named giving opportunities within the facility. If the campaign is for endowment or equipment, there may be no need for a facilities manager, but it is advisable to have a program person on the committee who can help prioritize the needs and determine timelines and budgets for the program or equipment needs.

Because it is critical to assess the organization's internal readiness for a campaign, it is often recommended that a full-blown development audit be conducted before the actual study begins. The steering committee will help decide if a development audit should be completed. Many organizations find an audit useful if they have recently had staff turnover, if they are concerned about their board's ability to run a campaign, if they have not had a strong annual fundraising program, or if they are involved in a strategic planning process. The steering committee may decide to do the audit first and then wait for these results before authorizing a feasibility/planning study. If a full-blown development audit is not done, the steering committee will want to ensure that counsel does an internal assessment as part of the feasibility/planning study.

This committee is usually the group who authorizes the study or presents the idea to the full board for approval. Once a study has been approved, the next step is selecting a consultant. Some organizations may opt for issuing a request for proposals (RFP) and then narrow the field of consulting firms down to a few who will be personally interviewed. The steering committee should be aware, however, that many consultants do not respond to RFPs. Often, the steering committee will talk with other nonprofits that have done studies and/or campaigns and get recommendations from them for consultants they wish to interview. The steering committee will generally contact these firms individually and determine if there is a good fit between the consultant and the organization and, if so, invite the consultant to present a proposal. Most organizations prefer to see the written proposals first and then invite two to four firms to make a formal presentation. Others may wish to interview all the firms first and then invite the ones they feel have the strongest presentation to submit a written proposal. In some cases, the organization may have prior experience or a personal relationship with a consulting firm and will base their decision to engage this firm on that experience or relationship, without contacting other consultants. The steering committee should be open with the firms and advise them of the process they will be using and should provide competing firms with the same information about the organization and the campaign in order to assure that all the consultants are all on equal footing.

Once the consulting firm has been selected, the steering committee will work with the consultant to develop the preliminary case statement and conduct the internal assessment, if a full-blown development audit has not already been done. The role of the steering committee in this process is generally to provide the consultant with the information they need to conduct the assessment and prepare the case and to approve the final case statement.

Another critical role of the steering committee is to select the people who will be interviewed. The committee will meet with the consultants and review the list of those to be interviewed, which has been developed by the organization, with input from the consultant, ranking them in order of importance. The steering committee should also provide the consultant with as much background about the potential interviewees as possible. Once the interviews are started, the role of the steering committee is minimal until after the report has been presented. Occasionally, steering committee members may be called upon to help obtain an interview.

The steering committee is usually the first group to see the report and will review a rough draft for accuracy of the information being presented (i.e. spelling of names of interviewees or people mentioned by the interviewees as possible donors or volunteers). This group will also determine the format of the presentation to the full board (i.e., will it be the full report or just an executive summary?). Many boards do not want all the detail that is in the full report, but just want to see an abbreviated version, most particularly the consultant's recommendations. Often, a PowerPoint presentation summarizing the findings will be presented to the full board.

The steering committee should act as a liaison to the board; therefore, it is critical to have at least one board member serve on the steering committee. Having a peer introduce the consultant who will present the report and encouraging the board's full participation in the campaign on various levels—emotional, physical, financial, spiritual—will assure their involvement. Once the board has had the report presented and votes to proceed with a campaign, the steering committee should plan to keep them abreast of the plans for the campaign and recruit their involvement on the campaign cabinet where appropriate.

The steering committee will work with the consultant to develop a realistic timeline, establish a final goal, and recruit the campaign cabinet. Their input will be valuable as they are also working with the architect and/or project manager and will be up to date on any changes that could affect the campaign. They will also be the most likely persons to have the ability to recruit top-notch campaign volunteers.

CHIEF DEVELOPMENT OFFICER

The role of the development staff in the study is very important. Organizations that do not have development staff should not panic at the thought of a study; however, it is important to secure or reassign a staff person to fill this role at least for the duration of the study. After the study is completed, the organization may wish to consider engaging a temporary or permanent development director to manage the campaign.

While the development officer's role is important, at times during the study his or her role is minimal. The development officer's role is heaviest at the beginning of the study. She or he may write the case statement for review and editing by the consultant. Usually, this is the situation in a larger, more mature development office. In other instances, the consultant does the actual writing of the case, but the chief development officer must supply the consultant with all the information he or she needs to write the case. Typically, the kind of information that the development staff person should prepare for the consultant includes:

- Mission statement of the organization.
- Vision statement, if there is one.
- A summary of the organization's programs and services.
- Financial information about the project to be funded by the proposed campaign.
- Building plans and sketches, if this is a bricks-and-mortar campaign.
- A list of key staff people.
- A list of the board of directors or other governing body.
- Information about the organization such as brochures, annual reports, newsletters, and the like.

It is important for whoever writes the preliminary case statement to have full access to the information needed, and for all parties to be open about the issues that may detract from a compelling case statement. Often, organizations are better served when an outside person writes the case statement, so they can benefit from the objective viewpoint, but the development officer can shed light on the organizational personality, which is helpful in presenting its case.

Another key role of the chief development officer is to serve on the steering committee and to work with this committee and the consultant to develop the list of potential interviewees. The development officer should review the list of current donors and prospects and provide giving history to the consultant or consultants who will be conducting the interviews.

The development officer also must provide the consultant with all the information needed for the internal assessment and should plan to meet one or more times with the consultant to answer questions he or she may have about the information obtained in the assessment.

Another role that sometimes falls to the chief development officer is assisting to set up interviews for the consultant. While some consultants prefer to schedule their own interviews, most ask the organization to do this for several reasons:

- In most cases, the interviewees know the organization and respond better to a call from them than to one from a consultant whom they probably do not know.

- If the consultant is not local, he or she may not know the area, and driving distances may be difficult to estimate, so a local contact person is better equipped to plan the details of the scheduled interviews.

- The development staff generally knows its major donors well and can schedule extra time for those interviewees they think may be more talkative, or arrange a convenient location such as a restaurant for someone they know will respond better to the suggestion of meeting over coffee, and so on.

The role of scheduling is often assigned to an administrative person, but sometimes the chief development officer steps in to get interviews where perhaps someone else has failed. The chief development officer should maintain close contact with the consultant and the scheduler during the interview process to see if there are any problems in scheduling interviews, and whether there are additional names to be added to the interview list. Consultants often find that as they are doing interviews, some names will surface that had not been on the original list, and the consultant will ask the organization to send out additional letters to these new prospective interviewees. It is important that the development officer stay on top of the progress of the interviews, although it is equally important that they not ask the consultant to divulge any confidential information he or she has received during the interview process. If there are problems scheduling interviews, it is usually an indication that the organization may have a public relations problem or that perhaps the original interview list was flawed and there may be a need to bring the steering committee together again and rework the list.

Once the interviews are completed, the chief development officer and the rest of the steering committee will generally meet with the consultant to review a draft of the report. Scheduling meetings for the initial review and the board presentation is usually a task for the chief development officer, along with assuring that the consultant has everything he or she needs for this presentation, such as audiovisual equipment and the like.

Chief Executive Officer

The CEO of the organization also has an important role to play in this process. As part of the steering committee, he or she will be involved from the beginning in the selection of the consultants, decisions about the project that will impact the case statement, selecting interviewees, and participating in the internal assessment.

The CEO must be an effective leader in order for the organization to portray a credible image in the community. The CEO should be a visible and visionary person, whose leadership is recognized by the community, enabling the organization to be granted interviews with key people in the community. Even if the CEO is fairly new in the organization, he or she should bring a reputation for excellence that will enhance the organization's image. He or she should also have a good working relationship with the board of directors and with the staff, particularly the development officer. A mutual trust relationship between staff and board will be critical to the success of the campaign study.

These qualities will generally be apparent to the consultant during the internal assessment process and the consultant will want to have the CEO complete some form of self-assessment. The consultant will need to meet with the CEO one on one in order to determine the quality of leadership the CEO provides for the organization and his or her commitment to the project. The CEO may also be asked to facilitate interviews with other key staff people, such as the chief financial officer (CFO), facilities director, program directors, and so on. He or she may also be called upon to facilitate meetings with board members or key volunteers, depending on the relationship of these persons to the organization and the staff.

In addition to the CEO's role in the internal assessment part of the study, he or she should also be highly involved in the process to select prospective interviewees. Often, the CEO has a close relationship with major donors or potential major donors to the campaign and may be instrumental in securing interviews for the consultant. Generally, the CEO or the board chair is the person who signs the initial letters requesting an interview. Although often the consultant drafts this letter, the CEO may want to add her or his personal touch to the letter.

As with the chief development officer, the CEO should maintain a close relationship with the consultant during the study and should be made aware of any issues that might affect the outcome of the study, such as problems in obtaining interviews. The CEO is also part of the group to review the draft report from the consultant.

ADMINISTRATIVE SUPPORT STAFF

Administrative support is important during a campaign, but there are key roles for the support staff person during the study process as well. The support staff person should be included in the meetings with the steering committee from the beginning of the process so they understand the importance of each aspect of the tasks they will be asked to perform during the study. This staff person records and distributes the minutes of steering committee meetings, prepares agendas and handouts, and sends out meeting reminders. Once a campaign is started, this person often assumes the title of campaign assistant.

During the study, he or she may be asked to gather information for the internal assessment, for example, sending out questionnaires to board or staff members, gathering information about the organization's donor history, or scheduling meetings with key staff and volunteers. The support staff person also prepares lists of prospective interviewees to be reviewed by the steering committee and so forth. Once the list of prospective interviewees has been finalized, the support staff person is responsible for preparing and mailing letters to these people before they are contacted by phone or e-mail to schedule an interview.

Usually, this person also schedules the interviews. The interviews are a crucial part of the study and an efficient and enthusiastic performance of this role is critical to the study's success. The consultant should provide the support staff person with some important items to ensure that they can complete their tasks on time, such as:

- A schedule of dates when the consultant is available to conduct interviews.

- A proposed "script" for the staff person to use when making his or her calls.

- Texts for the letter to be mailed as appointments are scheduled, confirming the appointment date, time, and location.

- Preliminary case statements to be mailed along with the confirmation letters.

Regarding the letters, the consultant generally prepares a draft letter for approval by the CEO or board chair and provides this letter electronically to the support staff person, who then prints the letters on organization letterhead, obtains the appropriate signature(s), and mails the letters. The consultant may also provide an e-mailable version of the letter and case statement to be sent to interviewees who may schedule appointments without sufficient time to mail these materials.

It is vital to have a person making calls who is able to obtain interviews. The support staff person must have a pleasant phone manner and good computer skills. He or she will also be asked to maintain the master schedule of interviews and keep the consultant up to date on any schedule changes. Most consultants will prefer doing this by e-mail so they can be up to the minute on the schedule. If the consultant is not local, the support staff person should ask for directions and provide the consultant with a map. The staff person may meet with the consultant at the beginning of each trip or each day of interviews to review the schedule and answer questions about driving directions. Often, the support staff provides MapQuest directions for the consultant to facilitate the interview process.

Once the interviews are completed, the support staff may be asked to send a thank-you letter and/or follow-up materials requested by the interviewees. The process of scheduling interviews can be quite demanding, and the support staff should be prepared to spend a large percentage of her or his time on this process for several weeks. Once the interviews are completed, the support staff role is minimal, although he or she may be asked to assist with the distribution of the final reports and make arrangements for meetings at which the report will be presented.

The good news for all the staff members is that their role in the study process is minimal. However, they must all be made aware that, once a campaign is launched, the roles will take a dramatic shift away from being consultant driven, to being staff and board driven, with the consultant in the role of coach and the board and staff that of the players.

THE BOARD

As with the staff, the role of the board during the study is minimal compared to their role in a campaign. Some board members serve on the steering committee and therefore have a greater role than the rest of the board. All of the board members, however, can participate in developing the list of potential interviewees, and some may be called upon to assist in setting up interviews, using their personal contacts with the prospective interviewees to gain an appointment where perhaps the staff person is unable to reach the prospective interviewee.

Some board members may also be involved in the internal assessment, particularly the board chair and the chairs of the development committee, facility committee, and the finance committee. These board members have insights that are helpful to the consultant in evaluating the organization's internal readiness for a campaign. Board members might also participate in helping to develop the case statement, providing input into the need for this project and the costs associated with it.

All board members should participate in the presentation of the report and make every effort to attend the meeting where the report will be presented. The report, as discussed later in this chapter, is a critical rallying point for the staff and board to make decisions about the future of the campaign, so it is vital that board members attend this report meeting, review the report carefully, and ask key questions that will help them better understand the rationale for the consultant's recommendations and the role they are expected to play in the campaign, or in preparing the organization for a campaign.

Once the report has been presented, the board sometimes meets as a group to decide the next steps, or they may base their decision to move forward on the recommendations of the steering committee and the consultant. Whatever method they choose, it is important that all board members understand what is involved in launching a campaign and what is expected from them, financially and in time and talent. The board should adopt a resolution to move forward with a campaign if that is the recommendation they have accepted. It is important to have this vote in writing and to have full approval of the board for going forward with a campaign.

THE INTERVIEWEES

One of the most important groups in the study process is the people who are interviewed. The outcome of the report is based on the quality of the interviews, so it is critical to interview the right categories of people. Typically, people who are interviewed include:

- Key board members
- Key staff members
- Major donors to the institution
- Selected volunteers
- Prospective donors
- Government officials
- Community leaders

Usually, not every board member is interviewed. By the time the organization has reached the study phase, the board should already be "on board" with the campaign. In some cases, where a larger number of people are interviewed, or where board members are all major donors, or when board members may not be as aware of the campaign as they should be, the organization may choose to have all its board members interviewed. However, in every case some key board members will be interviewed, such as the chair of the board, the chair of the facilities committee, the chair of the development committee, and the chair of the finance committee. Often, there are other board members who are major donors to the organization, so they should be interviewed as well as any board members that the organization feels may not yet be fully aware of or supportive of the campaign. It is important to get a cross section of ideas about the potential success of the campaign and not just to interview those who are the eternal optimists, so if there are any naysayers on the board, they should be interviewed to determine the cause of their concern.

In many institutions, key staff members could also be major donors, for example, a university professor, a physician on the staff of a hospital, or an artistic director of a performing arts organization. Even if the organization does not have any potential major donors on its staff, many of the staff members, particularly those directly involved with the program may have insights and connections to major donors, so it is wise to interview selected staff members. Many organizations do not realize the "gold mine" they have within their own organizations, and the study is a good time to draw staff into the development process.

Those who have been major donors to the organization in the past should always be interviewed. The best candidates for a gift to the capital campaign are usually those who already support the organization. The organization should be able to easily prepare a list of the top 10 percent of its donors, keeping in mind that, as a rule, 90 percent of the campaign donations come from 5 to 10 percent of the donors to the campaign. If the organization does not have a software system that can easily track the top 10 percent, some research must be done to determine who these people are. Another group that should not be overlooked is the loyal donors—those who have supported the organization consistently but perhaps do not fall into the top 10 percent. It could be that these folks have never been *asked* for a major gift or that there was never a case exciting enough to motivate them as donors. The development staff should work closely with the consultant to prepare the list of donors who will be interviewed.

Key volunteers of the organization should also be interviewed. Some organizations hesitate to ask their volunteers for monetary contributions, thinking that they are already giving of their time. But, in most cases, if a person is volunteering for the organization, it is because he or she really cares about its mission and is committed to its programs. If this passion is there, the person is likely to also make a donation to the organization when asked. The list of dedicated volunteers should be reviewed, and some volunteers should be included on the interviewee list, particularly if there are those who could be major donors, or who have a lot of community contacts that could lead to a major contribution to the campaign.

Volunteers who have been involved in fundraising activities might be particularly helpful. For example, a volunteer who has worked on a special event or an annual fund drive might have insights into potential donors for the campaign. However, it is not just fundraising volunteers that may be prospective donors or campaign volunteers. For example, a museum may have a major donor prospect in one of its docents; a hospital auxiliary member might be the person who holds the key to a lead campaign gift from the auxiliary itself or one of its members; or a volunteer who cooks for the soup kitchen might have a close relationship with someone who could be a key campaign volunteer.

While most of the people interviewed should already have a relationship with the organization, usually some prospective donors are interviewed as well. The level of involvement with the organization makes it easier to get an interview, and the steering committee should try to first interview those who are most likely to support this campaign. However, many organizations do not have a strong history of fundraising, so there may not be a sufficient number of donors to be interviewed. This makes the interviewee selection process a bit more challenging, but there are usually prospective donors in every community for each organization. The steering committee should carefully review who the best prospective donors would be. They should look first to those who would have a natural affinity with the organization: alumni, current or former recipients of service and their families, vendors, companies located in the community the organization serves, foundations that have an interest in the organization's work.

Government officials are often interviewed during a study, particularly if the organization is hoping to secure funding from governmental sources. The organizations should evaluate those officials who might be most helpful to it in obtaining funding, whether they are at a federal, state/provincial, or local level. While elected officials may not always be helpful in the actual fundraising efforts in a campaign, they can provide the leverage to help obtain government funding from various sources. There are also some appointed officials who may be helpful in securing funding within the departments in which they work. Usually, elected officials also have a good insight into the community and know of companies moving into the area as well as the financial status of companies and individuals within the community, particularly if they are individuals or businesses who may have supported their own election campaigns.

Government officials can also be useful in helping the organization navigate zoning departments, planning commissions, and other political mechanisms the organization may have to deal with as their project moves forward. In many instances, they may also know of land or buildings that are available for purchase, lease, or even donation from various governmental sources, and skilled interviewers often uncover some interesting options for the organization to consider.

Community leaders sometimes comprise a large segment of the interviewees, particularly where the organization does not have a pool of wealthy donors on its board or among its volunteers or donor base. Community leaders might include CEOs of local businesses, executives of the local chambers of commerce or other trade associations, foundation leaders, union leaders, or key people from local service organizations. Like government leaders, input is sought from these people, sometimes not so much because of their personal wealth, but because they have a good feel for the community and will be able to share vital information on the local economy, the local business community, and local volunteers who might serve on a campaign cabinet.

A WORD ABOUT THE REPORT

Once the interviews are completed, the consultant prepares a report for the client. A few words to address this report and the people who are involved in the report process are worth noting.

First, the consultant prepares the report independent of any input from the organization's insiders. It is important to have an objective, impartial view of the organization's internal readiness combined with the community's assessment of the likelihood of a successful campaign. No one within the organization should attempt to influence the outcome of the report one way or another.

However, consultants often prefer to meet with the steering committee, which should include the CEO of the organization, the chief development officer, and the board chair, along with other key leaders of the organization, both staff and volunteer, to review the report before it is presented to the full board. The purposes of this review are to confirm that names are spelled correctly and facts are recorded accurately, and to ensure that key organization leaders are not surprised by the final report. During interviews, the interviewee often provides names of potential donors or volunteers, and sometimes the person providing this information does not have accurate spelling or other information to share. Moreover, in the internal assessment process, it is important to report accurate information about the organization. However, those participating in this review should not expect the consultant to change her or his recommendations because the organization may want things presented in a more favorable light. Basically, the consultant tells the organization, "It is what it is," and a good consultant will hold fast to his or her recommendations even if the organization does not want to hear this news.

Usually, the consultant prepares an executive summary of the report that is generally the version of the report that is shared with those outside the steering committee. Some organizations prefer that their full board see the entire report; others want the board to see the executive summary only. In either case, the consultant should present the report in person to the full board, because this is a perfect time for the consultant to make clear to the board what their responsibility will be going forward, whether the consultant recommends proceeding with a campaign or not.

Many consultants also recommend that the executive summary or some type of summary of the findings be sent to those who took part in interviews as well, since these folks have given of their time and input and are usually eager to hear the results.

Summary

While there are many people involved with the feasibility/planning study, each of these has a different, but critical, role in the process. To sum up these various roles:

- A study should always be done by an outside consultant, not the organization itself.
- The consultant must be prepared to accept the idiosyncrasies of the organization, balancing these with accepted campaign principles.
- The staff of the organization should provide the consultant with as much information as possible about the organization, the project, and the people to be interviewed.
- The board should hear the results of the report from the consultant and be ready to accept the recommendations on the basis of the consultant's knowledge of their organization and of accepted campaign principles.

- The interviewees must be carefully selected and should represent the organization's constituency, with an emphasis on those who would most likely be major donors and/or volunteers in the campaign.
- The organization must provide support staff to assist with the implementation of the study.

CHAPTER 6

Listening to the People — Selection of Interviewees

J.A. Tony Myers, CFRE

INTRODUCTION

It is all about the people!

One of the very first things I learned as a fundraiser was that philanthropic fundraising is all about "people giving to people." How many times have we heard this? Well, when it comes to the fundraising feasibility study, it too is all about the people. It is about getting the right people to talk to the right people for the right reasons at the right time and with the right questions in hand.

We've already talked about who should conduct the study and the interviews in Chapter 3, and it provided some confidence in our ability to move forward on that front.

This chapter is all about choosing the right categories of people to interview, finding the appropriate mix of people in each of those categories, and choosing the right number of people to ensure your fundraising feasibility study provides you with reliable information you can use.

Once the right individuals and the right number have been selected, then the challenge is to ensure that you ask the right questions and then, of course, listen to and hear the responses given. Hearing an interviewee is only the first step in the multifaceted activity of acquiring information that will form the very basis of the study's report.

The interview script is the starting point for the conversation that will take place between the interviewer and the interviewee. The script and script development is discussed in some detail in Chapter 7.

Setting the right environment and establishing an immediate rapport and a high level of trust is essential to meeting the challenge of drawing the best qualitative answers from interviewees. Establishing the right environment and context is essential if the fundraising feasibility study is to realize its goal of giving voice to the constituents.

CHOOSING THE RIGHT CATEGORIES OF PEOPLE: GIVING VOICE TO CONSTITUENTS

Constituent is a great word to use in a fundraising context. Many of us learned the word in school in connection with the political process, and then, as we got older, we may have experienced the meaning of *constituent* as voters engaging in the democratic process. We are constituents because we have a stake in the outcome.

Constituents in a fundraising context are those who contribute their time, talent, and resources to a charity or cause, and in the process, they too gain a stake in the outcome. Constituents are also those people involved with your products or services either directly or indirectly.

In the fundraising feasibility study, your constituents are the people you want to provide you with their views on your agency, its reputation, and the anticipated success of the campaign or fundraising initiative you have in mind.

As much as campaigns and charities differ in size, purpose, and formation from one geographic and political region to another, so too does the list and number of people we decide to interview. However, there is a fairly well established starting point for putting together a list of people to interview for a fundraising feasibility study.

The standard interview list of major prospects, key influencers, potential campaign leaders, and key community contacts include the following categories of individuals (*remember these as the standard categories of interviewees because we'll refer to them later on in the chapter*):

- Board members (chair, leaders, influencers, skeptics).
- Fund development committee and other volunteer members of important committees (fund development committee, finance committee, volunteer committee).
- Campaign cabinet or campaign planning committee (campaign chair, leaders, influencers, powerful, wealthy).
- Chief executive officer (CEO)/executive director and other relevant professional staff members, particularly fund development staff (give insight as to strengths, weaknesses, commitment, expertise, and readiness).
- Major donors to previous related capital and annual giving campaigns (determine appetite for the campaign, link current donors with prospective donors).
- Prospective donors (gauge community receptiveness of case to potential new donors).
- Other potential campaign leaders and influencers (seek input and opinion from others in the community including civic leaders).

- Corporate, foundation, and government executives.
- Other individuals who may provide guidance, support, and connections to the campaign.

If we look at the preceding list more closely, we can see that the list of people we want to interview begins with those most closely associated with our organization and ripples outwardly in a series of concentric circles, not unlike the constituency model identified by Hank Rosso in his classic work *Hank Rosso's Excellence in Fundraising,* 2nd edition (Eugene R. Tempel (ed.), San Francisco: Jossey-Bass, 2003). The total number of interviewees varies depending on the size of the campaign, the history of the charity, and the budget allocated for the fundraising feasibility study. Tony Poderis's book *It's a Great Day to Fund Raise!* (Willoughby Hills, Ohio: FundAmerica Press, 1996) covers a wide spectrum of information on fundraising and feasibility studies. His Web site www.raise-funds.com/library.html contains a "Fund-Raising Forum and Library" in which he suggests it will take six to eight weeks to conduct a fundraising feasibility study and write the report. My rule of thumb is that the study should include interviews with 35 to 45 constituents in order to gather sufficient information on which to base relevant findings. Poderis suggests it usually takes about 25 days to complete the work required. At an estimated cost of $1,000 per day for a consultant, he estimates the cost of a study to be $25,000, plus expenses.

WHOM DO WE CHOOSE? (CONCERNS ABOUT STACKING THE DECK)

Let's assume, for the sake of discussion, that you've hired a consultant to conduct the feasibility study, you've outlined the plans for your feasibility study, you've got things in good order, and now it comes down to decision time. Now you have to select those whom you wish to interview. How are you going to choose? Whom are you going to choose? Who has what responsibility in this selection process?

The starting point, of course, is the standard category list discussed earlier in this chapter. The challenge is not only whom you pick, it also involves ensuring you have a balance. How do you avoid stacking the deck with people who will want to answer your questions in a positive and supportive manner? What you need are people who will give you honest answers and provide you with critical thinking, and in some cases analytical responses. You need a group of people who together can accurately reflect the views of the community. You do not need people who are going to tell you what it is you think you'd like to hear. If that were the case, there would be little sense in conducting the fundraising feasibility study in the first place.

Here is an approach that will allow you to get the best people to interview and at the same time allow you to avoid stacking the deck.

- List those who are "must" interviews. This list will likely include:
  - Your top donors and donor prospects.
  - The most likely campaign volunteer leaders (in the event you have not chosen that leadership yet).
  - The most powerful influencers and members of your nonprofit organization (staff and volunteers).
  - The most powerful influencers in your community, including civic leaders.
  - The most powerful detractors in your community (whether that is inside or outside of your organization).
- Prioritize each of the five lists just mentioned. For each list, put the person you most want to interview at the top of the list, add the name of the next most valuable person second, and keep going until you have the list completed.
- Determine what standard category each of your interviewees fits into.
- Once you have the name of each person you've identified placed in one of the categories outlined above, prioritize the names in each of the categories. If, for example, you've identified eight of your top donors and donor prospects, put that list in order of importance.
- Ensure that there is a balance of interviewees in each category.
- Where there is not a balance, seek further interviews in the standard categories that have not yet been filled.

Exhibit 6.1 may be helpful for drafting the list of interviewees and ranking them in order of importance.

You can take some comfort in the fact that the fundraising feasibility study consultant is responsible for providing you with criteria to keep in mind when selecting interviewees. However, the consultant may not be in a position to tell you whom to interview unless they happen to know your charity and donors unusually well. The decision is ultimately the responsibility of those who best know their organization and their community, and that decision usually lies with the development director, the executive director, and the fundraising committee of the board.

If you follow the process outlined above, a number of things will happen:

- You will get those most important to the success of the study involved.
- You will bring to the study a balanced approach.
- You will include attractors and detractors engaged in the process (best to keep your critics and detractors close to you).
- You will enhance the credibility of the study.
- You will ensure that those who can make a difference are heard.

Just because you identify the right people to interview, you can never take it for granted that they will be heard and understood. "Hearing" is only the first stage of

EXHIBIT 6.1   PROSPECTIVE INTERVIEWEES

Fundraising Feasibility Study

Category	Must	Should	Could
Donors and donor prospects (individual, business, corporate, foundation, and government)			
Potential leaders and key volunteers			
Internal people with influence and affluence (current and former board, staff, and volunteers)			
External people with influence and affluence in the community, including civic leaders			
Detractors and critics			

a five-step process involved in truly listening to what is being said. If you miss a step anywhere along the way, you will miss getting the information you need to complete a comprehensive fundraising feasibility study.

LISTENING DEEPLY

If we do everything else well, including selecting the right people to interview, but then fail to "listen deeply" to what is being said, then our likelihood of success diminishes considerably.

Listening deeply combines a developed skill and a refined process. Let's begin with the process and then talk about the associated skills. The process, according to Alder and Towne, goes something like this:

- *Hearing what is said.* Though this is a physical activity, it should not and cannot be taken for granted. If you do not "hear" your interviewee, the communication fails at the start.
- *Attending to what is said.* This is the psychological process of selection. We select based on our interests, desires, background, and many other factors.
- *Understanding occurs when we are able to make sense of what is being said.* Ensuring that we share the same understanding requires the interviewer to check in with the interviewee often to ensure that messages being sent are the same as those being received. Understanding increases with responsiveness.

- *Responding is an essential component of an interview.* Responding verbally and non-verbally provides clarity, encourages conversation, and builds confidence and trust among conversational participants.

- *Remembering.* If we can't remember what the interviewee has told us, we won't have much upon which to build our report. Recording the interviewees' responses is a critical element of our work. Some research suggests we forget half of what we've heard immediately, and that reduces to about a third within eight hours.

Here are some tips on listening effectively:

- Write it down.
- Clarify ambiguous messages. Don't pretend to understand—be sure you understand.
- Provide constant and consistent feedback by paraphrasing what it is you understand.
- Ask questions, even of the obvious, and always do so by respecting the dignity of the interviewee.

How do you know if the consultant you hire to do the feasibility study is going to engage in deep listening? There is no secret to this answer. It is actually quite simple to determine. All you need to do is to take notice of how they listen to you. You are their customer. If they don't listen to you, question for detail, probe for understanding, paraphrase for clarity, then it is not very likely that they will practice those skills when they meet with the people you've identified as being so critical to your capital campaign success.

ENSURING THOSE WHO CAN MAKE A DIFFERENCE ARE HEARD

If the goal of the fundraising feasibility study is to determine to what extent your campaign may be successful, then you need to talk to those constituents who

- Have time, talent, or treasure to give, or
- Can influence those with time, talent, and treasure to give, or those who
- Know where the time, talent, and treasure are located in the community in which you plan to fundraise.

ACCESS TO WEALTH: HOW MONEY IS CREATED AND DISTRIBUTED IN OUR CULTURE

It seems to me that time spent talking to those constituents who fall outside of the categories identified above is not all that fruitful. Ultimately, if the campaign is intended to raise money and other forms of capital in support of the charity, then time must be spent in finding out where the money and resources are in the community and determining those most likely to give as well as those most likely to influence giving.

As a young man, I worked for a government agency responsible for economic development. It came as a revelation to me that money came from profit, and profit came from investment and risk, and those who led that kind of activity were usually the businesspeople we call *entrepreneurs.*

Though governments can and do participate in the process of generating wealth by providing the right kind of regulatory and economic environment, it is not generally the role of governments to create wealth, but rather to distribute wealth once it is created in an entrepreneurial and business setting. Profits produce taxes, taxes are collected by governments, and thus governments engage in the redistribution of wealth, not necessarily the creation of it.

As a representative of a charity, my role as a stakeholder in a fundraising feasibility study is to determine the sources of wealth in my community who are most interested in investing in my organization. We need to determine who those individual people, organizations, businesses, foundations, and funding agencies are that will believe in us and will help us further the mission and vision of our charity based on our goals, objectives, and priorities as outlined and articulated in our case statement.

MOVERS AND SHAKERS AND THE REPUTATION OF YOUR ORGANIZATION

We call them movers and shakers for a reason! They are the people who, for better or for worse, are involved in your community and who pass judgment on the performance or your organization. The ominous "they" are those who shape the reputation of the work you are doing and how well you are doing it. The potency of opinion shapers in the creation and maintenance of the community's perception of your organization must never be underestimated.

So how are perception and reputation created in the first place? Working with numerous small and large organizations and charities, I have learned that our reputation is based on four primary factors: how we treat others; how well we perform the tasks, duties, and responsibilities associated with our vision and mission; how we deal with problems and challenges we face along the way; and, finally, how we choose to speak about (represent) ourselves and our organization in the community.

Treating our staff and volunteers with respect and dignity and providing them with meaningful opportunities to make a difference allows those working most closely with our clients to contribute to our service in a positive manner. When we treat our staff and volunteers well, they treat our clients well and our reputation is enhanced.

Treating others well isn't enough to enhance our reputation if the quality of our work is poor and if we are doing work that is not consistent with our vision and mission.

Reputation is formed by how you treat others, how you perform your tasks, and also whether you perform the tasks you promised to perform. Doing great work and working on things outside of your vision and mission is not helpful from a reputational or a fundraising perspective.

In a study I conducted with Guy Mallabone in 2000, we interviewed 1,203 donors about motivations and barriers to giving. We were able to determine that the number one reason why donors stop giving is that charities or nonprofit organizations "don't do what they said they were going to do."

Our personal and organizational reputations are profoundly influenced by how we deal with problems and challenges we face in the course of our activities. American industrialist Henry Kaiser once said that "problems are only opportunities in work clothes." At the large, research-intensive university where I used to be director of public affairs, we received complaints from time to time. On most occasions we made an effort to meet personally, face-to-face with the person making the complaint. Every time we did this, we learned more about the person, we learned more about the complaint, we were able to deal with the matter personally, and we were able to defuse the emotion or angst surrounding the situation. By doing so, we found we are able to maintain our reputation individually and at the same time enhance the reputation of the department and the services we provided. Our experience is that the same holds true for charities and nonprofit organizations working in a community as it does for departments in large organizations.

Finally, reputation is established, built, and maintained by what we say about ourselves and as an organization. Attitude is everything. Our feeling of well-being about ourselves and the role we play in our organization as a leader, as an employee, or as a volunteer influences what we say and the tone we bring to conversations and representations.

Marketing and communications departments carry the responsibility of establishing, building, and maintaining reputations while at the same time promoting and assisting in the "selling" of services to the community. Board members, who themselves will either be movers and shakers or have access to opinion makers in the community, have a profound influence on an organization's ability to tell its story in a positive and forthright manner.

There is no substitute for the power of positive thinking. Every positive statement made about an organization has the potential to add to our reputation as a contributor in the community. Every negative statement will more than offset the positive.

Consider the last time you were treated well by an individual or organization. You were happy to share this experience with others and perhaps did so with a few close friends and acquaintances. Now consider the last time you were treated poorly. For whatever reason, it seems to be human nature to place emphasis on the negative. Some have suggested that if we are treated poorly, we're likely to share that information far more often that if we have been treated well.

The more good news we share with others, the more positive stories we tell about the work of our organization, the more opportunities we present for the community to think and speak favorably about us and our organization.

MAKING SURE THAT POTENTIAL AND CURRENT VOLUNTEER LEADERS ARE GIVEN AN INSIDE SEAT

Volunteer leaders are among the rarest kinds of donors because they are hard to find, difficult to recruit, in high demand by other charities, and once they've agreed to join your initiative, they need to be supported and challenged.

The primary role of a volunteer leader is to bring community perspective to the charity and help it set direction with the community perspective in mind. Once direction is set, the role of the volunteer is to help the organization meet its goals and objectives by providing access to resources and volunteer expertise. Expertise in helping solve strategic challenges is among the most valuable contributions volunteer leaders can make.

Active volunteer leaders have a significant role to play in the overall success of the fundraising feasibility study because they bring with them a community perspective and viewpoint, they can serve as valuable interviewees, they can provide access to potential interviewees not currently connected to the organization, and they can offer credibility through their personal reputation and involvement.

Martha Piper, former president of the University of British Columbia and a leader in research and education for almost two decades, has consistently asked volunteers and staff alike for their advice and counsel. This approach to engaging volunteers proved to be incredibly effective. It gave volunteers a sense of value: their opinion was sought after and listened to, and even though it was not always acted upon, it was considered, thereby bringing volunteers closer to the organization. There is power in asking for advice and counsel.

CREATING AN ATMOSPHERE AND AN OPPORTUNITY FOR LEADING CONTRIBUTORS TO HELP IN THE DEVELOPMENT OF POTENTIAL CAMPAIGN MOMENTUM

It begins with the case for support. The case outlines in an urgent and compelling manner the vision, mission, and priorities of the organization, and at the same time identifies the projects and initiatives that fundraising is intended to support. Few other documents influence the outcome of a campaign as much as the case for support. Not only does it provide feasibility study participants with a foundation upon which to offer opinion about a prospective campaign in the feasibility study interview, it also gives the charity or nonprofit organization a clear focus that ties its vision, mission, and priorities with the strategic initiatives included in its fundraising efforts.

Once the case for support is developed, its value continues through every step of the fundraising feasibility study, from identifying potential interviewees to making the phone calls to conducting the interviews and following up with a thank you and an executive summary of the study.

The feasibility interviews can serve as an initial cultivation event in attracting donors, leaders, and volunteers to the fundraising effort. The interviews in fact set the stage, create the environment, and help identify the tone for the entire campaign.

Because the fundraising feasibility study interview is so important to setting the tone for the campaign, the selection of the consultant who will conduct those interviews is no small matter. The selection of consultants for fundraising feasibility studies is discussed in some detail in Chapter 12.

Timing of the fundraising feasibility study will have an influence on setting the tone for the study and the campaign that follows.

Consideration for the interviewees is paramount. Common sense strategies to avoid major holiday seasons and national holidays, busy and stressful times for interviewees will provide a more positive response to requests for interviews and will provide the interviewees with a more favorable environment in which to respond to questions.

FINDING ROOM FOR CRITICS AND GADFLIES

We ignore criticism at our peril. We're not saying that we should act on all the criticism we get. We are saying that we need to hear, listen to, and take into consideration all the criticism that we get. If we ignore the critics of our services and/or reputation, it denies us the opportunity to deal with the criticism and either answer it with informed facts and opinion or act on it as a means of enhancing our services and reputation.

Our critics should be valued and respected. At the same time, they need not be given an undue platform or undue influence in the direction of our organization. They are valuable because they bring a different perspective and sometimes an opposing view that can help us balance the work we do and the case for support we present, and can assist us in preparing for potential opposition from the community before it gathers momentum.

We were involved in a major campaign to raise money for a large public university shortly after the government announced cutbacks in funding. Our critics told us that it was the government's job to fund us. This early warning sign, picked up in feasibility study interviews, allowed us to deal with the criticism very early on in the campaign. As a result, we ensured that all future communication talked about academic competition and about the importance of excellence. The government was required to provide education to a "standard." Our campaign was dedicated to providing educational excellence and moving our university to the next level, allowing us to compete on the international stage. The argument was focused and truthful and resonated with our donors.

It changed the discussion from "Why doesn't the government take on this funding?" to one that emphasized the need for the private and public sectors to work together for the benefit of the university and the city to provide "excellence" in education for our children and future generations.

We ignore critics at our peril!

Again this speaks to the importance of including our critics in the fundraising feasibility study. We need to identify them and actively seek them out as part of the interview process. It provides us with an opportunity to hear, to listen, to respond, and to educate. The strongest converts to a cause are sometimes recruited from the ranks of the most opposed to the cause. Opponents care enough to carry an opinion about your cause or organization. If they care enough about your opinion, they care enough to argue it and learn from the argument.

So invite your critics to participate. Consider their criticism. Respect their feedback. Listen to them. Respond to them with information and perspective, and when appropriate, act on their advice and counsel.

Gadflies

A gadfly is a persistently annoying person. Then why would we want to include them or even consider them for inclusion in a feasibility study?

In communities and organizations, people identified as gadflies, if managed correctly, can provide a communication channel for getting out information. They spread good news and bad news. So the key is to communicate the good news to them, respond to their questions, treat them with respect, and give them an opportunity to work for you rather than against you.

A gadfly differs from a critic in the sense that the gadfly shares good news and bad news.

We are not suggesting that there is a need, a requirement to include gadflies as interviewees in the fundraising feasibility study. We are, however, encouraging you to recognize that there are gadflies in every community, and some are likely associated with your organization. They have a purpose that may have a positive or negative influence on your organization. So consider how you can interact with them and how they might be beneficial to your cause.

You may consider sharing your campaign initiative with them and ask whom they think you might interview to get both favorable and opposing views on the organization and its case for support. You may wish to ask them to keep an "ear to the ground" and let you know if they hear anything in the community.

In short, make them your friend, and keep them close to you and your organization . . . but not too close.

FITTING THE DESIGN OF THE STUDY TO THE ETHOS AND CULTURE OF THE ORGANIZATION!

Have you ever sat down at your computer, put the name of two different organizations at the top of an empty page and then jotted down under the name of each the characteristics of the organization. Let's try it and see what it looks like (see Exhibit 6.2).

It is obvious that the two organizations, both of which rely heavily on the community for support of their activities, are very different. They are different in size, in structure, in approach, and in the services they provide. One, a large and complex organization dedicated to the academic pursuit consistent with its vision and mission, is much different from the other, which is committed to providing friendly, compassionate, and timely services to families who, because of their situation, are often under significant emotional and financial stress.

There are similarities as well. Both organizations have close associations with hospitals and the medical community. Both organizations provide services beneficial to the community. Both organizations rely heavily on community support to fulfill their mandates.

You'll appreciate, in conducting the interviews for the university, that the tone and approach may well be different than interviews involving Ronald McDonald House.

EXHIBIT 6.2   COMPARISON OF ETHOS AND CULTURE OF TWO ORGANIZATIONS

Major Research Intensive University	Home for Sick Children
Primary clients are students who are healthy and want an education.	Primary clients are families with children who are ill.
Primary purpose is teaching, research, and service to community.	Primary purpose is to provide a home away from home for sick kids and their families.
Administrative structure is complex, hierarchical, and multidimensional, supported by a large and well-educated professional staff.	Administrative structure is functional, efficient, and supported by a large and dedicated volunteer base.
Operates on an annual budget approaching $1 billion.	Operates on an annual budget approaching $2 million.
Interaction with its community ranges from the formal and academic to the friendly and familiar.	Interaction with its community is friendly, folksy, and compassionate.
Values individual, learning, discovery, growth, service, and citizenship.	Values family, wellness, community, mutual support, empathy, and consideration.
The case for support is based on the pursuit of excellence, the advancement of the human condition, and service to the community.	The case for support is based on the value of keeping families together in support of children when they are ill by providing housing and programs adjacent to major hospital facilities.
Its public persona is that of a large, complex institution, attentive to needs of community, seeking innovative solutions and strategic partnerships to enhance learning.	Its public image is that of a compassionate, caring organization providing important and valuable services to a segment of the population very much in need.

Because the nature of the organizations is different, so too will be the interviews and the interaction with the interviewees.

It is not unlikely that an interviewee for a Ronald McDonald House campaign may be a donor who found support for his or her family at a time of illness of a child, and who has subsequently lost that child. The sensitivity, consideration, and compassion involved in the interview in this situation are understandably much different than that required for the standard fundraising feasibility study. When done well, it represents the organization as authentic.

Authentic Leadership

In his book *Authentic Leadership: Rediscovering Secrets to Creating Lasting Value* (San Francisco: Jossey-Bass, 2004), Bill George, former chairman and CEO of Medtronic, argues that leaders dedicated to mission-driven goals, rather than financial goals, are those who create lasting value in their organizations. The value, he contends, comes from authentic leaders who foster the five essential dimensions of purpose, values, heart, relationships, and discipline.

In a book with a similar title, *Authentic Leadership: Courage in Action* (San Francisco: Jossey-Bass, 1993), Robert W. Terry shows how a shift in perspective carries enormous consequences for consideration of courage, vision, ethics, and spirituality as they relate to leadership. He argues that the central organizing principle of leadership is authenticity, and he shows how authenticity and action, when joined together, form a solid foundation for effective leadership.

Staying true to our ethics and culture is the foundation on which we build credibility for our organization and the impending campaign as we interact with interviewees. Ensuring that the case for support and the priorities are consistent with the ethos, mission, and vision is the third step. Finally, ensuring internal support before conducting interviews externally will go a long way toward bringing consistency of message to the community and demonstrating how our organization is distinctive.

The Attractiveness of Developing Greater Distinctiveness

One of the greatest challenges our organization faces is positioning itself and its cause in the minds of donors and donor prospects. Positioning itself in a manner that is compelling, urgent, and distinct will attract interest and draw support.

Though the purpose of a fundraising feasibility study is not to market the nonprofit organization, a potential outcome of the study is an improved knowledge, understanding, and appreciation of the charity and its services. Interviewing people of influence and affluence and members of a community who have clout allows the charity to tell its story face to face and one on one. The opportunity the fundraising feasibility study provides to further understanding, develop appreciation for the cause, and further potential support is unique.

When completed, the fundraising feasibility study will demonstrate to what extent a proposed campaign and campaign initiatives are distinctive. Interviewees and community members will let you know what they think. They will tell you to what extent your project is distinct and to what degree it overlaps with other community initiatives. Listening to interviewees views about the distinctive nature of your campaign and its initiatives will go a long way toward helping you position your case for success.

SUMMARY AND CONCLUSIONS

Selecting the right people to interview is among the most critical decisions to be made in the process of conducting a fundraising feasibility study. Get this right and your likelihood of success increases dramatically. It starts with identifying the categories of individuals you want to interview. Once the categories of interviewees have been determined, it is essential to get the right people in each category starting with (1) those who must be interviewed, then (2) those who should be interviewed, followed by (3) those who could be interviewed.

Selecting the right folks to interview is a process. If you follow the process as outlined in this chapter, chances are that you'll get it right.

Selecting the right consultant is equally important to the interview process (see Chapter 5). In conducting the interviews, the consultant's behavior will not only reflect on the charity, but it will also set the initial tone for the campaign. The consultant's ability to hear, listen, record, report, and provide feedback to the interviewee will have a profound influence, not only on getting the campaign off the ground, but more importantly, on providing the information necessary for deciding whether to proceed.

If you have the right people to interview but hire the wrong person to interview them . . . well, you know the rest of the story! The fundraising feasibility study will be only as good as the person you engage to do the interviews and the report of the findings.

The findings will be only as good as the information brought to it. The information brought to the report can be only as good as the information recorded and interpreted by the person doing the study. And the information recorded for interpretation can be only as good as the questions asked of the interviewees. And, finally, the answers to the questions will be only as good as those who are chosen (and agree) to be interviewed.

The selection of the interviewees for the fundraising feasibility study is among the most critical elements to ensuring that the study is on a firm footing and provides the information necessary to make a responsible decision for the benefit of the campaign, the charity, and ultimately the community it serves.

Now the fun begins. You've hired a consultant, you've identified the people you want to interview, and now you're ready to begin the task of setting up and conducting the interviews.

CHAPTER 7

Coming from Donors— Conduct of the Interviews

Betty Ann Copley Harris, FAHP

Introduction

In this chapter, we will explain the detailed process of planning, preparing for, and conducting the feasibility study interviews, sharing the perspective of the organization as well as the prospect. The best feasibility studies are done by consultants taking a donor-centered approach to the process (i.e., if you were the donor, how would you like the process to unfold?).

Capturing the Interest of Donors to Participate in Your Study

Letter of Invitation to Participate

A letter should come from the organization inviting the participation of the preselected study prospects. The letter describes the intent of the organization to plan for a capital campaign and its desire to get the views and opinions of key leaders in the community before embarking on the plans for the campaign. It should have a brief paragraph that describes the project around which the campaign will center. The letter should also introduce the consulting firm that has been retained to conduct the study and the name of the individual with whom they will be asked to meet. It should state that a representative from the organization will be calling to schedule an appointment for the prospect to meet with the consultant, and a time frame for the meeting should be given (e.g., within the next two weeks). A sentence in the letter should confirm that the purpose of the meeting is not to solicit their support of the project, but rather to elicit their *confidential* views and opinions about the organization and the project to provide help in their planning. Finally, the letter should be signed by a person of considerable influence within the organization, preferably the president and/or the chairman of the board.

Scheduling the Interviews

To facilitate the process of scheduling the one-hour appointments with the busiest, most influential people in your community, it is advisable to have your consultant provide you with a scheduling grid confirming the dates and times that he or she is available to meet with your donor prospects.

With the scheduling grid in hand, the most important factor in assuring your success in getting a "yes" when you ask for the appointment, is to have the right person make the call requesting the appointment. It might be the president of your organization, or a board member who personally knows the individual. Don't presume that it is a call that can be made by the secretary. These phone calls are important opportunities to catch up with the prospect to learn about news in their lives and an opportunity to share news about your organization. It should be treated as a prospect cultivation call, with notes carefully taken as to key messages shared and uncovered during the course of the conversation.

Many influential donors receive calls to participate in feasibility studies more than they would care to recall, so you cannot assume that they are eagerly awaiting your opportunity. If the individuals you are going to call do not already have a relationship with your organization, they may not want to participate because they are smart enough to know that the feasibility study interview will eventually lead to a solicitation for their campaign.

You need to ask for their participation because of its importance to the outcome of your planning. Let them know how much you value what they have to say about your organization. You might also let them know that you are impressed with the consultant who has been hired to help your organization in planning for the campaign and that you can assure them it will be time well spent on their part.

When requesting a date and time, offer two suggestions for them to pick from. Then you should ask whether they would prefer the meeting to take place at their home or office. If there is a spouse involved in the charitable decision-making process, you are well advised to recommend that both parties participate in the interview. If they indicate that they are not going to be in town during that time, ask them to give you a date when it would work best for them.

Anticipating Questions and Objections from Invitees

Before launching the call to your prospective study participants, you should anticipate some of the many questions they may ask about the process. You should also be prepared to hear some people being somewhat critical or sharing their concerns about your organization. Your goal is to make the prospective interviewee feel comfortable with the study process.

Preparing for the Interview

Three days before the scheduled appointment, a confirmation phone call should be made by the organization restating the appointment time, date, location, and the name of the consultant who will be coming to visit. This is also a good time to offer a gentle reminder to the study participant to read the case statement materials sent in advance of the meeting. If you must leave a message, be sure to provide a phone number for the individual to call and reconfirm. This confirmation phone call provides yet another opportunity to thank the individual for participating and for their help in this important project.

Prior to going to the study interview, your consultant should have had ample time to review the research materials provided by your organization about this prospect. A good feasibility study interview requires that your consultant know as much as possible about the individuals with whom he or she is meeting. I like to take the process of learning about the individual a few steps further by doing my own version of Internet research a few days before the meeting. Important discoveries come about when you learn all there is to know about a potential study participant. These discoveries help the consultant shape the line of questioning and direct thoughtful opening conversations that put the prospect and the consultant at ease with one another.

Conducting the Interview

A wide variety of interviewing styles is utilized by the fundraising professionals who conduct feasibility study interviews. Remember, you have already done your homework by screening and selecting just the right consultant to meet with your most important donors. You chose them based on their personality style, their appearance, and their successful track record working with other nonprofits. You will need to trust their instincts for how the interview should go, based on their years of experience.

First, you must expect the consultant to arrive on time for the scheduled appointment. Since most of the interviews take place in donors' homes, there are always risks to being punctual, including traffic delays and difficulty with directions. Make sure your consultant has telephone numbers to be able to reach each interviewee in the event there is a mishap along with way. With today's global positioning system technology, the consultant whose car has onboard navigation is more likely to be on time and never get lost!

Second, you should expect that your consultant knows as much or more than you do about your interviewees. Assuming you have already provided the consultant with a donor profile worksheet and knowing they have most likely done further research on the individuals they are meeting with, the consultant should already have a strategy in mind for opening conversation points and appropriate donor-centered questions that will leave the interviewee with a comfortable sense that the consultant is well prepared for the meeting.

Third, you should have already reviewed and approved the study questionnaire that will be used by the consultant to shape the line of questions asked during the interview. There is nothing worse than a consultant who asks the questions robotically without regard for messages and clues they have picked up during the course of conversation with the interviewee. Your prospect should enjoy *conversing* with the consultant rather than feeling like he or she is being *questioned*.

In the opening comments of the interview, the consultant should provide an introduction to the meeting by introducing him/herself and the firm they represent. It is also a good time for the consultant to offer a reminder of the purpose of the feasibility study and why the organization has retained him or her to complete this important project on their behalf. The consultant should also take this opportunity to remind the interviewee that the conversation is confidential and that comments heard during the study interview will be referenced in the report but without attribution to the source of the comments made. The consultant might share the names of other individuals who are being interviewed, and he or she should also tell the interviewee that a summary report of the study outcome will be provided to them upon completion of the project.

Many times, issues are uncovered by the consultant based on criticism or negative experiences the interviewee may have had with the organization. It is helpful for the consultant to suggest to the interviewee that he or she would like to bring the matter to the attention of the organization's chief executive officer or executive director so appropriate corrections or actions can be undertaken. Because the consultant has just assured the interviewee that the meeting is confidential, it is important to confirm that the interviewee wishes to have his or her comments remain anonymous. The point is, when there is an objection or concern uncovered, it is beneficial to bring the matter to the organization's attention.

The consultant must uphold the promise kept in the letter of invitation to participate in the study by not breaching the agreement that "this is not a solicitation." There are effective ways to ask a study participant about their likelihood of giving without soliciting them. This is an area that you will want to probe when considering the selection of fundraising counsel. A good question to ask your prospective consulting firm is, "How do you find out how much a person will give to a campaign without soliciting them in the feasibility study interview?" The answers provided by your consultant should serve as a great indicator of how effective they are likely to be having thoughtful conversation with your top prospects.

The style and approach used by your consultant in the course of conducting the interview is where your feasibility study's success is determined. Ideally, you want each and every individual who meets with your consultant to be impressed, to feel that the hour they have just devoted to talking about your organization was time well spent. Ultimately, you want your feasibility study participants to:

- Know more about your organization after the meeting than they did before.
- Tell you where your organization fits on their list of philanthropic interests.

- Offer important clues as to what it would take to elevate the position of your organization among their top three charitable interests.
- Have heightened interest in the work of your organization.
- Offer constructive advice about the case for support and how it can be improved.
- Be eager to become more involved and possibly serve as a campaign volunteer.
- Offer the names of other philanthropists who might be willing to support your campaign.
- Be willing to attend information sessions offered in the months ahead.
- Offer to host a cultivation reception in their home to introduce your organization to their circle of friends.
- Anticipate making a generous gift to your campaign.

You should be counting on your consultant to come away from each interview with solid recommendations for how you can better engage and develop the interest and likelihood of generous support from each prospect. While you cannot expect that every interview will yield a generous donation to your campaign, the feasibility study interview is the most significant opportunity you will ever have to shape the cultivation and solicitation strategy for each potential campaign prospect. Without breaching the confidentiality agreement, the consultant can offer you important insights about strategic steps you can take to build a stronger relationship with each study participant—now or at some future date.

CHAPTER 8

Telling Our Story—Use of the Case for Giving

WILLIAM L. CARLTON, ACFRE

THE STATEMENT OF NEED

The preliminary case for support that is used in the fundraising planning study process is called the statement of need. The statement of need is a written document usually no more than three or four pages in length, often accompanied by attached exhibits, including a listing of the client's board of trustees or directors, a single page that metricly outlines the parameters and financial requirements of the proposed project, and perhaps, if available, an architect's site plan or preliminary elevated drawing to give the interviewee a sense of what the facility might look like after it is constructed, if that is appropriate.

The document is created by the institution, often with guidance from and in collaboration with fundraising counsel. The statement of need is a precursor to the more fully developed case for support document, which is usually drafted after the fundraising planning study and before a major capital/endowment campaign begins. The statement of need is sometimes called a case for giving, as distinguished from the case statement or case for support document.

OUTGROWTH OF STRATEGIC PLAN

The statement of need document is ideally an outgrowth of an organization's long-range strategic plan. It not only articulates the institution's mission, but also describes the strategic direction of the organization and, most importantly, why the proposed project must be successfully completed now and, accordingly, what special benefits will be derived from the completion of the project for the community or for the constituency that the organization addresses. Therefore, the statement of need focuses on the resulting bene-fits for the community, the constituency, and less so on the institution itself. The state-ment of need focuses on the difference the proposed project will make on the life and welfare of the community and the constituency served.

Therefore, the statement of need must convey a thoroughness of planning, a sound logic, and an urgency sufficient to demand the attention of those best able to lead and provide major-gift resources to make a campaign viable. At the same time, the descrip-tion of the project must generate enthusiasm, excitement, and anticipation to a broader audience.

The statement of need in the fundraising study process is a "talk piece" used by the interviewer to set the agenda and tone of the interview and seeks to elicit candid reactions regarding the quality, priority, attractiveness, and logic of the fundraising plan. The statement of need is often sent to the interviewee before the interview session so he or she might become familiar with the document before the interview begins.

Certainly, there is no guarantee that those who receive such information ahead of time will indeed take the time to study and become familiar with it. It is important, therefore, that the interviewer be thoroughly grounded with the case and able to speak about it with deftness, conviction, and in a spirit of advocacy. If fundraising counsel is used in the process, this is exactly the role that the interviewer will assume when con-ducting the interview.

CONSENSUS OF THE "FAMILY"

It is vitally important that the board of directors or trustees become familiar and reach a consensus on the statement of need before "external" interviewing begins. In more closely knit communities, people will be well aware of certain board members and might have the occasion to ask them "What's going on?" and what they think about the pro-posed project being tested. It will be important that every board member can speak convincingly, enthusiastically, and knowledgeably regarding the case that is being initially presented through the statement of need.

It is also essential that the chief executive officer (CEO) of the institution have a heavy hand in developing and approving the statement of need. Together with the director of development and fundraising counsel, the CEO should articulate in his/her own words what they want the institution to become and how the success of the pro-posed project fits into that mission.

DISTINCTIVENESS OF THE DOCUMENT

It is the role of the fundraising counsel to guide this process and often to write the case based on the input of the CEO, board, director of development, and those most passionately involved with the institution. Since the statement of need document represents the institution, the document must reflect careful preparation and professionalism. The document is to be prepared without error and put in an attractive, readable format. The document should be on distinctive paper and not just on the run-of-the-mill stationery that institutions use every day.

If the document winds up on a desk full of papers, the backseat of a car, or a packed full briefcase, the distinctiveness of paper quality, color, and format should help it stand out among a sea of other materials. It should be of such quality that people can pass it along to others without sarcasm or embarrassment. At the same time, the statement of need should encourage conversation and input while not leaving the impression that the matter is perfunctory or that the program has already been decided upon.

Appended to the statement of need document can be a board list, a page devoted to a financial summary of the project's scope and costs, and perhaps an architect's rendering. Since time is increasingly valuable, it will be important that this document not exceed three or four pages.

The statement of need, therefore, must be painfully concise (three or four pages of copy does not allow for a rambling narration). This is particularly true if the typeface is large enough and bold enough to keep the attention of a wide variety of age groups and attention spans.

A Common Guide Outline

The following outline can serve as a common guide to what may be included in a case statement or a statement of need document. It places the proposed program in context with the institution and also with the community constituency it serves.

What are the institution's accomplishments?

Founding and purpose

Historical highlights

Important contributions to the community (current or past)

What are the priorities?

What is missing? How to service affected, limited, or impaired?

What opportunities are available?

What process was employed in identifying these strategic issues?

What is the rationale for the project?

What is the institution considering doing about its needs and opportunities?

What are the proposed plans?

How will this help?

How will service to the community be improved in quality and/or quantity?

Who benefits?

Why is community support needed?

> What are the estimated costs off the project?
>
> What funds are available? From what sources?
>
> How much would the organization like to raise among its constituents?
>
> Why is community support important?

Who is in charge? Can I have confidence in the people who are asking for this gift?

> Why am I being asked to give?

Provide logic and emotion.

> Engender confidence that needs, plans, and proposed costs are sound.
>
> Stress the benefits in terms of people; not buildings, programs, or institutions.
>
> Identify key voices and messages to be conveyed.

Professional counsel often finds that extraordinary time is demanded in compiling and creating the statement of need. This is exactly as it should be.

Nothing less than the best should be created when capturing the attention of those that are ideally most suited to assume key leadership roles and provide major gift investments in the event a major campaign program takes place.

After the interviews are completed, and hopefully with the right people, concerns or suggestions about the statement of need can be the basis for modifying the project as presented and provide a clear guide in the articulation of an expanded case for support statement that outlines the parameters of the project in greater detail.

Therefore, the statement of need can be pivotally important in capturing the attention of those best able to assure the proposed program's success. As importantly, it can become and often is the basis for the expanded case for support document, which is an extensively refined and amplified definition that then becomes the resource document for public relations materials such as the major brochure and individual, corporate, and foundation proposals.

ANTICIPATING CONCERNS

The statement of need therefore becomes the "elevator speech" for every board member, the CEO, the development staff, and other passionate parties who wish to rally behind the proposed project. The statement of need is the opening salvo, the first shot across the bow, the first piece of commercial advertising for the project contemplated. It demands the utmost care in its preparation, format, and interpretation.

Another important area is the role of fundraising counsel, who can be helpful in addressing anticipated questions and reactions based on past experience. Some of these critical issues must be addressed directly in the statement of need document. These issues might have to do with a perceived duplication of existing facilities within the community or the expressed desire for collaboration with other agencies with the same mission. Some concerns may be expressed about competing fundraising programs and their impact on the likely success of this proposed campaign.

Some may inquire about using other forms of financing, including borrowing, issuing of bonds, or use of existing resources in reference for the institution to self-finance the project. Transparency with regard to finances will include a disclosure of assets, debt, scope of operating budget, and general operating performance over the past few years.

Some interviewees may want to talk about skeletons in the closet or past scandals or problems that are lingering and have yet to be resolved. Issues regarding the endowment component of the statement of need will surface, such as what the proceeds of an endowment would yield and how endowment support can be distinctly translated to projects and programs.

Another aspect of the statement of need is to answer the question, "What's in it for me?" The statement should allude to commemorative and recognition opportunities for volunteers and major gift donors.

Much of volunteering today is a leisure-time activity, and special attention should be directed to the positive benefits that will accrue to the volunteer and those who might give to make the project viable. Certainly, everyone who is interviewed and reviews the statement of need should have a sense that the program is important and how each volunteer and donor can truly "make a difference" because of their involvement and investment. In other words, the statement of need should give a sense that the proposed program will be personally fun and meaningful.

A First and Lasting Impression

Needless to say, the statement of need document should be readable, attractive, and eye-catching. As importantly, it must be free of typographical errors, be unusually neat in appearance, and, of course, clearly written, using the best grammar possible. The statement of need should be on the highest grade of paper, using a typeface and point size that can be easily read, especially by an older audience.

Some statements of need are elaborately packaged using tasteful graphic design and color, and some are laminated. The goal, of course, is to capture the reader's attention and sustain it through the reading of the document, so that he or she comes away with a favorable impression of the institution, if not a genuine understanding of the case as presented.

CHAPTER 9

Sifting and Sorting— Compiling of the Data

S. SANAE TOKUMURA, APR, ACFRE

What we are involved with here is journalism, pure and simple. And as a professionally reincarnated reporter, I am here to tell you that raw data that is objectively and responsibly gathered in primary research must be handled objectively and responsibly in transition to a malleable format so that its eventual interpretation will be sound. After all, it is your job to finally report unvarnished truth, no matter how much it may hurt or gladden the leaders of an organization. The honest nonprofit organization that is doing the responsible thing by ordering this work to be done is investing in learning about its true circumstance. It is ethically critical to precisely translate data from a raw notes format to interpreted information in order to validate the trust that both organization and interviewees placed in the process. Simply *everything* depends on the integrity of the feasibility study. Results, if used to full potential, can change an organization's service delivery and leadership and can influence many more matters than whether or not to conduct a capital drive and what goal to set if a campaign looks positive.

Compared with the drama of carefully selecting key questions, skillfully phrasing them within the interview setting, completely recording all responses including body language nuances and other clues within the context of the local social, political, and cultural subtexts, *compiling and interpreting the information is hellish drudgery.* Because, once past the careful phrasing of a question, there is little room for creativity. There is only accounting of what is given to be accounted, and clearly expressing these facts. The following chapter should describe the fascinating art and science of basing conclusions on these interpreted facts.

This chapter, however, will describe the process of assembling many detailed notes into one comprehensive, organized mass of information. Do not expect spiritual enlightenment in this chapter. Basically, I will be describing how to manipulate a Word file. We are talking about aggregating a cohesive, consistent, workable group of statements, percentages, and lists from stacks of interview notes. From there, we will distill the facts we need to determine whether or not an organization can commence with a capital or annual campaign and/or what needs to be accomplished in order for them to do so, both in terms of infrastructure and in the arena of the greater community.

Garbage In, Garbage Out

It goes without saying. If your interviewer is a bad conversationalist, has no idea what your organization's history has been and where it wants to go, has a bad list of topics to discuss, and is really, really bad, you will most likely get minimal or even faulty information after all of that questionable data is aggregated. Please, before investing in the time-consuming acts of data compilation and earnest interpretation, make sure that the conversation guide is sound, that the interviewer is personable, objective (preferably completely unrelated to the organization), armed with a solid case for support and has memorized facts about the organization and its programs. Make sure the interviewer is competent and documents all information that is discussed in the format that is required, and can at least manage decent note taking.

The volume of interviews I've done in my studies has ranged from 30 to 75 and more per study. Most interviewers find that they begin getting repeated comments after about the twelfth interview. Even so, those of us conducting interviews should remain diligent in recording precisely what is represented, 100 percent, to the last subject discussed and take absolutely nothing for granted. Although some studies have sole interviewers, there are also studies that require a troop of us to be involved, perhaps because of geographic, language, cultural, or other considerations. Whether I am personally interviewing or sharing interviewing duties with colleagues, all of our "conversation guides" are identical. Questions and subquestions are clearly articulated on the guide, and we are all briefed to understand the case, the facts, and our interviewees.

The Next Step

As the interviews are completed, all documented information is "processed" as soon as possible, and all hard copies of notes are destroyed. A master list of interviewees is kept, however, although interviewee comments are unable to be traced to interviewees from this point.

Processing is a gentle word for the thankless, horrible job of entering thousands of bits of data into an electronic document so that the person who has to make sense of it all can manipulate and sort the information into accountability. However, be grateful, you young'uns: in my day, I remember compiling raw data manually with a typewriter!

I counted responses with stick figures! I had to have an entire living room floor carpeted with interview forms just to find out if we could raise a million dollars! And I had to walk to work two miles in the snow!

In my ultra-modern and techno shop today, in order to enforce the objectivity mandate, a separate department inputs our handwritten notes (and some of us are nice and actually type or use block letters) into a computer database and removes all identification of the interviewees from the responses. We use Excel, but there are other databases that could probably accomplish the same thing. Basically, both numerical and complete descriptive sentences and quotations are sorted into separate subject headings.

Depending on the type of information I am specifically researching, I also have the data segregated and grouped according to constituency group (board, staff, politicos, media, parents, patients, and congregation, whatever is appropriate and pertinent for the organization), income bracket, age, sex, religion, profession, and so on. Each constituency's respondent and members of other groups are counted and percentages are calculated accordingly. Percentages are attached to all categories of responses in general "positive," "negative," or "no opinion" categories.

Once we have obtained an aggregated state of data, and all the math is done, we turn the whole darn thing into a Word file. Obviously, the easiest compilation can be made of questions that can be answered with multiple-choice responses. However, if that had been your intention, it would have been far easier (also far less expensive and time consuming) to have mailed a survey to your most important opinion leaders—"use black ink please,"—and zap responses through a machine to add up the score. To do so, however, would have deprived you of the face-to-face, human encounter opportunity that has the amazing power to correct misunderstandings, add to a constituency's knowledge base, and revive or create relationships. Information is the same as rental cars: you get what you pay for, unless the counter guy is your friend, but that's another analogy.

Naturally, within a human interaction, there are many unexpected variables and therefore many intricacies in its note taking. Understandably, there will be a heavy price to pay in focus and skill required during data interpretation of such an encounter. Although each one of a study's topics will be covered throughout this type of personal interview, there are infinite avenues to take along the way that would result in the revelation of deeper, more significant information that may substantially affect a campaign. Notes on each of these side roads must be taken and later compiled right alongside the standard questions. The more skilled the interviewer, the higher the quality of responses, and the more complex the accounting for these responses will be during interpretation.

INTERPRETATION

The final interpretation of it all is as simple and as honest as a doorknob. The process to get to the doorknob is not rocket science, but a nightmarish, tedious grind. Lucky for us, I have a great data guy who lacks human emotions. Once I have clean data stored in a format that I can manipulate in Word, I begin by separating the easy stuff: numerical, "yes" and "no" responses, and answers capable of being conveyed with "very satisfied," "somewhat satisfied," "not satisfied," or "no opinion." Then I turn with steely eye to the unreasonably expansive responses of the deadly open-ended question. These are the monsters for which I have my reliable "positive," "negative," or "no opinion" general categories of attitude to help me slay.

I've found that compiling each of these (wordy) responses under each question for each of the interviewees into categories of answers is most efficient. Each time I delve into the response, I go more deeply into subcategories until I distill the entire response. Being careful not to change any language, using my good old Associated Press stylebook, I group all the responses for each question, using quotes as much as possible, since I insist on note taking verbatim quotations for each response during the interviews. The result is a good representation of the interviewee's attitudes toward a number of issues that I identify in order of popularity in the interviews. *Note:* I do not use a recorder. I've found that it causes my interviewees to feel pressured to be grammatically and otherwise "correct." Responses are less natural, much less spontaneous, and, most importantly, much less honest.

Then, I use my "cut and paste" function to organize responses in order of frequency from most popular responses and attitudes to single responses and attitudes, and calculate percentages. (After all this work, and our conclusions summarized, I am loath to consign such juicy material to a file no one will read. Therefore, at the end of my feasibility studies, I provide a whole section comprised of each question with statements organized according to their frequency. This also tends to hold us accountable. It is quite thoroughly read as board members seek out their own responses to see if we are indeed as accurate as we say.)

From this point, I've found that keeping my eye on the horizon of truths we are seeking keeps me from losing my mind each time I analyze a study's completely organized responses. Through statements and other clues that have been recorded and aggregated, these truths include:

- The community's affinity and respect for various parts of the organization.
- Confidence in the organization's programs and leaders.
- Belief in the case for support.
- Philanthropic readiness of all parties.
- Whatever prevailing issues may be involved with the organization or project.

Affinity

Affinity with an organization, its mission, and its work is an important indicator of natural acceptance and emotional support. Since we are interviewing opinion leaders of various constituencies, we must assume that the groups these leaders lead feel much the same way, or that the leader can/will influence his or her network to feel the same way. Voluntarism and philanthropic support follow the heart. If there is a natural attraction between the community and the organization, a solid case for support is easier to convey, and a successful campaign more likely. I will attempt to detect within my organized data the *level of affinity* people in various constituencies feel for:

- The organization as a whole.
- The mission of the organization.
- The programs of the organization.

Respect

Comments that reflect respect for a charitable organization, its leaders, staff, and programs indicate that the group has impressed the community with its scope of programs, quality of programs, or integrity. Hopefully, it is admired because its work has benefited the community. Obtaining key campaign leadership, major gifts, and general community support will be more likely if the organization has earned its reputation this way. I must determine leaders' *level of respect* for:

- The governance body of the organization.
- The executive body of the organization.
- The program staff of the organization.

Case for Support

A corporation's prospectus describes all the reasons an investor should invest in it. Tested by psychologists and marketers, its extensive and artfully executed content is powerful and persuasive. Our case for support, which we share in draft during our interviews, attempts to do the same thing. We are testing it in this process. What is this organization? Who runs it? Is it run well? What is the great big problem that this group is attempting to solve or gap that it is going to fill? Will the proposed project effectively address and provide solutions? Can we prove that what it will cost is worth it? Is the leader being interviewed willing to step forward to support the organization based on what is represented in the case?

In order to determine the *level of strength and potency of the case for support*, I need to judge each interviewee's response to its presentation by assigning values for:

- The urgency of the case.
- The rationale for the case.
- The financial goals and other numerical details of the case.

Confidence

A community's confidence in an organization, its leaders, and likelihood of campaign success is a huge part of the set on the stage of an over-the-top drive. Community confidence in an organization's and project's leadership and philanthropic strength, campaign strategy, popularity, and infrastructure can be a campaign's self-fulfilling prophecy. Lack of community confidence will have the opposite effect on every part of the campaign's mechanisms.

I must judge statements to decipher the *level of confidence* interviewees have in:

- The attainment of the dollar goal.
- The organization's capacity to handle logistics and details.
- The philanthropic advocacy of the board.
- The community's candidates for campaign leader.
- The chief executive officer (CEO)/executive director (ED) leadership to support the campaign.
- The commitment of the campaign planning group/campaign cabinet.

Philanthropic Readiness

Are we really together on this? I mean, really together? Are our leaders committed enough to make sacrificial gifts toward the project? How much our core constituency gives toward the project is an indication of whether the project is truly a solution. Poor results in this area may indicate that the project may not have resonated with the organization's truest supporters—a good sign that the rest of the community will not buy in either. Add up the dollars. Are we there yet?

Most easily accomplished is determining the *philanthropic level of readiness* of:

- The CEO/ED.
- The board president.
- The campaign planning group chair/campaign cabinet chair.
- The development staff or, if none, administrative staff.
- The development committee chair.
- Those most likely to become campaign volunteers.

Issues

Statements about these booby traps will come at an interviewer from anywhere at any time during the conversation. Methodical distillation of all statements will reveal repetitive representations if real issues are present. Most of the time, issues will be present.

The question is, are they legitimate? If so, can they be mitigated? If so, how, and how long will it take? Usually, there will be issues such as overcontrolling, destructive CEOs or other managers; CEOs or other managers who are not "present" enough; board members who are micromanaging, board members who don't do anything, past debacles that just won't be forgotten, and so on. Whatever the issue(s) may be, each one must be described and a determination made of its prevalence. Campaigns can be undone with one unidentified issue or an issue that has been left unaddressed.

Most interesting and challenging is to identify the *presence and depth of any issues* interviewees may express about the:

- Relevance of the mission.
- Focus and performance of the board.
- Competency of the programs.
- Effectiveness of the administrative staff.
- Performance of the program staff.

Finally, depending on the ultimate goal(s) of the consultant, the analysis may or may not include information from other disciplines, such as organizational development, nonprofit governance, strategic planning, human resources, accounting, and other areas.

Onward now, to the application of all of these facts!

CHAPTER 10

Tell Me What I Say—Findings, Conclusions, and Recommendations

EUGENE SCANLAN, CFRE, PHD

AN END AND A BEGINNING

In a sense, the consultant's report to the organization represents the end of the consulting process but the beginning of the next steps for the organization. Reports I have seen or written range from a seven-page feasibility study report that basically said, "You're a great organization—go out and raise a lot of money," to an over 100-page report. The latter was prepared for an organization exploring a comprehensive campaign for its many sites in a major urban area.

THE QUALITY REPORT

However, as college instructors sometimes say, "It's not the length but the quality that counts." Actually, the best feasibility study reports should not only demonstrate quality but also several other elements that will help ensure their acceptance and usefulness by the organization. These include:

- *Responsiveness* to the key questions that the consultant and the organization agreed to address at the beginning of the feasibility study process (these are often defined in the contract). These questions should go far beyond the simple "go–no go" question and should include areas such as the image of the organization with its constituents, the appeal of the proposed campaign and its various elements to these constituents, the effectiveness of the case for support, potential objections to providing support, the overall environment in which the campaign will be conducted, potential leadership and leadership structures, and critical issues that must be addressed before the campaign gets under way or during the campaign.

- *Cultural sensitivity* to the uniqueness of the organization and its needs. Reports— and the entire consulting process—should be attuned to the organizational culture, including its mission and vision, its leadership, those it serves, its donors, its services and programs, its uniqueness, and the environment in which it operates. Each organization has its own culture, and the best reports reflect this culture. Information, conclusions, and recommendations should be presented in ways that will be accepted by the organization because the consultant has shown that there is a basis of understanding of who and what the organization is and does.

- *Honesty and openness* in presenting information. The report should, within the bounds of both confidentiality and cultural sensitivity, present information in an open and honest manner. Conclusions and recommendations provided by the consultant should be direct and to the point. Problem areas and issues should be presented in ways that will not create defensive reactions by the organization or, worse, result in rejection of the entire process, but rather presented along with ways to overcome these potential obstacles. I once presented a feasibility study report with the primary conclusion that the proposed endowment campaign should not proceed because of some major issues with staff leadership; this was certainly not the conclusion the board leadership desired. At the conclusion of the presentation to the board, I received a round of applause; when I asked the board why, the board chair responded, "Because you told us what we needed to hear, not what we wanted to hear."

- *Clarity of information and next steps.* Feasibility study reports should clearly present information and next steps in ways that the organization will understand and will help ensure their use and follow-through. Complex, long, and detailed data analysis may not be what the organization needs if in fact their primary interest is focused on a few key questions related to the planning and execution of a campaign. The consultant should always ensure that his or her opinions are clearly separated from information obtained in interviews or through other sources. Quotes or information drawn from organizational materials, whether internal or published should include citations of sources. I was once challenged by a staff member of a client about a statement made in a feasibility study report, with the staff member commenting, "We would never describe our organization that way." I showed the staff member that the statement was a direct quote from the organization's current annual report.

- *Protection of confidentiality of interviewees and, if necessary, other sources of information.* Confidentiality of the interviewees and their opinions can be one of the most sensitive issues when presenting information in a feasibility study report. Sometimes staff members or board members of an organization will want to determine who specifically said something, especially when there is a criticism or a high gift potential indicated. The report should protect the identities of interviewees and ensure that any identification is only as generic as possible, such as "a board member stated . . ." or "one of the 12 foundation funders interviewed said . . ."

- *Separation out of the report of information that should be shared with only a few staff or board members, or that may not be directly related to the study.* Some consultants provide such information in a confidential memo to management or through other methods (sometimes only verbally) to ensure that this information is given to appropriate persons but not more widely shared as the report will be. An example from my experience is a concern that was raised by several interviewees during feasibility study interviews that there was a potential conflict of interest at the organization because the board chair and the business manager who were two of the three people authorized to sign checks were husband and wife.

- *Combining the needs and interests of the organization with the experience of the consultant.* This relates to the earlier comments about the culture of the organization as well as the need to clearly separate the opinions of the consultant from the other information collected during the study process. One of the values of using a consultant is that his or her experience and insights can benefit the organization and help it move forward. However, there is also the danger that, if the consultant does not understand the culture and uniqueness of the organization and what it is really seeking through the feasibility study process, the experience brought by the consultant will be too generalized or generic to mean much to the organization. There is always some ambivalence on the part of both the consultant and the organization around this issue. One of my favorite comments encountered in many marketing calls is, "You need to understand why we're so unique and special," followed by "what other organizations like us have you worked with?"

- *Reflecting the highest standards of ethics.* Some consultants offer to carry out the feasibility study and campaign as part of a single package. This presupposes that the study will indicate a go ahead for a campaign and offers the potential for a study biased in favor of a campaign to ensure continuation of the contract. Ethically, I strongly believe that the study contract should be a single and separate entity from any campaign consulting contract, and the former should focus entirely on the study process and outcomes, not on execution of the campaign. The contract, work of the consultant in carrying out the study process, and the report should reflect codes of ethics and standards, such as the Association of Fundraising Professionals Code of Ethics and the Donor Bill of Rights. Starting with the marketing process, the consultant should provide accurate and factual information on his or her background, past and present clients and work, successes and failures, and other related factors.

- *Providing conclusions and recommendations specific to the client.* This might seem like an obvious point, but I have seen more than a few reports by other consultants that were heavily weighted with generic information that had little to do with the organization's specific situation and needs. National data on giving, "cut and paste" information on campaign structures, and so on may not have anything to do with a particular organization and its environment. Even some of the "tried and true" principles and techniques of the consulting and fundraising professions may not be appropriate. For example, the usual donor pyramid did not apply to a study for a $3 million capital campaign when the first gift prospect identified was for $1.7 million and an additional nine prospects could—and did—round out the campaign.

These, I believe, are the broad parameters for a quality report. Now, let's look at the report itself and the report process.

THE REPORT PROCESS—IT'S MORE THAN PAPER

The wise and experienced consultant will want to ensure that all of the work, time, and energy put into a feasibility study report does not result in nothing more than the filling up of shelf space in the office of the organization's CEO or executive director (ED). So, while the report itself is critical, how and where it will be presented to the organization can be almost equally as critical helping the organization take action and move forward. Consultants may, and probably should, define the report process and expectations of the organization in the contract. Ideally, once the report is completed in draft form, it should initially be reviewed by a staff member or two to be sure that basic information and descriptions are correct and that any sensitive information is presented in ways that should be acceptable to the organization.

At this or a later point, the reviewers might want substantial changes in the report; this can be a point of contention with the consultant, especially if the changes involve removal of information or recommendations that the consultant feels are critical to the study outcomes and next steps. As was covered above, sensitive information and confidentiality issues should already have been addressed appropriately. Changes desired by initial reviewers might reflect their own biases rather than the needs of the organization and the information collected through the interview process or from other sources. Sometimes, for example, a reviewer might ask or even demand that key statements from interviewees cited in the report be removed, or that basic conclusions drawn by the consultant be changed. Ethically, the consultant may have to "stick to his or her guns" and remind the client that these are critical points or conclusions that reflect the work done, information collected, and analysis carried out.

A "worst case" conflict occurred when an ED presupposed a campaign should be carried out and would be successful, and was only seeking justification for his point of view, which was not supported by the board, who preferred to remain neutral until the study was completed. When the study came back with the conclusion that major-donor relations had become so bad that the campaign should not proceed and would fail if attempted, the ED demanded that the conclusions be changed to give the go-ahead for a campaign. The consultant refused to do so, and when the report and conclusions were presented to the board, the ED proceeded to undercut the process carried out, even though he had approved it and been involved every step of the way.

After the initial review, a revised draft may be submitted to a group such as the board development committee or a study committee, if one was established. Once this group has met with the consultant and completed their review and approved the report, it can be presented by the consultant to the full board (this may not be necessary or appropriate in some organizations). Strategically, the smaller group can help serve as advocates to the board for the report and its conclusions and recommendations.

The presentation by the consultant to the full board should be a focus of the meeting, not just another point on a heavy agenda. The leadership of the organization needs to realize the importance of the study process and outcomes and the potential impact of a campaign decision on the future of the organization. Board members should receive at least an executive summary of the full report prior to the meeting, and time should be allowed for questions and discussion. Many consultants ask that the board formally vote on accepting the report at the meeting after the presentation and discussion. In some organizations the development or fundraising committee might serve these functions in place of the board, but in most cases the full board should be part of the report process.

THE REPORT AND VARIATIONS ON A THEME

Exhibits 10.1 and 10.2 present two examples (A and B) of listings of tables of contents for consulting reports that I prepared for clients. While there are many similarities in the contents of these two reports, note that in example A the findings section was one of the appendices while in example B the findings section was included in the body of the report. This difference reflected the needs and culture of the client as well as the specific review process that was carried out in each case. Also note that "generic" items as well as study-specific items were included in the appendices; "generic" items were clearly marked as such in the reports. In one case, sample gift acceptance policies were included, as this was an item the client needed to develop.

The structure, contents, and items included in the feasibility study and other reports can vary considerably from consultant to consultant. But a more important point is that an individual consultant's reports should vary from client to client and must reflect the unique needs and culture of each client, as well as the consultant's own experience, which has been brought to that particular study process. For example, some organizations have a primary concern with the qualitative information collected during the interviews, while other organizations might be more concerned with the quantitative information. As discussed later, there must be some balance and a clear understanding of the implications of each, but the emphasis might shift from client to client.

In addition to a cover, acknowledgments, and a table of contents, typical elements in feasibility study reports are listed below and discussed. Remember that these elements

EXHIBIT 10.1   TABLE OF CONTENTS, TYPE A

Table of Contents

may be combined, called something different, or be more or less focused on, depending on the consultant and the organization.

Element 1: The Executive Summary

Not all reports contain an executive summary. In some cases, the executive summary might be an entirely separate document or, in a few situations, an executive summary may not be necessary. However, a brief executive summary can be a valuable tool for providing focus and direction to larger groups, especially to board members who may want to hear the key outcomes of the feasibility study process rather than wade through the details. In my experience, board members from the business world may not have the time or patience to review a detailed 70-page report and prefer the quick 6-page executive summary with the highlights of the full report. Volunteer leadership, senior staff, and others, such as major supporters, may want to see the full report and should be offered this opportunity by the staff and board leadership, if appropriate. Distribution

EXHIBIT 10.2   TABLE OF CONTENTS, TYPE B

Table of Contents

of both the executive summary and full report should be a decision made by the organization, not the consultant.

The executive summary is usually brief (five to six pages is a common criterion, but the length should again reflect the needs of the organization and who will be receiving it) and focuses on a few key areas. These can include:

- *The consulting goals, key questions or areas addressed, and the process.* It is important for anyone reading the executive summary to understand up front the rationale behind the study process and what the organization wanted to know, as well as what the agreed-to process was (materials review, meetings, study process materials that were developed, numbers interviewed, categories of interviewees, etc.).

- *Findings—a quick summary.* In some cases it may be desirable to recap the findings in an executive summary. However, this can raise issues of how to effectively include both quantitative information and qualitative information in ways that will not lose the fine points or cause readers to focus on the wrong things. For example, if quantitative information regarding those in favor of doing a capital campaign versus those opposed is the only such information presented without the details and amplifications, it may appear to be a "vote" rather than an indication of what opinions people have based on a given point in time and current information available to them. Some executive summaries prefer to leave out the findings and move directly into other sections.

- *Analysis—another quick summary (see also Conclusions).* As will be discussed in greater detail later, some consultants include an analysis section in their feasibility study reports. This section is where the consultant brings his or her general experience and understanding of the organization together and applies them to the findings or "raw data" of the study process. Again, this is usually a lengthy section in the full report and may only be summarized briefly or just alluded to in the executive summary.

- *Recommendations.* The executive summary should have as its primary focus the recommendations for action by the organization. The recommendations included in the executive summary should, in most cases, just be the capsule recommendations without the extensive details and rationales provided in the full report. Many consultants provide fairly brief statements for each recommendation, all of which should address the primary questions of the study process and any related areas. These statements are then expanded upon with a justification, rationale, or more detailed explanation.

- *Conclusions.* In some cases, a consultant may use this term to cover what other consultants call the analysis section. In other cases, the conclusions section may just be a summary of the major recommendation, such as "In conclusion, the XYZ organization should proceed with its capital campaign in accordance with the recommendations, action plan, and timeline presented in the recommendations above."

Element 2: The Consulting Process

This section is often drawn from the detailed contract or letter of agreement between the consultant and the organization and presents in detail:

- The key questions addressed by the study.
- The goals and desired outcomes of the study process.
- Roles and responsibilities of the organization and the consultant.
- Organizational materials and information reviewed by the consultant.
- The interviewee selection criteria and process.
- Discussion of materials developed for the study and the process for developing them (the materials themselves, such as the interview questionnaire and the case, may be included as appendices).
- Numbers and categories of interviewees (and possibly their names, which alternately might be included in a separate appendix).

- Sources for other information collected for the study process.

- Other groups or committees of the organization involved in the study process or specifically set up for it, such as a study committee, including who they were and how they were involved.

- Factors that may have changed the study process, changed the originally projected timeline (such as the unavailability of key interviewees during the original time frame), or required additional or unanticipated work by the consultant.

- Other information or events that may have impacted the study process (staff turnover, death of a major-gift prospect, etc.).

While it may seem repetitive to include a detailed section on the study process, it is important to restate the original understanding (contractual arrangement) between the organization and the consultant, the focus of the feasibility study, and the different parts of the process. Remember that not everyone in the organization was involved in the original negotiations and contract development/approval, nor would they have a complete understanding of the details of the arrangements or possibly even what a feasibility study process is, its rationale, and how it proceeds. Also, it is always good to remind even those close to the study process of the original focus and key questions that were addressed.

Additionally, as the study proceeds, other events and things beyond the control of the consultant, the organization, or both may impact the process. It is important to point these out in the report, and the consultant should reflect on their impact on the study and the potential campaign. For example, the original list of prospective interviewees may need to be supplemented if it turns out that some of those interviewed were not as appropriate to the criteria for interviewees as was first thought.

Element 3: Findings

As was mentioned above, the findings are the "raw data" collected during the feasibility study process. Findings can be quantitative, qualitative, or both. There are pluses and minuses to each type of data that should be taken into consideration even before the study process begins or the consultant is retained to carry out the study.

- *Quantitative data.* Quantitative data can be presented as simple numbers ("23 interviewees agreed, 7 disagreed with this statement") and/or with statistical analysis ("the median potential gift for those interviewed was $25,000"). Quantitative data can be useful to get some general sense of information provided by the interviews but may not reflect specific situations and actual campaign potential. For example, the use of a mean or average may cloud the potential for major gifts for a campaign. If an average potential gift was $25,000, based on the interviews, it might obscure the fact that one person interviewed indicated a willingness to consider a $500,000 gift, while many others would consider only much smaller gifts.

○ Raw quantitative data can thus be counterproductive if not presented within some context. It may provide far too much information for a casual reader or to someone seeking answers to the major questions addressed by the study process, or it may put the focus on the wrong areas, raise concerns that are not warranted, or just confuse the readers about the relation of the information to the outcomes and recommendations of the feasibility study process. It can also hide important nuances emerging from the interviews, such as an interviewee who responds to a question about whether or not he or she would support a campaign, with a statement such as "I would not support it unless I had the following information . . ." This person might just be counted as a nonsupporter.

○ If raw quantitative data is presented, it should be presented consistent with the key questions addressed by the study process and the culture of the organization as well as in a form and style that promotes understanding. Grouped data and analyses should be stated in a logical manner and should be consistent with the other parts of the report and with consideration for factors that can make a campaign successful. This type of data is only a first step toward understanding the current readiness for a campaign and should be presented and used very carefully so that it does not become the sole focus of the organization.

• *Qualitative data.* Qualitative data in feasibility study reports is often presented through statements or summaries of statements provided by interviewees and other sources, or through results of statements provided on written surveys. A qualitative statement might be "I really like this organization because I see the kids they work with changing their behavior in positive ways." Another less positive qualitative statement might be "I'm not sure what that organization really does, but in terms of my giving priorities, it's not high on my list." Now either of these could be grouped with other statements to become quantitative measures. For example, if 22 people made similar statements to the first one, a quantitative statement might be "22 interviewees (73 percent of those interviewed) spoke favorably of the work of the organization."

○ Like quantitative data, qualitative data has both pluses and minuses associated with it. Merely listing all of the statements or responses given to each question, based on the interviewer's notes, can cause the reader as much overload as providing detailed analyses of quantitative data. Grouping qualitative statements moves them into the realm of quantitative information. And yet not using qualitative information can lose the richness of people's perceptions of the organization including its mission, effectiveness, and plans. Donors in particular may make emotional statements during interviews about why they are associated with a particular organization and support it. These can provide valuable insights for future versions of the case, for the campaign materials, and for future development efforts of the organization. Some consultants use qualitative statements from interviews in a selective manner to highlight groups of responses to key parts of the study process. For example, if the analysis of the responses and information supports moving ahead with a major capital campaign, this conclusion might be highlighted by citing a statement such as "Doing this campaign and building the new center will transform this organization and better serve the community." —A major donor.

- *Quantitative + qualitative.* The best reports should probably include both types of information, but use them in ways that keep the focus on the key questions addressed by the feasibility study rather than just on the information itself. The experienced consultant will help ensure this happens by using the data to provide answers to three major questions:

  - What does the data tell us? Raw numbers and data analyses don't really tell us much about individuals and can cover the emotional elements so important in the gift giving process. It is the job of the consultant to take both the quantitative and the qualitative information and distill it in ways that are meaningful and appropriate for that particular organization.

  - What can we draw from the data? The consultant should be able to guide the client organization in constructive ways to the important points supported by a combination of the data, the current state of the organization, and his or her professional experience and expertise. This question should be answered in the analysis section (sometimes referred to as the conclusions section). Please see below for further discussion of this section of the report.

  - What should we do about it? This question leads to the action plan or recommendations section, where the consultant brings together all of the elements and presents the organization with an action plan with specific next steps that are realistic for the organization; have designated roles and responsibilities for volunteers, staff, and others; and have timelines and benchmark points outlined. If there are reasons a campaign should not proceed, it is incumbent upon the consultant to present the specific reasons why and what steps should be taken to address these issues, as well as a recommended timeline, roles and responsibilities, desired outcomes, etc.

Element 4: Analyses (or Conclusions)

Here is where the consultant brings together all of the information and his or her experience and develops the underlying basis for the next section, the recommendations. He or she assembles the pieces and builds the foundation for the suggested action plan, drawing from the data what is most important for answering the critical questions addressed by the feasibility study process. As indicated earlier, the data in most studies may not give definitive answers to these key questions and may in fact obscure those factors that are most likely to contribute to the success of a campaign. The findings can be one indication of the direction the organization can take, but the experienced consultant will be able to add other elements into the mix to give a much more definitive set of answers as well as define a plan of action. The analysis should cover the contrasting points of view presented by the various sources of information, and should seek to determine what principles and best practices of development and fundraising are most likely to result in a successful campaign.

The consultant should, in this section, also be able to look at all of the key elements of the organization individually (board leadership, staff leadership, mission, vision, programs and services, constituents, donors, development and fundraising and sources of support, public relations and marketing, the environment in which the organization operates, history, and planning, including the proposed focus of the campaign) and present detailed analysis of each as well as the relation of each to the proposed campaign. Ideally, the analysis/conclusions section should give the consultant's views on the entire organization and its relation to the campaign, as drawn from the study process and the consultant's experience and skills.

The analysis presented should be realistic but presented in ways that will encourage appropriate action by the organization rather than cause defensiveness or rejection of the entire report. The consultant should discuss areas that need strengthening, adjustment, or enhancement in the organization in order to ensure and improve its effectiveness, not only in terms of the study but overall. Good feasibility studies take a comprehensive look at an organization even though they have a specific focus, because there is a recognition that all aspects of the organization are related to the success or failure of a campaign effort.

The analysis section should also ensure that the organization understands what are current best principles and practices that can be directly applied to their situation and proposed campaign effort, but the consultant should not attempt to force the organization into a particular mold or develop unrealistic expectations. The best consultants recognize that their work and recommendations must build on where the organization is now, but also encourage them to stretch to achieve goals that might otherwise seem just beyond their reach. These consultants also recognize that, as the title of this book indicates, the best feasibility studies and outcomes reach far beyond the simple question of "Can we raise $X?"

The analysis section should also introduce the element of the strategic values of the campaign into the discussion. Campaigns and the uses of the funds are only means to other ends, including better enabling the organization to carry out its mission and better meet the needs of those it serves. Effective campaigns can bring in new leadership, new donors, reenergize an organization, create higher levels of annual support, enhance its value to the community, and, in the best sense of the word, transform the organization. If all of these are the outcomes of a campaign, the success is measured in much more than the dollars raised.

This section can also become a resource for the organization. Just as the findings section can serve as a resource for the materials and messages of the campaign, in the analysis section the consultant can give observations and suggestions to help enhance the organization and prepare the way for the campaign and the future.

All of the analysis presented should provide additional critical information for decision makers at the organization and should cut through what may be the clutter of information collected during the study process to begin to give a sense of direction and purpose to what follows. While the findings may be ambiguous at times, those reading the analysis section should come away with a much clearer sense of how to proceed and should feel comfortable and accepting of the recommendations that follow.

Exhibit 10.3 shows a brief example of both findings and analysis (excerpted and shortened from an actual report).

Element 5: Recommendations

Recommendations in a feasibility study report can vary considerably from consultant to consultant. Some consultants prefer to give fairly general recommendations, while others give very detailed recommendations that may represent specific steps or an action

---

EXHIBIT 10.3   FINDINGS AND ANALYSIS

Findings: Interviewees have a positive impression of XYZ's board of directors. They feel the board is doing a good job, is genuinely interested in the council's work, and is engaged in the organization. Interviewees felt that the primary roles of the board were oversight, policy direction, fiduciary responsibilities, strategic planning, and fundraising. As to other roles the board should fulfill, most respondents did not feel there were other roles. However, several interviewees suggested the board work on ways to get XYZ members involved through committees. Of those who had knowledge of the various committees of the board, several interviewees commented that the committees need to be strengthened with roles and responsibilities of members clearly defined.

Analysis: XYZ needs to continue to attract the same high caliber of board members it currently has. To ensure that, it is important that there is sufficient professional staff to assist them with their duties. As the council moves ahead in building its development program, it will be necessary for more board members to be actively involved in fundraising-related activities. Later in the report, we make several recommendations as to ways XYZ's board can play an important role in the development program.

One of the best ways to identify potential board members and cultivate donor relationships is to involve members on committees. We agree with the suggestion of several interviewees that the board work on ways to involve more members in the organization and, in particular, on committees. The role of committees and the roles and responsibilities of committee members need to be clearly defined so that serving on a committee will be a worthwhile experience for an XYZ member. Committees can also serve as a means of evaluating the interest, commitment, and leadership capabilities of individuals before they are placed on the board.

plan for the organization to follow in planning for and executing a campaign. Here are some suggested key questions to ask about the recommendations section of the report:

- Are these recommendations specific to your organization or are they generic and applicable to many organizations?
- Do they show a comprehensive understanding of your organization and where it is now?
- Are they appropriate to your organization's culture and resources?
- Are they realistic overall or will they possibly place a major burden on the organization that it might not be able to handle?
- Do they effectively deal with issues that might block a successful campaign?
- Do they show how staff, board, and others should be involved in a campaign (their possible roles and responsibilities)?
- Will additional staff or outside resources be needed to succeed?
- Do they provide advice on a possible campaign structure and leadership, with specific suggestions for campaign leadership?
- Do they provide phases for a campaign and possibly goals?
- Do they recommend any policies and internal procedures that are needed for the campaign?
- Do they recommend recognition programs for the campaign or a procedure for establishing these and some ideas for a recognition structure?
- Do they provide a recommended timeline for the campaign?
- Do they recommend campaign-related materials that might be developed?
- Do the recommendations cover strengths and weaknesses of the case and a procedure for improving it (if not covered elsewhere in the report)?
- Do the recommendations address overall strengths and weaknesses of the organization and how these might impact a campaign, as well as ways to build on strengths and improve areas needing enhancement?
- Do the recommendations provide ways to enhance relationships with current donors as well as acquire new donors?
- Do the recommendations provide advice on various fundraising methods (person-to-person solicitations, group activities, direct mail, planned giving, etc.) and how they can be used in the campaign?
- Do the recommendations cover integration of the campaign with the annual giving program and other fundraising-related activities of the organization?
- Is the donor pyramid presented in a way that shows there are sufficient prospects to make the campaign successful?

- Are possible donor objections provided as well as recommended ways to respond to these?
- Are all of the key questions that were to be part of the study process covered by the recommendations?
- Is the specific overall goal realistic and achievable?
- Do the recommendations provide the "how" needed to do the campaign or do they just comment on readiness?
- Are there other areas that need to be or could be covered in the recommendations that will help enhance your organization's chances for a successful campaign?
- If the primary recommendation is that your organization should not proceed with a campaign, does the report provide steps to address the issues and lay the groundwork for a future campaign?

The above is a fairly comprehensive list of possible questions. Each organization's particular needs regarding campaign information and planning should be addressed by the specific recommendations provided in the report. Not all of the above points may be covered or even relevant to your organization. Some of the above items may not be included as part of the recommendations, but may be addressed in the analysis/conclusions section, or in the memo to management. Again, each consultant will have his or her own style for presenting recommendations; the important point during the contract phase of negotiating with a consultant is to be sure your organization knows what it will get at the end of the process.

Organizations should be careful not to accept generic or very general recommendations, such as the "You're a great organization and can raise the money to meet your goal" mentioned earlier—this is a paraphrase of an actual recommendation that was part of a seven-page final report for a feasibility study. Recommendations should also show sensitivity to the ability of the organization to carry them out. The consultant should avoid presenting recommendations that will overwhelm the client organization or that will have it conclude the recommendations are impossible to fulfill, given the workload and resources of staff and volunteers. It is better to focus on a few critical recommendations rather than a long list of recommendations that try to cover every detail. My feasibility study reports generally have 10 to 15 recommendations, although the client's needs and the key questions addressed by the study can cause considerable variations in this number.

A recommendation not to proceed should be accompanied by a detailed justification or rationale as well as steps the organization can take to better prepare for a future campaign. The consultant should be honest and open about any issues that can be shared, with more sensitive issues being presented to the organization in the memo to management.

Element 6: Attachments

The table of contents examples provide some insights into possible attachments to feasibility study reports. Some organizations prefer that the very detailed information be separated out and attached so that the report itself focuses on the most important points. Others prefer the detailed information be included in the body of the report. Again, this is a matter that is best agreed upon by both the consultant and the organization before the report is written. Attachments might include:

- Quantitative information details, with only summaries provided in the body of the report.
- Qualitative information details, such as sample comments by interviewees or even detailed comments from interviewer notes.
- The list of interviewees, possibly including categories ("board member," "staff," "major annual donor," etc.).
- The interview questionnaire.
- The case.
- Sample letters to prospective interviewees and sample thank-you letters to those interviewed.
- The donor pyramid, either in generic form or with prospect information (not names) by potential giving levels.
- A sample or recommended donor recognition program.
- Sample gift acceptance policies and procedures.
- A recommended campaign structure.
- Recommended campaign leadership.
- Roles and responsibilities for board, staff, and other volunteers in the proposed campaign.
- A campaign action plan with timelines.
- A recommended list of materials needed for the campaign with possible samples.
- A statement of or example of campaign phases with specific goals for each phase (may also be part of the action plan).
- Sample job/position descriptions for recommended additional staff needed for the campaign, if any.
- A campaign budget, including projected time requirements for senior staff.
- Other items that might be appropriate to assist the organization with its campaign planning and execution.

As with other elements of the report, the attachments can vary considerably based on the nature and depth of the study and report, the organization itself, the issues being explored by the study, and the consultant.

OTHER CONSIDERATIONS

One question that often comes up about feasibility study reports is: Who owns them? Is it the consultant or the organization? In my opinion, the feasibility study report is the property of the client organization. It is up to the organization to distribute it and use it as the organization wishes. Much of the information in the report may be of the nature that the organization wants to keep it "in house." The organization may wish to share some parts of the report, such as the executive summary, more widely. At times, organizations offer to share the executive summary or even the full report with interviewees, who at least should be informed that the study is complete and the organization has made its critical decisions about proceeding with the campaign.

Some consultants may specify that certain materials, such as the interview questionnaire or other items, or that certain techniques used during the study process are proprietary and are not to be shared by the client outside the organization or too widely without the consultant's specific permission. It is important to be clear on who owns what, and what can and can't be shared at the start of the consulting process; statements about these areas often are included in the contract.

An effective consultant and a comprehensive interview process will provide rich information resources on possible major campaign donors and leadership. Often, organizations will want to access this information—if not in writing, at least through conversations with the consultant. However, the consultant is obligated to maintain the confidentiality of the interviews and those interviewed. This can sometimes cause tension, but if this point is made early in the process, there will be fewer problems. At times, interviewees may, in the course of the interview, say something like, "I don't mind if they know who said this, . . ." or even, "Let them know I said this . . ." The consultant should clarify immediately what part of the interview this specifically applies to and, once this is clear, may wish to include the comment in the report with attribution. However, before doing so, it is often best to check back with the interviewee to ensure that the comment(s) are accurately presented and the individual is still willing to be cited as the source.

Also, identification of interviewees linked to comments should not be so specific that they can easily be identified, even without their names being attached. Attributing the comment to a "housewife on the board," for example, might pinpoint the respondent if there is only one housewife on the board. Or saying a response came from a "major foundation donor" can narrow down who said it if there are only very few foundation donors.

CONCLUSIONS

The feasibility study report and recommendations is really, for the consultant, the culmination of the study process. It should effectively bring together all of the organizational elements related to the possible campaign, as well as the experience and expertise of the consultant. It should also directly respond to the key questions the organization wanted addressed in the study process. Like the entire study process, the report should be educational and provide a realistic starting point and road map for a successful campaign.

CHAPTER 11

What Strengthens Our Institution— Integrating Results

LINDA LYSAKOWSKI, ACFRE

Okay, the study is done, now what? How does an organization use the findings its of the study to move forward? What if the organization is not ready for a campaign? Was the money paid for the study wasted? How soon should the study findings be implemented? How long is the study report valid before findings are outdated?

In this chapter, we look at integrating the results of the study into the organization's campaign plan and/or its overall goals.

SUCCESS FACTORS

There are many factors that will help ensure the success of a capital campaign, among them are four critical factors:

1. Full and early commitment of the board to the campaign.
2. A compelling case for support.
3. The availability of effective volunteer leadership.
4. A pool of major donors likely to support this campaign.

If the study has not been able to answer these questions, it was somehow flawed. The internal assessment and the interviews with selected board members should provide a good indication of the board's willingness to get involved in the campaign, and the level of financial commitment that might be expected from the board should be based on the board's responses to the interviews. The responses of interviewees to the preliminary case statement should be a good indication of whether the organization has presented a compelling case to key people, one that will motivate and inspire leadership gifts. And there should be a list of potential major donor prospects that have been identified during the study. Another critical role that the study should provide is the identification of effective, enthusiastic volunteers who are willing to serve in a leadership capacity on the campaign cabinet.

The consultant, in the report, should recommend a goal for the campaign, if indeed the recommendation is to go forward with a campaign. A preliminary timeline for the campaign should also be included in the report. The consultant should also identify any problems or issues that may have been uncovered, which would hinder the chances of a successful campaign. As noted earlier in this book, the typical procedure for the presentation of the report is usually as follows:

- Consultant completes internal assessment and interviews.
- Consulting firm develops report with input from all consultants who conducted interviews (if more than one).
- The steering committee meets with the consultant(s) to review the report and have any questions answered about the firm's recommendations.
- The consultant prepares final copies of the report, after assuring that there are no inaccuracies in the report.
- The report is presented to the full board, along with recommendations for moving forward.
- A summary report is sent to those who were interviewed, thanking them for their time and input.

A typical report is in written format, often with graphs and charts showing results of the interviews. Some consultants provide some educational materials along with the report, outlining basic capital campaign principles that are helpful to the board in understanding what can be expected during a campaign. A typical report contains:

- An executive summary.
- An analysis of the internal assessment.
- A copy of the preliminary case for support.
- A list of people who were interviewed.
- Campaign recommendations and/or other recommendations.
- A narrative justification for the stated recommendations.
- Quantitative and qualitative results of the interviews.
- A list of potential campaign donor prospects.
- A list of potential campaign volunteers.
- Notes about any issues that might adversely or positively affect a campaign.

- A proposed campaign timetable, or a timetable listing steps needed to prepare the organization for a campaign.

During the presentation of the report, it is important that all board members feel free to ask questions about the results of the study and especially about the recommendations for moving forward.

TYPICAL STUDY PROCESS ISSUES

While every organization is unique, there are some typical issues that often arise during the study process. These may include, but are not limited to:

- The board is not committed to the campaign.
- The board does not have the community recognition or fundraising strength to successfully carry out a campaign.
- The organization has a low profile or a lack of public awareness about what they do.
- The organization does not have staff experienced in conducting a campaign.
- There is a lack of staff or staff is overinvolved in things like special events, and will not have sufficient time to devote to the campaign.
- The chief executive officer (CEO) does not recognize his or her responsibility in a campaign.
- Leadership gifts sufficient to assure success have not been identified.
- The organization has a weak infrastructure, lack of policies and procedures, a good software system, or other internal systems needed to manage a campaign.
- The community does not think the organization has a compelling case.
- The consultant has not been able to uncover a sufficient number of people willing to get involved in the campaign as volunteers.

Public Relations

Occasionally, an organization will have a serious public relations issue to deal with, such as fraud or embezzlement of a former staff member, a board chair who is not well respected in the community, or a scandal involving a staff member. Fortunately, these occasions are the exception rather than the rule. More often, the issues that are uncovered during a study can easily be resolved, and the consultant should provide solutions for these issues that will enable the organization to move forward with a campaign, even if a delay is recommended.

Another area that may surface during the internal assessment is that of board issues. Among the most often seen weaknesses in this area are the size of the board, the fundraising strength of the board, credibility of the board, or lack of board commitment.

If board size is an issue and/or if the board is not made up of people who can help the organization during a campaign, the organization should begin a board development program immediately. The consultant may be able to provide assistance in this area, or can recommend a board development specialist to assist the organization in increasing the size of the board and assuring that the board has the appropriate skills and talents needed by the organization. If the board is in serious need of total reorganization, it will take some time, perhaps a year or more, to put into place a strong fundraising board, but often the board just needs some education and encouragement in order to get them ready for a campaign. If the board is not committed wholeheartedly to this campaign, the organization should consider a board training program, inviting an outside consultant to come in and review with the board what their responsibilities during the campaign will be and talk about the general roles and responsibilities of board members. This training must include the discussion of the board members' financial commitment, which is critical to a successful campaign. Sometimes this process results in the organization's losing some board members who are not totally committed to the organization or this project, and that may actually be a desirable outcome. Although larger boards are usually recommended for fundraising purposes, especially during a campaign, sometimes it is better to have a smaller board committed to the organization than a larger one that has a lack of committed people.

Staffing

Another area of infrastructure that may be weak is the staffing of the development office. Often, even where there is a development staff, they are overly involved in things like special events or grant proposal writing, leaving little time to devote to managing a campaign. And even if the organization plans to hire a consultant, its leaders need to be aware of the time requirements of staff during a campaign. Often, the CEO of an organization spends 50 percent of his or her time during a campaign focusing on cultivating and soliciting donors, strategizing with volunteers, and attending campaign meetings, while the development staff may spend virtually all of its time managing the campaign. Support staff will also be needed to manage some of the day-to-day aspects of the campaign, such as producing reports for the volunteers and board, sending out meeting notices, entering gifts and pledges, sending acknowledgments, and so on. Often, the study recommendations include the need to hire additional help as the organization prepares for a campaign.

Donors and Volunteers

Among the big issues that sometimes are discovered in the study process is that there are not a sufficient number of donors or volunteers available to support this campaign. Often those interviewed will state that they think this campaign can be successful and that the goal is realistic, yet when asked about the projected level of their own support, they respond with much lower numbers than are needed to meet the stated goal. When this happens, the organization must look carefully at whether the goal is realistic. Although as a rule people generally respond low during the study process, when asked to give during a campaign by someone they know and presented with a finalized case, they may increase the actual amount of the gift significantly over what they had indicated in the study interview. However, the organization cannot count on this support as it plans the campaign. Usually, even those who do not respond with the likelihood of a leadership level gift from themselves or their company, will offer a number of other possibilities including individuals, businesses and foundations that they believe the organization should approach for a gift. If these names are not already on the list of prospective interviewees, the organization should attempt to contact these prospective donors before the study is completed to find out if they can be interviewed in order to determine what their anticipated level of giving might actually be. Sometimes, after the report is presented, additional interviews may be recommended with selected people who have already been interviewed or names that have surfaced during the study. In addition, there may be some research recommended that can help determine the range of giving that might be anticipated from these donors.

Likewise, there may be a lack of key community leaders willing to accept a leadership role in the campaign. This is often because there is a lack of community awareness about the organization and its case for support for this project. The study can help develop awareness in some of the key community leaders and in fact, this is one of the key benefits of doing a study. It is often said that the study helps to "presell" the case to the right people. If an organization finds during the study that its lack of community awareness is going to be a challenge, it must start immediately to develop these relationships, since cultivation efforts take time.

Overcoming the Obstacles

How does the organization deal with these issues and the recommendations to overcome them?

If indeed the organization does have a more serious issue, such as a scandal, the consultant will probably recommend delaying the campaign until such time when these issues have subsided. A problematic board member or individual staff member may be removed for cause, but it might take the organization a long time to recover from the effects of this issue. The size of the community, the organization history, and how its leaders have dealt with the issue from the time it surfaced, will all have an effect on how long it takes the organization to recover sufficiently to launch a major campaign. If, however, the entire board is known to be ineffective or problematic, it may take longer for the organization to recover because it will probably have to completely overhaul its board and start anew building the community's confidence.

Most organizations, if aware of serious issues, do not even get to the point of doing a study until these issues have been resolved, but occasionally there are issues of which the organization is not aware. More often, the organization is ready to start planning the campaign even if it has some minor issues with which it needs to deal.

First, let us look at the organization that is ready to launch its campaign. The study report should show a timeline for implementation of the campaign. Generally, the first steps in the timeline include:

- Refining the case for support.
- Developing a campaign plan.
- Recruiting a campaign cabinet.

The case, having been tested in the study, usually needs some "tweaking" before it is considered to be in its final form. Often during the study, community members will offer different insights than the organization may have had when the preliminary case was developed. For example, the organization may have underestimated the cost escalation of the building project, may not have allowed enough campaign funds to be put into an endowment fund, or may have offered named giving opportunities that are not appealing to donors. Or they may have focused on programs in which there is not much interest and neglected to focus on programs that the community feels are important, necessary, and fundable.

In addition to refining the case statement, the organization should determine early in the campaign what materials it will need to prepare for the campaign. Sometimes during the study a whole new constituency may arise, such as civic and professional organizations, which may require a different approach, using different formats for the case statement. Another factor that may be decided based on input from the study interviews is how much should be spent on materials, and how "glitzy" should they be. Interviewees may have strong opinions, on either side of the issue, about the value of the organization's spending money on campaign materials. Although many of the materials used in a campaign will not be needed until the public phase of the campaign, the organization must allow ample time for design and production of materials, particularly if the design or production is going to be donated. Therefore, the case statement should be finalized and a complete list of campaign materials should be developed in the early stages of the campaign, based on input from interviewees during the study.

THE CAMPAIGN PLAN

If the consultant's report comes back saying the organization is ready to move forward with a campaign, the next step is to develop a campaign plan. This plan should include:

- A campaign timeline.
- A campaign budget.

- The scale of gifts and numbers of prospects that will be needed at each level.
- An organizational chart for the campaign cabinet.
- Position descriptions for all campaign volunteers and staff.

Campaign Timeline

The timeline will be based on several key factors contained in the report. The availability of top level gifts and the number of key community leaders who are available and willing to serve in campaign positions will affect how long it will take the organization to develop the campaign cabinet, fill committee positions, and develop its leadership gift list. The level of awareness of the organization on the part of potential key donors will determine how much time needs to be spent on cultivation events and activities.

Some information from the study that can be helpful in developing the timeline will be information on other campaigns in the community that might affect this campaign, the internal readiness of the organization, the level of board commitment, the number of prospects the organization has in its database already, and the number of prospective donors identified in the study, along with the number of potential volunteers that have been identified. All of these factors will affect how soon the organization can and should move forward with its campaign. If there are other major campaigns being conducted at the same time, the organization needs to carefully weigh whether this organization's constituents are likely to overlap with its own donor base. Just because there are multiple campaigns running simultaneously in a community, however, does not necessarily mean that this campaign cannot be successful. The organization must take into consideration how many of its own constituents will be affected by these other campaigns. For example, a major university campaign may not directly impact the constituents of the local synagogue that is contemplating a campaign unless its key members are also graduates of that university and likely to be tapped for major gifts to the university's campaign. However, a campaign for the local Boys and Girls Clubs may affect a campaign for Girl Scouts because some of their corporate donors may support both organizations and will most likely have an allotted amount of support set aside annually for capital campaigns.

The timing of other campaigns is important to note—are they in the silent phase, just getting ready for a campaign, or wrapping up a campaign? It will be important to research other nonprofits in the community and talk with their development people about their campaigns. Keep in mind that most campaigns have three- to five-year pledge payment cycles, so even if a major campaign in the community has already been completed or is in the final phase, donors may have multiple-year pledges to pay on these campaigns, diminishing the likelihood of a major gift to this campaign or perhaps a request for an extended pledge payment period. The key to determining the effect these campaigns will have on a new campaign is to analyze the number of donors who have solid ties to the organization in question and what these donors' relationship is to the other organizations that are running campaigns. If the relationship with its donors is solid, the organization will not be as affected by other campaigns, as would an organization whose donor relations are weak or whose donor history is limited.

Campaign Budget

The study should also prove helpful in the development of the campaign budget. Issues such as the need to hire additional staff or purchase software that are contained in the study recommendations will dictate how much of the campaign budget needs to be spent on beefing up the organization's infrastructure. Also, during a study, interviewees may express differing views, and sometimes strong opinions, about what type of materials should be used to promote the campaign. If it is clear that the organization's constituents expect high-tech, high-quality, and/or glitzy materials, a higher budget may be needed for publicity materials. On the other hand, sometimes during a study, constituents may express strong opinions that the organization should be conservative in their budget for campaign materials. Occasionally, someone will step forward during the interview process to volunteer his or her company's time and talent to produce campaign materials, thereby reducing the campaign materials budget drastically. The number and type of cultivation activities that will be needed will also affect the campaign budget and the study should provide recommendations in this area as well that will help the budgeting process.

The report should also provide a guideline for how much guidance the organization will need from fundraising counsel. Whether the organization needs resident counsel, periodic counsel for selected activities, or a monthly retainer for a specified number of days will affect the costs of the consulting services in the campaign budget. At this time, the organization should also decide if it plans to use the same counsel that conducted the study or if someone else will be brought in to provide campaign counsel. Sometimes an organization prefers to use a firm from outside their immediate area for the study in order to get a more objective viewpoint, but may prefer working with local counsel for the campaign because they will be working with counsel for an extended period of time. A local consultant can offer the benefit of knowing the community in addition to keeping travel expenses at a minimum, which may be a large factor in the budget if counsel is not local or regional. Although consulting fees are not generally addressed in the study report itself, the experience of working with a consultant during the study will give the organization an idea of the costs likely to be incurred for campaign counsel.

Scale of Gifts and Numbers of Prospects

The next key finding from the study that will help determine if the organization is ready to move forward is the number of prospects in the organization's database. While many organizations have successfully run capital campaigns as their first-ever fundraising attempt, in general, those organizations that have a base of existing donors will be far better prepared to launch a major campaign. If the organization does not have a strong donor history, the recommendation might be to delay the campaign until such a time when the organization has had an opportunity to identify and cultivate potential donors for a campaign. However, if the case is compelling enough and good volunteer leadership is secured, a campaign can successfully implement the process of identifying, cultivating, and soliciting donors within a relatively short time period.

Integrating the results of the internal assessment should be one of the first things the organization tackles, even if the consultant recommends that the organization is not ready for a campaign. If, for example, the internal assessment shows weaknesses in the infrastructure, now is the time for the organization to correct these weaknesses before preparing for a campaign. If the consultant recommends that the organization needs a new software system for fundraising, it typically takes several months to allocate funds for the software purchase, investigate different software program options, arrange for live or online demonstrations of each of these programs, and research other program users before making a decision. Another infrastructure issue that may take several months is preparing gift acceptance polices and office procedures for handling gifts. This is true particularly in the case of gift acceptance policies, because they require board approval. Again, it will be important for the organization to research what other, similar organizations have in place in this regard, perhaps request sample policies from other organizations or through the Association of Fundraising Professionals and other professional networks, determine what components their policies should include, draft proposed policies, and allow time for several revisions before they go to the board for approval.

A finalized scale of gifts and numbers of prospects that will be needed at each level should also be part of the campaign plan, and these figures may help determine the goal of the campaign. The study report should provide enough information for the organization to determine if it has a sufficient number of prospects in each category of the top levels of giving. Generally, the organization will need three to four prospects for every gift commitment listed on the scale of gifts. If this number of prospects has not been identified in the study, more time may be needed in the cultivation phase of the campaign, and most likely additional funds will need to be spent on cultivation activities.

Organizational Chart and Position Descriptions for Campaign Cabinet

The campaign plan should also provide an organizational chart for the campaign cabinet and position descriptions for all campaign volunteers and staff. Information gained in the study will be helpful in establishing the number of divisions that will be needed and the number of volunteers that will be needed in each of these divisions. For example, during the study, it may become apparent that a new category of constituents, important for the future campaign, has arisen; for example, a health clinic may decide that it needs a physician division and a dental division; a school may decide to add a grandparent division in addition to alumni and parents of students; or a community center may find that there are a number of service and professional organizations in its community and it may want to add a division to contact these organizations during the campaign.

STUDY REPORT RESULTS

If the study report says, "go ahead," the organization should consider itself fortunate that it is well prepared to run a campaign and pay careful attention to the recommendations in the study report in order to successfully complete their campaign according to the recommended time schedule. But what happens when the organization is not ready to proceed? First, the organization should not consider itself a "failure." Many organizations find in the study process that they are not ready to proceed with a campaign; in fact, sometimes the consultants will recommend, after the internal assessment, that they are not even ready to proceed with the community assessment part of the study.

If the study report does come back saying the organization is not ready for a campaign, the consultant will provide a rationale for this recommendation, along with suggestions for what the organization must do to prepare for a campaign. If the consultant does not make these recommendations, the organization should press the firm for the recommendations that should be part of a study report. The organization needs to know why it is not ready, and what it can do to better prepare itself for a campaign. Sometimes the stated goal may have been too high and, in this case, the consultant will recommend a lower goal; occasionally, a higher goal may be recommended if the organization has aimed too low. If the goal seems unattainable, the recommendation may be to do a "phased" campaign, first raising money for the most pressing needs, as perceived by the constituents, and then raising money for the remaining projects in a later phase of the campaign.

Following Up on Recommendations

If the organization needs to beef up its infrastructure, the consultant should provide specific recommendations for what is needed—software, policies, procedures, staffing, donor base, board development, and so on. These recommendations, if followed, will assure that the organization has the basis for a viable development program, even if it should choose to not run a campaign at all.

Often, organizations fear that they will have wasted their money on a study if the report says they are not ready for a campaign, but this is shortsighted thinking on the part of the organization's leadership. A good planning study report will help the organization see its shortcomings in the light of an objective outsider's view and, using the report recommendations, it should be able to build a much stronger organization, whether it chooses to proceed with a campaign or not.

VALIDITY OF THE STUDY

How long is the study valid? Often, an organization is uncertain about when to do a study, particularly if its leaders feel that the report will come back with a recommendation that they are not ready. Generally, a study report is valid for about 18 months; after that time, much of the information may be outdated. Certainly, competing community campaigns will change as current campaigns are wrapped up and new ones begin. Interviewees' responses to questions about the likelihood and size of their own or their company's gift are likely to change as well, due to different economic climates, business fluctuations, and personal life changes. And the availability of key volunteers has a limited time span; while one may be available and eager to get involved at the time of an interview, if the organization waits too long to proceed with its campaign, the volunteer may have lost interest or committed him- or herself to another campaign. Conversely, an interviewee who is committed somewhere else at the time of the interview may be available at a future date. The perception of community needs may also change due to a variety of factors, so what was once a strong, compelling case may weaken as time goes by, or new circumstances may actually strengthen the case.

What if the study says "no," but the organization has pressing needs and the board wants to proceed in spite of a negative report? Of course, paying a consultant to do a study and not heeding his or her advice may seem like a foolish thing to do, but sometimes the organization has no choice but to proceed. In fact, this is why the term *feasibility study* is often referred to as a *planning study,* because often the organization doesn't need to know if the campaign is feasible, they know it must be done. In this case, they are more interested in using the study to better position themselves for a campaign.

Extenuating Circumstances

If there are extenuating circumstances that require the organization to go forward with a building project, there are some options that can be considered. The organization can try to finance the project through other means, such as a bank loan or bond financing. Then, at a later time, a campaign may be initiated to enable the organization to fund program needs or endowment. A word of caution: It is very difficult for most organizations to raise money to retire debt, so this option should be considered only as a last resort. However, sometimes an organization can run a campaign that includes debt retirement along with other needs such as capital, endowment, or program needs.

Another option would be the phased campaign mentioned earlier; running a smaller campaign that is successful will do a lot more to boost the community's perception of the organization than attempting a major campaign effort that fails. The organization should discuss all its options seriously with the consultant who has conducted the study and seek his or her advice on how it can capitalize on what it has learned during the study.

CHAPTER 12

Seeking Help—The Benefits and Burdens of Working with a Consultant

SIMONE P. JOYAUX, ACFRE

"**M**e. Me. I'm a consultant. Hire me!"

Is that what you expected in this chapter? Well, hold on just a minute. Here's my mantra: "Hire a consultant if you need one. But don't hire a consultant unless you really need one!"

This chapter provides you with general information about the benefits and burdens of hiring a consultant, tips for selecting a consultant, and what you might expect when working with a consultant.

WHAT IS A CONSULTANT?

The dictionary defines a *consultant* as one who gives advice; an expert who charges a fee for providing advice or services in a particular field. Synonyms include *adviser, expert, mentor, guide,* and *counselor.*

A *consultancy* is defined as a process. During a consultancy, you discuss and deliberate together.

Quick tip: Be careful. You don't ask your consultant for permission before taking action. It's your organization. You decide. You are accountable. But if you are working with a consultant, make sure that you seek his or her opinion on issues before acting. The consultant is there to help you make the best choices. You and your consultant deliberate together.

WHO DECIDES THAT YOUR ORGANIZATION NEEDS A CONSULTANT?

If you're thinking about hiring a fund development consultant, I think this is a board decision, not a staff decision. Why? Because fund development affects the entire organization.

Fund development is not an independent part of your organization, isolated from the rest of operations and governance. Instead, fund development is woven into the values, mission, and vision of your organization. Fund development infiltrates every area of activity, affects every area of activity, and is affected by every area of activity.

Your board is responsible for the health and effectiveness of your organization—that's the basic concept of governance. Your board makes the governance-level decisions regarding fund development. For example, your board decides the amount of money that must be raised for what. (That's the budgeting process.) Your board decides what kinds of gifts the organization will and will not accept. (That's gift acceptance policies.)

Each of your individual board members helps with fund development in some way. For example, some board members identify prospective donors and solicit gifts. Some board members nurture philanthropic relationships. Other board members serve on the board's fund development committee or work on the special events committee. And, I hope, every single board member gives a personal charitable contribution each year, based on his or her personal ability.

With all this in mind, it's essential that the board decide if the organization needs a fund development consultant—because the board needs to own the decision. The process of deciding whether to hire a fund development consultant builds understanding and ownership. And the process of choosing the right consultant for your organization assures a good match between the individuals in your organization (e.g., the board members and the key staff people) and the consultant.

The process of selecting the right consultant for your organization is discussed later in this chapter. For now, just remember: The board decides whether to hire a fund development consultant. The board decides the general scope of the consultancy (e.g., hiring a consultant to conduct a feasibility study for a capital campaign). Board members should participate in the screening and selection process. And, of course, your organization's chief executive officer and chief development officer provide leadership to the process.

Quick tip: Competent fundraisers and fund development consultants all know the body of knowledge. These professionals understand best practice and the standards and ethics of the business. You're not picking a consultant based on expertise. Anyone selling him or herself as an expert adviser better be a subject matter expert.

So what are you seeking? You seek the person who is the best match for your organization. Picking the best consultant for your organization is discussed later in this chapter.

When Does Your Organization Need a Consultant?

Consider these situations:

- Your organization needs an expert. You don't have the necessary expertise and experience on staff to provide leadership.

- Your organization needs additional resources. You don't have sufficient staff resources to take on one more project, especially one as big as a possible capital initiative.

- Your organization needs objective outside evaluation. You worry that your organization may be weak in some areas. Or you're sure that your organization is weak in critical areas and you need an outsider to document this and suggest solutions.

- Those who care most about your organization (e.g., prospective funders) believe that feasibility studies are essential. You must have a feasibility study report to ensure their future participation—and you cannot figure out how to explain that a feasibility study will not add value.

The next sections in this chapter explore each of these situations.

Your Organization Needs an Expert

If your organization needs an expert, hire one.

Why do so many organizations think that anyone can be a fundraiser? Why do so many people think that personal opinion is just as valid as expertise? The reality is quite different.

Fund development is a profession with a body of knowledge that documents facts, principles, and best practice. The profession is based on codes of ethics and standards of professional practice.

Keep in mind that opinions are not helpful unless they are based on experience, application of the body of knowledge, exploration, and self-examination. Anything less compromises the quality of discussion and decision making.

Perhaps those who volunteer in the sector have become overly confident about their expertise and understanding of the body of knowledge. Just because a person chaired a capital campaign does not mean that the individual actually is an expert in fund development.

My favorite definition of philanthropy comes from Robert L. Payton, the first professor of philanthropics. Bob defines *philanthropy* as voluntary action for the common good.

We need volunteers in the sector. We need board members, committee members, fundraising volunteers, office volunteers, and direct service volunteers. In fact, I think that fund development is moving too far from volunteers. Organizations hire staff to do the fund development and, too often, the staff don't engage volunteers enough as cultivators and solicitors.

But, generally, these volunteers benefit from the leadership and enabling of professionals. It's the professionals who transmit the body of knowledge and help the volunteers perform accordingly.

Your fund development consultant provides the expertise your organization may lack. Your consultant supplies the body of knowledge and best practice as the basis for your organization's fund development. Your consultant interprets and personalizes the body of knowledge for your organization and its particular challenges and opportunities. Your expert adviser helps you anticipate and prevent problems. Your consultant intervenes in situations gone awry and helps you get out of difficulties.

YOUR ORGANIZATION NEEDS ADDITIONAL RESOURCES

Maybe your organization already possesses fund development expertise. Your chief development officer is one of the best. Your board understands its role and engages in strategic dialogue and decision making to guide fund development. Individual board members take on activities and are effectively enabled by the staff.

But you want another brain. You seek added value. You want more perspective. You want someone to question your assumptions and challenge your thinking. You want a consultant to partner his or her expertise with your own expertise.

You want another set of hands. You're a busy organization. Your competent staff and engaged volunteers are working hard. Adding a consultant to your team will expand the labor pool to do the work.

YOUR ORGANIZATION NEEDS OBJECTIVE OUTSIDE EVALUATION

Your organization isn't operating as smoothly as it should right now. And you're worried about what will happen if you try to launch something as big as a capital program.

Your organization has a history of difficulties—perhaps known only to insiders, making them increasingly anxious. Or perhaps others outside the organization know of the difficulties, and these are the very people and businesses whose support you will need.

Consensus? You keep hoping, but it isn't happening. Your leadership isn't even clear about what information is necessary to make a good decision, and what process should be used to make decisions.

You hope that a consultant can help your organization work through all these issues. You need your consultant to conduct an evaluation and share the findings—the good, the bad, and the ugly. You need your consultant to facilitate discussion and decision making. You're counting on a quality process that builds understanding and ownership.

But Maybe Your Organization Does Not Need a Consultant!

Here's a thought: Maybe your organization doesn't need a consultant. Remember my mantra: "Don't hire a consultant if you don't need one!" And the corollary? "Save your money if you can!"

Consider the following:

Does your organization actually need a feasibility study? Let's pretend that land and a building were given to you. This is a great opportunity, and you have accepted the gift. You own the building, but it needs some renovation. You plan to do the renovation as money is available. It's the best decision for you.

So why do you need a feasibility study? Why waste the time and money? How about doing really good fund development planning and designing a plan to raise money and renovate as you raise money?

Maybe you need to do all the renovation simultaneously and immediately. You've borrowed from the bank and the renovations are under way. In this situation, why would your organization need a feasibility study? Instead, do good fund development planning, and raise as much money as you can. However much money you raise reduces the loan and the loan payments.

Yes, this nonfeasibility approach works in any number of situations. You just have to convince those community people and businesses that are used to the feasibility study model.

Talk to them about return on investment. Discuss the cost and time requirements of a feasibility study. Share with them the extraordinary results of a good fund development planning process.

For example, share these concepts:

- A good planning and improvement consultancy can address the same issues as a feasibility study—and address the problems immediately.

- Organization staff and board members can speak personally with most of the donor prospects and secure honest responses. And, if necessary, the organization can hire a consultant to conduct confidential interviews with selected individuals who may not speak candidly with organization representatives.

Perhaps you're ready to launch your capital initiative. You didn't conduct a feasibility study. Instead, your excellent planning process provided you with a great plan. You're ready to start raising capital gifts. Your own development office, board members, and community leadership are engaged and committed.

And so off you go—without a consultant. That's the right decision for you. Great!

Quick tip: A good consultant does not automatically assume that you need a feasibility study. The best consultants talk with you about whether you actually need one.

The best consultants are innovative. They modify the traditional feasibility study model. Sometimes consultants suggest that your organization doesn't need a feasibility study. Instead, the consultant recommends a good fund development planning process, provides advice about how to make immediate improvements to your fund development program, and then says, "Go ahead, start raising those capital gifts." The best consultants help you decide whether you need a consultant for anything at all.

IS YOUR ORGANIZATION READY FOR A CONSULTANT?

Now this is a really big question. And usually it's the consultant who is wondering this. Unfortunately, not many organizations assess whether they are ready for a consultant.

I think your readiness for a consultant is about your organizational culture. Organizational culture refers to your organization's personality and the way your members interact and behave. Organizational culture is "the set of rarely articulated, largely unconscious, taken-for-granted beliefs, values, norms, and fundamental assumptions the organization makes about itself, the nature of people in general, and its environment. . . . Organizational culture consists of the set of unwritten rules that govern acceptable behavior within and even outside of the organization" (I. Mitroff, R. Mason, and C. Pearson, *Framebreak: The Radical Redesign of American Business,* San Francisco: Jossey-Bass, p. 65).

Consider the questions below. These questions are all about your organizational culture and your receptivity to questioning, learning, and change. And that's what a true consultancy is about. The best consultancy is all about questioning, learning, and change.

1. Do your board and staff understand the value of questioning your own assumptions—each individual's assumptions and your assumptions as a group?

2. Are your board members and staff most comfortable with each other and uncomfortable with those they consider outsiders?

3. Does your organization have a history of internal focus and self-reliance?

4. Are your board members and staff respectful of criticism and suggestions?

5. Is your organization comfortable with candor and respectful of criticism and suggestions?

6. Are your board members and staff comfortable with disagreement and arguing?

7. Do your board and staff know how to conduct conversations— rather than lobby for one point of view or another—and make decisions together?

8. Is your organization committed to learning and innovation? Is your organization adaptive and committed to making change?

9. Is your organization continually trying to enhance its capacity to carry out its mission?

10. Does your organization have a pattern of doing what it thinks is best, regardless of expert advice?

11. Does your organization conduct regular assessments of all areas of operation, analyze and discuss the findings, and figure out how to make change?

12. Does your organization have a regular process to secure input from those outside the inner circle, including clients, donors and funders, other service providers, and community leaders?

13. Does your organization regularly evaluate its relevance to the community, and modify its mission and services as necessary?

These are tough questions. I wouldn't expect any organization to score 100 percent on any of the questions. But if you want a successful consultancy, you must confront these questions. Yes, confront them. Confront these questions in a board meeting. Confront these questions at the staff level.

Maybe you are ready. But perhaps not.

Quick tip: Remember, your consultant will help you cope with the resulting stress related to these questions. But your consultant cannot do a good job if your organization and its leadership are unable to pursue the paths required by these questions.

THE BENEFITS OF WORKING WITH A CONSULTANT

If you are ready for the consultancy, it can provide specific benefits to your organization.

Consider the level of risk as you think about a capital campaign. Your organization may need to raise more money than ever before. People inside and outside of your organization are asking really tough questions. Some of these questions are uncomfortable, and some of the answers might be very uncomfortable.

You know that board members and staff have different opinions. Perhaps your board and staff have difficulty speaking candidly about issues. You see conflict coming soon.

Often, a consultant can help. As an expert adviser, the consultant can analyze and interpret information. As a trusted adviser, your consultant can help develop organization-wide understanding and negotiate alignment across board and staff.

For example, using a consultant in capital campaign planning should accomplish the following:

- A well-coordinated and integrated inquiry that documents the perceptions and opinions of prospective donors regarding your proposed project.

- A careful analysis of your internal operations that highlights the challenges and outlines solutions.

- A careful analysis, both internal and external, that identifies opportunities and outlines how to take advantage of them.

- Recommendations about what to do next and how to do it.

The consultant is your confidant, coach, and mentor. The consultant makes sure that the questions are asked and answered as well as possible for your organization at this time.

The consultant runs interference and confronts the challenging people. The consultant keeps ego damage to a minimum and negotiates difficult decisions. The consultant fosters organizational learning.

But remember: These benefits result only if you are ready for the consultant and the consultancy.

THE BURDENS YOU FACE WHEN WORKING WITH A CONSULTANT

An effective consultancy requires full disclosure. Your organization has to make its internal and external processes open and understandable to the consultant, who is, at first, an outsider. Your organization must divulge any skeletons in the closet—and the consultant will make sure that all the elephants in the room are revealed.

The consulting process is risky. Your organization's best ideas and fondest hopes will be questioned. You may hear things you don't want to hear. You will be expected to face issues you do not wish to face. Certainly, you will be uncomfortable at times. Board members and staff may feel vulnerable. But only with full disclosure, candor, and questioning can the consultant help you achieve your desires.

In addition to the risk, there's the workload. Yes, part of the burden is more work. Your organization has to do its regular work while participating in the consultancy. You have to maintain your program quality, serve your clients, and conduct your typical management and governance activities.

Sometimes you'll tell the consultant, "No dice, we cannot do what you want us to do now." Other times, the consultant will say, "You really have to do this now or the consultancy cannot move forward." Your organization must balance both, and that's stressful and exhausting and often seems impossible.

Use your consultant to help you figure out how to balance your regular work and the consultancy. Come up with a work plan that accounts for your key dates and the expectations of the consultancy. Speak candidly with your consultant. Don't follow blindly. Yes, you've hired expert advice—but the consultant isn't walking in your shoes and needs your feedback.

But perhaps the biggest burden of all is change. And change is the biggest benefit, too.

THE CONSULTANT AS CHANGE AGENT

I believe that a consultant is a change agent, whether your organization wants change or not. Lots of consultants believe that. And some don't, I imagine.

What does change mean? To become different; to exchange, substitute, or replace something. To pass from one state or stage to another. Synonyms include *transform* and *revolutionize*. Transformation seems to inspire people, and revolution worries people. Your organization might benefit from either or both!

People decide that change is difficult and threatening. Despite the reality of a complex and uncertain world (and that means ongoing change!), many act as if change is unexpected, unwelcome, and undesirable.

My short answer to that is: Get over it. My longer answer is that your consultant should help your organization understand why change is necessary, overcome the anxiety, manage the stress, and devise the best change process.

And your consultant can hold your hand through the change process. Your consultant can provide you with ongoing advice, personal coaching, and mentoring. Your consultant provides a safe place for you to complain and whine, and then helps you go back out into the changing world and move forward.

How about those change naysayers? The ones who say "If it ain't broke, don't fix it." Or "the devil we know is better than the one we don't know." Or "we've always done it this way and it seems to work well."

One of my favorite articles ever is by Carl Sussman, "Making Change: How to Build Adaptive Capacity," published in the winter 2003 issue of *The Nonprofit Quarterly* (www.nonprofitquarterly.org). Sussman describes adaptive capacity as "the skill to take the initiative in making adjustments for improved performance, relevance, and impact. Fundamentally, it is the ability to respond to and instigate change."

Surely, all organizations want better performance, relevance, and impact. No one is perfect. All can benefit from improvements—and that's change. The most effective organizations understand that they develop adaptive capacity so they can make change.

I urge you to read Sussman's article. He talks about how to build your organization's adaptive capacity so that you can make meaningful change. Rest assured, the best consultants are focusing on that—how to develop your organization's adaptive capacity. The best consultants help you make changes.

Let me share with you some thoughts as a consultant. Do you know what I think about?

I think about quality customer service—and the definition that says, "meet the client's expectations." And I know that sometimes clients don't want my candid questions and comments. Clients don't want to hear about best practice because they don't want to do it.

But I believe that my job is to be a change agent. I think a consultant is a resource for the body of knowledge, a questioner, a confronter, a teacher, and a coach and mentor.

I have my ethics and standards of practice. And so I'll confront you. Even if it means that you fire me or I choose to quit.

I think about how I will find out if you are ready for a consultant. And I do that during the interview. I have questions and comments that I make to test whether you are ready for a change agent.

I think a lot about the change process. I think about how to help you define the change necessary to help you achieve your desires. I think about how to help you understand.

I think about how I will monitor the consultancy. I figure out how I will evaluate whether the consultancy is working. And sometimes, I have to figure out how to end the consultancy because you are not ready for a change agent.

Managing change means managing courage. Your organization has to manage its courage. And the consultant has to manage his or her own courage.

What Expertise Should You Expect in Your Consultant?

Of course, you need fund development expertise. Your consultant needs to know about prospect identification and solicitation, donor communications, solicitation strategies, management and reporting systems for gift giving, and much more.

This is a big, broad scope of knowledge. And there's a handy list to help you with the body of knowledge in fund development. Visit CFRE International (www.cfre.org) and review the test content outline. This describes the knowledge areas required for fundraisers. CFRE International developed this outline through a process called *role delineation,* which involves a professional testing service and surveys of fundraisers around the world.

As noted earlier in this chapter, fund development is not an independent function within the organization. Fund development is inextricably linked to every area of operation. Fund development affects every area of operation and is affected by every area of operation.

In my experience, most fundraising problems are not fundraising problems. Instead, most fundraising problems relate to other areas of operation. For example:

- Perhaps your organization is no longer relevant to the community served. Their allegiance has shifted to other organizations, and you cannot raise charitable gifts. This is a mission and services problem best fixed through strategic planning.
- Perhaps your board members are reluctant to help with fund development activities. Board members complain that they didn't join the board to do fundraising. This is a board recruitment problem best fixed through governance analysis.

I think the best fundraisers are both technicians and organizational development specialists. I think of consultants in the same way. Your consultant helps you solve the problems that affect fund development—even when they are not fund development problems. Take a look at my monograph about organizational development specialists, *Choosing Your Road: Organizational Development Specialist or Just Another Fundraising Technician,* at www.simonejoyaux.com/resources/free library/fund development.

A consultant needs other skills as well. As a change agent, the consultant needs to be a good communicator and a good teacher, a coach, and a mentor. The consultant needs to manage group dynamics, facilitate participatory decision making, and help resolve conflict.

What Kind of Consultant Do You Want? Here's What I Want

You need a subject matter expert. And remember, subject matter experts for fund development are not just great fundraising technicians. Great fund development advisers are also organizational development specialists. See the earlier section in this chapter, "What Expertise Should You Expect in Your Consultant?"

For fund development consulting, you need a process expert. Your organization's consultant must help board and staff members understand why, not just what. Your consultant must help you understand how to anticipate and prevent, implement and evaluate.

Does it matter if the consultant has worked with your type of organization? I don't think so. You're the expert in environmentalism or domestic violence or education or social justice. The consultant needs to listen well. The consultant needs to be flexible, sensitive, and adaptive. But you are responsible for your specific body of knowledge. Together, your leadership and the consultant personalize fund development for your organization.

Does it matter if the consultant knows your community? Why would it matter? You know your community. And the consultant probes what you know, helps you learn more, and then helps you apply this information to your organization.

Does it matter if the consultant has raised millions in other capital campaigns? I don't think so. The basic principles of fund development are the same, whether you want to raise $50,000 for operating support or $50 million for capital.

But this is such a huge difference in amount! Certainly, something about dollars raised must make some difference. Consider finding out the following about the consultant: What kind of expertise does he or she have in working with diverse donors, including those whose assets are very, very large and also very small? How experienced is the consultant in working with staff and volunteers who have solicited gifts at various levels? What is the consultant's level of sophistication regarding negotiating gifts of diverse sizes?

What else should you look for? There are lots of great subject matter experts available in the marketplace. There are lots of consultants with diverse expertise and experience. Many consultants have helped many organizations raise thousands and millions of dollars. All of these consultants can give you expert advice.

Here's what I consider when picking a consultant: Yes, I want a subject matter expert. I expect a fund development consultant to be able to do and explain everything in the role delineation of CFRE International. I expect diverse experience, specifically, different types and sizes of organizations.

I expect the consultant to have *experience working with the evolutionary stage of the particular organization.* This is very important. I've cleaned up too many messes made by experienced fund development consultants who couldn't work effectively with small organizations, limited staff capacity and capability, inexperienced board members, and a start-up development program.

Think about cultural competence. People — including consultants — have different levels of comfort with diversity. And organizations have different comfort levels, too. My favorite definition of diversity references the fact that people experience life differently. And sometimes people who experience life differently cannot work well together. For example, is your LGBTQ organization comfortable working with a straight consultant? Will your Latina organization feel comfortable with a white male consultant?

I think that cultural competence also refers to organizational culture. For example, does your organization prefer a more traditional corporate style or a more folksy grassroots style? Does your organization make top-down decisions?

To a very significant degree, picking the right consultant is about the match between your organization's culture and the consultant's approach, style, and behavior. Why? Because the consultant is so much more than an expert adviser to your organization.

But I still want more in my consultant. When it comes to fund development, strategic planning, management, and governance, I want more. These are all issues that probe the depth and breadth of an organization. These are the high-risk issues that worry both board and staff. These issues require a personal and intimate relationship between the organization and the consultant, and the organization's leaders and the consultant.

Can your leadership imagine confiding in the consultant, sharing worries and aspirations? Will your leadership be at ease with the consultant for long periods of time — whether the meetings are long or the consultancy extends over months or even years?

There's a wonderful book called *The Trusted Advisor* by David H. Maister, Charles H. Green, and Robert M. Galford (New York: Free Press, 2001). The authors describe the trusted adviser as the highest level of consulting. The trusted adviser is "the person the client turns to when an issue first arises, often in times of great urgency: a crisis, a change, a triumph, or a defeat" (p. 8).

The trusted adviser operates at a different level than the expert adviser. "The trusted adviser acts variously as a mirror, a sounding board, a confessor, a mentor, and even, at times, the jester or fool" (*The Trusted Advisor,* p. 10).

The authors propose various characteristics of a trusted adviser. Here are some of my favorites:

- Sees the client as a partner and equal in the consultancy journey.
- Focuses on problem definition and resolution, recognizing that this is more critical than mastering a body of knowledge.
- Constantly seeks new ways to be of greater service to the client.
- Focuses on doing the right thing (and I would add doing it the right way, e.g., the end does not justify the means).
- Pays attention to what is most effective for the particular client, and uses and personalizes (or discards) models, methods, techniques, and processes accordingly (*The Trusted Advisor,* p. 14).

Your organization chooses what kind of consultant it wants. Think carefully. Review the consultant's materials and highlight what you learned. Schedule interviews and ask the right questions to find out what you want to know. Check references.

Then think about those two words, "trusted adviser." That's the kind of consultant I want to hire. That's the kind of consultant I want to be.

USE THE INTERVIEW TO HELP YOU PICK THE RIGHT CONSULTANT FOR YOUR ORGANIZATION

Yes, you must interview the consultant. A face-to-face interview is great. But sometimes that isn't possible. You can make a telephone interview work. Then check references well—and you can hire someone without ever meeting personally, face-to-face.

Remember what I said earlier: Board members must participate in the interview of a consultant. Here's my idea of a great interview team for a feasibility study consultancy: your organization's chief executive officer and the chief development officer, the volunteer who will be board chair during the consultancy, the volunteer who will chair the fund development committee during the consultancy, and maybe a couple more board members.

Plan the interview in advance. Outline the questions you plan to ask. The consultant outlines his or her questions, too. Pay attention to the questions that the consultant asks—these questions tell you a lot about the consultant.

The interview is a conversation, not just questions and answers. The consultant tells you stories about his or her work with other organizations. What stories will you tell about your organization?

Quick tip: As a consultant, I'm carefully picking the stories that I tell you because these stories will help you understand how I work. If you don't like the stories, then you won't like working with me. I'm testing you.

I'm telling you about my style and my approach and my values. I don't need to tell you my subject matter expertise; you should see that in my background information on my Web site or in printed materials.

Another quick tip: Remember that while you interview the consultant, the consultant interviews you. The successful consulting engagement requires mutual selection. The consultant picks you and you pick the consultant.

Have you ever wondered how a consultant decides whether or not he or she wants to work with you? You should wonder and you should ask!

"Hello, Ms. Consultant: How do you decide which organizations you want to work with?" In 20 years of consulting, no more than 10 organizations have ever asked me this question. And yet, this is definitely a two-way interview. You think you're interviewing me? Well, I'm interviewing you, too. I'm asking you questions and, based on how you answer and what you answer, I'm thinking about whether we would be a good match.

CHECK REFERENCES!

Make sure you check references. And talk with both staff and board members who worked with the consultant.

Ask the consultant to provide you with references that somehow match with your organization. And evaluate how appropriate the references are for your organization. You want to talk with organizations that may be similar to you culturally (and remember that cultural competence itself is diverse). You want to speak with organizations that used the consultant for similar work.

Remember to avoid "yes" and "no" questions. Probe if you don't understand the answer or want more information.

Consider the following kinds of reference questions:

1. How well did the consultant listen to you and the others participating in the consultancy?

2. How well did she understand the various aspects of your organization's situation and the nature of your organization's work?

3. How comfortable were you sharing your organization's successes and failures, worries and questions?

4. How effective was she at personalizing information, strategies, and recommendations to your organization?

5. How effective was she at managing the diverse personalities within your organization?

6. How effective was she at managing conflict and negotiating agreement with the diverse players, departments, and so on within your organization?

7. To what degree did you feel you could entrust her with everything and anything?

8. What kind of reservations would you have about hiring this consultant again?

9. Tell me about the consultant's ethics and integrity, candor, and responsiveness.

10. Tell me about the consultant's inquisitiveness, innovativeness, and adaptability.

11. Tell me about the consultant's perception, insightfulness, and enthusiasm.

Summary

Your organization faces both benefits and burdens working with a consultant. Careful consideration is critical.

For certain issues, including a fundraising feasibility study, the choice to hire a consultant and the selection of the consultant is a shared decision. Your organization's leadership—both board and key staff—decide together. For example:

- Whether you need a consultant.
- Whether the benefits outweigh the burdens of working with a consultant.
- Whether your organization is ready for a consultant and prepared for change.

This chapter provides perspective about organizational needs and readiness, and consultant expertise and approach. The consultant is described as a subject matter expert, coach, mentor, and confidant. The consultant serves as a trusted adviser and change agent.

Picking the right consultant depends on your organization's self-awareness. Through the interview process and reference checks, your organization and the consultant must find the right match to create a viable partnership.

Think carefully. Talk to other organizations and multiple consultants. Plan well.

Hire a consultant if you need one. Find the right consultant for your organization. Don't hire a consultant unless you really need one.

CHAPTER 13

Taking It Home—Applying What You Learned

MARTIN L. NOVOM, CFRE

INTRODUCTION

In the first 12 chapters we covered the entire range of activities and processes of the fundraising feasibility study. At this point you might be asking yourself, "What do I do with all this information?" or, "How do I get started?" This chapter seeks to answer such questions and it covers these areas:

- Further exploration—when there is little pressure to pursue a study.
- Considerations for consultants—those current and future.
- Applying the subject matter—when a feasibility study seems likely.

FURTHER EXPLORATION—WHEN THERE IS LITTLE PRESSURE TO PURSUE A STUDY

There are lots of reasons why you might seek out, obtain, and read this book. You may not have sought it and its contents because of a pressing need for your organization. You might have just wanted to know more about this fascinating diagnostic tool. While my contributing authors and I have worked hard to include as much applicable information as possible, we have also been mindful of the need to keep the book to a reasonable length. It has been a balancing act. To reach the right balance, we have not covered every aspect to the maximum depth. Perhaps there is a specific topic, or topics, that you are interested in that would benefit from further exploration.

If you are someone who seeks to broaden his or her general knowledge of the campaign process, we encourage you to continue in your exploration by collecting and compiling all the samples related to capital campaign planning and the feasibility study that you can find. Whenever I get interested in a new subject, I get started by setting up a three-ring binder to collect and organize all that I can find on that subject. In this way, I create a living archive of the topic I am studying. You could begin your further exploration by reading some of the resources we have included in the bibliography. Personally, I am partial to the real stuff, actual examples of materials that are or have been in use with nonprofit organizations.

I have had real success by looking out for materials that friends and colleagues in other nonprofit organizations are using and willing to share with me. My experience with professional philanthropic fundraisers is that most are quite willing to share materials as long as they are not confidential. In this manner I have examined internal and external campaign and campaign planning materials, including feasibility study reports. It is important to be sensitive to the situation other organizations may be in, as well as candid about your reasons for wanting to read such documents. Timing also matters. It is much easier to get a positive response for your request to see a feasibility study report once their campaign is over.

Why Look Beyond This Book?

To produce this book, I purposely brought together a range of professionals experienced with the feasibility study process. The authors represent a wide geography, from Calgary to Las Vegas, and from Hawaii to Vermont. Their collective experience covers virtually all types and sizes of nonprofit organizations, including those found in urban, suburban, and rural locales. Nevertheless, I think I speak for all of us in saying we want to encourage in you an attitude of healthy skepticism. Don't believe what we have written just because it is printed in these pages. Take the time to think through what you have read, compare it with your experiences, and then make up your own mind. This means that we, the authors, do not view this book as the final word on the fundraising feasibility study but, rather, just the beginning of an open discussion and dialogue.

Reading books and collecting material is not the full extent of what you can do to broaden your knowledge and experience. If you are fortunate enough to be a staff member or volunteer leader in an organization that is in campaign planning mode, you could be right in the thick of it. In that case, it is more likely than not that a fundraising feasibility study is or will be in your work plan. If you are not so fortunate, you can chose to volunteer for an organization that is planning a campaign. If you live in or near a larger city, you may have more chances to do so than someone who lives in a smaller city. Being able to get involved, as a volunteer, in a campaign, or in campaign planning depends largely on how watchful and persistent you are. Nothing is as instructional for campaign planning as direct experience.

While it is unlikely as a new volunteer that you will be allowed to be the fly on the wall for serious strategy discussions, I can imagine the earnest student of the feasibility study can gain exposure to working documents (draft case for giving, table of gifts, etc.) or even a summary of the feasibility study report. Depending on the level of your involvement, as well as the size and complexity of the organization, you may or may not get to view a full feasibility study report. If you are a curious person, like me, who wants the exposure, the worst thing that can happen is that your offer to volunteer will be declined. There are always other places to try.

CONSIDERATIONS FOR CONSULTANTS

Based on the reactions I received from consulting colleagues prior to publication, I will assume that you have found this book at least partially instructive. My hope, and that of my contributing authors, is that by making this step to openly discuss what has been for far too long a quiet or secretive part of the fundraising consulting world, we will encourage you as a colleague to discuss openly all aspects of the fundraising feasibility study process.

As you know only too well, opportunities to discuss the unique challenges of fund-raising consulting are far too infrequent. If you are a member of a consulting firm that belongs to either the Giving Institute (formerly the American Association of Fund Raising Counsel, AAFRC) or the Association of Philanthropic Counsel (APC), you are fortunate indeed. Both of these organizations place open dialogue between member firms a part of their mission. If, like me, you are member of the Association of Fund-raising Professionals (AFP), or any of the other associations focused on fundraising, such as the Association for Healthcare Philanthropy (AHP) or the Council for Advancement and Support of Education (CASE), you may have had the occasional opportunity to network with other consultants. I encourage you to do as much formal networking in that regard as you can. Perhaps you can set something up similar to what the AFP of Northern New England has done and create a regular dialogue group for fundrais-ing consultants. We named it Consultant to Consultant and AFP-NNE (the chapter covers the states of Vermont, New Hampshire, and Maine) has been providing this opportunity for consultants to meet and discuss their unique questions and issues at the annual November conference since 2001. These sessions have been a very lively source of exchange and are widely appreciated by New England fundraising consultants involved in AFP. You could do the same or something like it in your geographic area.

Whether you engage in open group dialogue with other consultants or not, there is much you can do to further and deepen your familiarity with the range of approaches that experienced fundraising consultants are currently employing. I urge you to reach out, with a collaborative attitude, to your fundraising colleagues. The more we share, the more we know. The more we know, the more knowledgeable our nonprofits can be.

The more knowledgeable the nonprofit sector is at large, the more effective we can all be at working on societal issues and cultural improvement.

A note to new consultants, or those new to the feasibility study: Perhaps you purchased this book because you hoped that it would be useful to you as you consider becoming a fundraising consultant. It could be that you are already functioning as one but you have not been, as yet, offering your services to do feasibility studies. In either case, I have some suggestions for you to consider.

For the person who is thinking about moving into consulting, my recommendation for you is to focus your new consulting practice on what you already know, where you already have demonstrated your mastery. Does this mean that there is some kind of exclusive "club" or impenetrable barrier between you and your first feasibility study? No, of course not. Once you have developed a track record as a successful consultant, either on your own or as part of a firm, then it might make sense for you to move thoughtfully into work involving a fundraising feasibility study. In any case, I strongly urge you to work with a consultant experienced with feasibility studies. There are a couple of ways you might to do this. If you are on your own or planning to be on your own, you could find an experienced fundraising professional who does feasibility studies who might welcome your help in conducting interviews. Of the senior consultants I know, most appreciate an opportunity to help newer members of the profession. Not everyone will see you as a competitor.

Some men and women seeking entry into the fundraising consulting field go to work for a consulting firm whose organizational framework is structured to include people new to the field. This is how many fundraising consultants get their start. Often, the consulting firms that utilize people new to the field are offering their campaign and campaign planning services to nonprofit clients on what we call a residency basis. A consultant working under a resident arrangement lives in close proximity to the client organization, on a temporary basis, for the duration of the contract. This contrasts with another model, called the periodic basis. The main distinction between residency and periodic basis is the volume of time the consultant spends per month or per week with the client institution. A resident consultant can spend three or more days per week with the client, and the consultant works primarily for just that one organization. A periodic consultant arrangement has the consultant coming to the institution periodically, for example a few days a month. While the consultant in that instance may stay overnight, he or she does not take up a temporary residence and is probably working for a number of client institutions.

One final word of caution: Relying solely on the reading of this book does not, in and of itself, automatically prepare you to conduct a fundraising feasibility study as a consultant. It's just a good start.

APPLYING THE SUBJECT MATTER—WHEN A STUDY SEEMS LIKELY

If your organization is, or if you think it should be, contemplating a capital campaign, then it is most likely time for you and your colleagues to begin by first taking stock of the situation facing your organization. In awareness of this need to take stock, I offer some questions for you to consider in the spirit of organizational self-reflection.

Why does a campaign seem so attractive?

Could it be that your organization may be rushing toward the idea of a campaign because of internal or external financial concerns? Does your current roster of philanthropic support programs lack luster or depth and the notion of a campaign seems to offer some relief? Is the excitement of a potential campaign being perceived as possibly making it easier to raise money or making your organization more attractive to your donors?

Only those of you with a strong and intimate connection to your organization can provide meaningful answers to such questions. You won't find the answers in a book, certainly not in this one. Regardless, it is important for you to understand what might be at the root of why a campaign is appealing to your leadership and, possibly, to your major contributors. With this kind of background, you are in the ideal starting position to determine if the pursuit of a potential capital campaign, and therefore a feasibility study, is in your best strategic interests.

How widespread is the belief among your key leadership that a capital campaign is a viable option, either as one of the funding mechanisms or the sole funding mechanism, for the project under consideration?

Are you alone or do you hold the minority view, in your organization in thinking about a capital campaign? Is the opposite true—that many in your organization are ready to start investigating a campaign but you are holding back? Where on the continuum of "for it" to "not for it" do you think your organizational leadership currently rests? Has debt financing and financial reserves, as well as a potential capital campaign, been examined as possible funding sources for the project? For this piece of self-reflection, we should be less concerned with final answers than we are in the quality our knowledge and understanding of the attitudes and beliefs within our organization.

What is the overall tone or perspective in your organization regarding philanthropy?

Is there a general view within your organization that charitable giving happen, but not significantly? Does your organization have a track record of effectively raising gift money? Is there a desire to obtain charitable gift support but a reluctance to do the work or invest the necessary resources? The range of perspectives and attitudes held by nonprofit organizations in this regard is very broad. What is most important is acknowledging the unique perspectives with regard to philanthropy that live in and around your organization.

GREEN LIGHT, RED LIGHT

To help make the point, I will answer the above self-reflective questions in two quite contrasting ways. I will answer them:

1. Imagining the most positive and supportive situation.
2. Picturing a very negative and unsupportive situation.

By examining these admittedly extreme positions we can arrive at a clearer picture of what you might be facing, in view of what you have taken so far from this book. Obviously, nothing is usually so black and white, and most situations are somewhere in the middle.

The Most Positive Situation

Let's imagine the following scenario: The attraction to the idea of a campaign is based on the full knowledge of your choices for funding options for your organization. It appears that a capital campaign might make good strategic sense as a likely funding source. There is some amount of resident knowledge of the extent of the work required, both in terms of the level of intensity and in duration, for your organization. This is a situation where the possibility of conducting a campaign, as a viable funding option, is a widely held view among your leadership. Finally, the general tone in your organization regarding philanthropy is one that encourages donors and friends to participate in stewarding your mission, and seeking their charitable support is a natural extension of that open approach to stewardship.

To recap, we have an organization considering campaign funding based on knowledge of possible funding sources, reflecting a widespread perception among its leadership and consistent with ongoing efforts fostering philanthropic relationships.

Now let's contrast that with a vastly different picture.

The Most Negative Situation

Imagine an organization where the attraction to the notion of a campaign is based on misconceptions, unrealistic expectations, or partial information. Further, in this worst-case scenario, picture a divide in the level of support for investigating a campaign, with advocates both strongly for and strongly against investing resources in campaign planning.

Worse still, imagine an organization, which does not appear to embrace philanthropic relationships, nor does it raise charitable gift dollars either regularly or of any significant size.

These are two strongly divergent scenarios. In the first case, I painted a picture intended to give a green light for moving forward to investigate campaign planning. In the second case, it is obvious that more work should be done before one might feel comfortable with such an organization investing time and resources to investigate a potential campaign.

A Solo Inquiry or One with an Institutional Authority

There is an important distinction built into this notion of first determining the terrain. Any amount of investigation by your organization of a potential campaign should be conducted both consciously and with some form of mandate from an authorized body. There is a vast difference between an individual educating him or herself about capital campaigns, and fundraising feasibility studies, on the one hand and beginning a serious inquiry on behalf of an organization on the other. What you learn on your own is valuable and certainly gives you an increased understanding as you move forward. However, just because you think it is an important and worthy activity does not automatically give you the authorization to operate on behalf of your organization. Reaching conclusions or choosing pathways for your organization is best done as part of a clearly articulated assignment on behalf of the organization. In some institutions, it is considered a group activity.

Know how your organization makes decisions before you start plowing ahead. The adventurous solo inquirer, toiling on behalf of an unasked organization might not be appreciated or even given any value. Study and ponder on your own if you want, but remember it is education work when done solo. It only becomes organizational work when it is done by formal request or assignment.

Utilizing the Information in This Book

I have purposely placed this particular section of the chapter last. If you're like me, the need to know something can be an extremely strong motivator and so can the tendency to cut to the chase. I placed this here in the chapter to ensure you had the benefit of the discussions contained in the previous sections. They offer you and your colleagues useful and, possibly, vitally important information.

Perhaps you acquired this book with the expectation of pursuing a feasibility study all along. Having glanced through or thoroughly gleaned the previous 12 chapters, you remain convinced that your institution needs to consider conducting a feasibility study.

What's next for your and for your organization? Assuming that you are equipped with the knowledge of the landscape setting of your institution, let us proceed.

Determining Readiness for an Expenditure of Organizational Resources

Everything you do from this point on has some amount of commitment of resources and, therefore, some level of risk attached to it. The potential risks include disappointment, less-than-expected return on staff and/or volunteer investment, and less-than-optimal return on expenditures. Because of these risks, I urge you to think through the next steps carefully *before* rushing ahead.

In order to attain a productive feasibility study, and to minimize the risk factors, you should have affirmative responses to most, if not all, of the following questions:

1. Is the need or opportunity (the case) clear, and does it have general agreement?

2. Does the case fit into your organization's strategic plan?

3. Has your board discussed and generally embraced the notion of a potential capital campaign?

4. Has your senior management discussed and generally embraced the notion of a potential capital campaign?

Moving Slowly or Moving Rapidly

Without knowing your specific situation it is difficult, if not foolish, for me to make blanket statements about the next steps connected with a possible feasibility study for your organization. There are many variables to consider. However, it might be useful to look at the conditions surrounding the two "speeds" of moving ahead, slowly or rapidly, to help clarify your choice of actions.

Moving Slowly

Moving slowly offers some you and your organization some important advantages. You want to move slowly if you need more time to continue to build support within your organization and within your key volunteer leaders. It may be that there are certain aspects of your case that need additional time to become clarified. You might have a "chicken and egg" issue with an outside legal entity (a city, country, state, or even federal authority) whose approval is required sometime prior to the completion of the project for which the money would be raised. You need their approval, but the timing and the sequence of approaching, and of formally requesting their approval, may have to be accommodated. Moving slowly may allow you to incorporate their timeline and approval process into your schedule.

Moving slowly might also support any need you have to accommodate internal planning or staffing issues. It is possible that your institution needs this project completed tomorrow. However, there can sometimes be competing internal timelines with regard to staffing key positions, or with succession and grooming issues related to board leadership. Perhaps there are building and/or land design issues whose resolution it is not possible to speed up. For these and many other reasons, moving slowly can reflect the recognition that your institution will benefit from a smooth and continuous development of what will become the essential parts of a successful campaign.

Moving Quickly

Moving quickly has an entirely different set of dictates. It may be that there are issues or situations connected with your organization that demonstrate that the best interests are served by moving quickly. Perhaps there is a specific window of opportunity connected with acquiring a particular parcel of highly desired land. It may be that your organization's current site requires immediate action. Perhaps ongoing discussions or activities have continued for so long that there is a possibility of losing valuable volunteer leadership or donor support unless things move ahead in a brisk manner. Perhaps you have an extremely valuable volunteer leader, such as a potential campaign chair, who is able to play an important leadership role only within a specific time frame. Again, there are many instances where real life situations support the decision to move quickly.

In terms of considering a feasibility study, the difference between moving slowing and moving quickly probably has more to do with how much time you allow between the each of the steps to consider, select, conduct, and integrate results from a feasibility study.

WHO DECIDES?

Contacting potential consulting firms often seems like the first step. However, I would suggest that you need to be sufficiently clear about who is making the decisions within the organization on the big questions and who is doing the legwork on the small details. Every organization has its own leadership configuration of who leads and who follows. For some organizations, the chief executive officer or executive director operates in the forward position, leading the discussion and even the decision making. In other institutions, it is the president of the board, or the board as a whole. I have seen situations where the chair of a standing board committee, such as a development committee, is so respected and influential that they are, in essence, providing leadership in this process. Simone Joyaux makes the very strong and appropriate argument, in Chapter 12, for the importance of the board making such decisions. My comments here merely reflect the fact that there is what we would like to strive for and then there is often the situation we actually have. In any case, you will have seen elsewhere in this book the statement that you need staff and volunteer leadership involvement for the process to be effective.

In recognition of the risks present, it is important to be clear about:

- What criteria will be used for the selection of fundraising counsel for a possible study, and who is included in the decision?
- What is the sequence and timing for arriving at the selection?
- Where will funds come from to pay for the study?
- What is the draft timeline for a study and for a possible campaign?

Having agreement about these basic questions will go a very long way to help you as you begin your next steps with confidence and clarity.

Networking with Other Organizations

Just as I encourage fundraising consultants to be in dialogue with each other, there is much to be gained from conversations between nonprofit organizations. If you are the top administrative or executive person, you can gain tremendous insight by being in contact with other nonprofit executives. Look first to your particular niche, other organizations like yours (environmental, educational, social services, arts, religious, health care, at-risk populations, etc.). If you are at a loss of where to turn, contact your local community foundation. They often have a very clear, and sometimes deep, sense of which organizations in your area have done a fundraising feasibility study.

Summary

In this final chapter, we covered the various ways you as a reader might make use of the material provided by our team of authors. For those readers who are gathering further information and expanding their knowledge, I am encouraging continuing exploration with further reading, gathering of documents from nonprofits, and volunteering in campaign planning situations. For those who are consultants, I point to the importance of maintaining an open dialogue with other consultants. For the new or future consultant, I recommend seeking out an experienced consultant as a mentor.

For the reader ready to pursue a possible study, I point to the need to engage in some preliminary organizational self-examination, to know your institution. I stress the importance of obtaining an institutional mandate for the exploration of a possible study.

You will minimize the risks attendant with investing time and money in a study process if you begin with general support from the board and management, if the case fits into your strategic plan and is sufficiently clear. I characterized two distinctively different kinds of situations, one where you might want to move slowly into a study process and one where you might need to move rapidly. It is important to both know and acknowledge who determines the key questions pivotal for engaging a consultant. I end with encouraging nonprofit staff and volunteer leaders to network with other organizations.

MY FINAL THOUGHTS—WE CAN MAKE IT MUCH MORE THAN A DIAGNOSTIC TOOL

Most everyone I have spend longer periods of time with will admit to having one or more major "aha" moments in their life. Descriptions of such moments vary a great deal from person to person. I have heard colleagues and friends speak of visual experiences ("the room almost blacked out accept for that one spot I was focusing on"), audible experiences ("there was no sound, just that one voice"), even descriptions of vivid daydreams. For me a major "aha" moment came when I was doing a feasibility study for a client. It was in the reporting stage of the process and at the time I was conducting several sequential group presentations. I had decided to try something new, and to my knowledge completely unique. I had arranged with the client, a K through 12 Waldorf school in Vancouver, British Columbia, to have all the interviewees invited to hear a special presentation of the results. I specified that no one else was to be invited or allowed in the room to hear this particular presentation. It was for interviewees only. The results were so powerful; I have since made this, an interviewees-only meeting, a standard part of my feasibility study reporting process.

On that particular evening, there were several long-time supporters of the school present, including a few people who had during their interviews revealed to me some difficult and unresolved issues with the school from the past.

At the end of my presentation for this group, I did what I usually do with presentations and opened the meeting for questions and discussion. It began as a relatively benign question-and-answer period, but became something else. Without my directing or shaping it in any way, several of the interviewees zoomed right in on a couple of the issues alive in the school. They began to self-identify with parts of the report. ("You know that comment on page 34, well I was the one who said that.") This brought a mood of candor and trust into the room. Even more impressive, two individuals who had been on opposite sides of a divisive issue from many years earlier acknowledged to each other and the others in the room the role they each played toward each other in terms I can only describe as wholesome and healing. Without being overly dramatic, I was witnessing a moment of resolution, connected to the history of the organization, made possible by the acceptance of the feasibility study report as a reflected image of the school and the conduct of the participants. It was at that moment that I realized the power of the feasibility study was like an undiscovered gem. Yes, we can weigh and measure for the important answers of depth of overall support, sufficiency of leadership giving, strength of volunteer leadership, potency of the case, and awareness of any organizational or programmatic issues. However, it is my belief that the power of the feasibility study to also be a mirror for organizational self-knowledge is only beginning to be understood. A major reason for the creation of this book is my vision that, particularly with nonprofit organizations that want to grow and improve, the fundraising feasibility study can be an important vehicle for organizational self-understanding, self-diagnosis, and even self-healing.

Appendices

Please note:

1. These samples are provided by several of the authors and the editor.
2. They represent different working styles.
3. They are presented here without the accompanying oral or written instructions.
4. Their full value is in the collective samples, not in each specific item.
5. In the two feasibility study reports, confidential information has been masked.

The following is a listing of the appendices you will find in this book:

Planning Study Action Plan

Event or Action	Person(s) Responsible	Date
Decision to launch study	The Salvation Army of Licking County	04/26/06
Study organizational meeting	The Salvation Army of Licking County and *Carlton & Company*	07/14/06
Request for suggested interviewees	The Salvation Army of Licking County	07/14/06
Deadline for compilation of interviewee list	The Salvation Army of Licking County	07/21/06
Study team to review process, prioritize list, discuss case	The Salvation Army of Licking County and *Carlton & Company*	07/14/06
Case preparation information and material to *Carlton & Company*	The Salvation Army of Licking County	06/16/06
Letters requesting interviews	The Salvation Army of Licking County	
First draft of case for support	*Carlton & Company*	07/06/06
Begin scheduling interviews	The Salvation Army of Licking County	
Send confirmation letters with final draft of case for support as appointments are scheduled	The Salvation Army of Licking County	
Compile appointments and personal data forms	The Salvation Army of Licking County	
Begin interviews	*Carlton & Company*	
Complete interviews	*Carlton & Company*	
Compile findings; draft report	*Carlton & Company*	
Final report presentation	*Carlton & Company*	

Letter Requesting Names
of Interviewees

<Date>

<Inside Address>

Dear _____ :

As you may know, we have retained the consulting firm of Ketchum to conduct a planning study in advance of the major fundraising campaign we have been discussing. A representative of Ketchum will be conducting confidential interviews, and we need your help to ensure that a representative group of those upon whom our success depends are interviewed in this study.

Please provide us with ten or more names no later than <insert date>. We have enclosed a form for you to use, as well as a return envelope. The origin of these lists will be held in the strictest confidence, and all names will be screened by an ad hoc committee assembled for this purpose.

Study participants should be prospective major donors, either personally or through the corporation or foundation they represent, or they must have the capacity to influence others to make a major investment in <organization name>.

This study seeks to gain factual information to determine if our proposed campaign can attract the necessary volunteer leadership, if and from where funds are available, whether the timing is appropriate, and whether the overall reaction of our constituency is favorable. When determining the priority of the names you suggest, please highlight individuals whose responses can directly address these key issues. Please be assured that no funds will be solicited during these interviews.

Your help is greatly appreciated.

<Appropriate Closing>

KETCHUM

www.ketchum.viscern.com

Potential Participants Form

Please list the names and addresses of those you believe should be interviewed in the upcoming planning study. These should be individuals who are prospects for major financial support and/or candidates for leadership positions in the campaign. In the last column, please give us the benefit of your knowledge of these candidates by dividing them into three categories: "A"—those who MUST be interviewed, "B"—those who SHOULD be interviewed, and "C"—those who COULD be interviewed if circumstances are convenient. This list will be checked against our other suggestions to avoid duplication. Your suggestions will be held in the strictest of confidence.

Name	Address		Phone	A/B/C
1.	Business:			
	Home:			
2.	Business:			
	Home:			
3.	Business:			
	Home:			
4.	Business:			
	Home:			
5.	Business:			
	Home:			

Name	Address	Phone	A/B/C
6.	Business:		
	Home:		
7.	Business:		
	Home:		
8.	Business:		
	Home:		
9.	Business:		
	Home:		
10.	Business:		
	Home:		

Name of person providing information:

KETCHUM

www.ketchum.viscern.com

Planning Study Interview Schedule

Consultant: _____ Day: _____ Date: _____		Interviewee Name/Title	Address Phone Number	Relationship to Institution, Directions, and Other Comments
From:	To:			
From:	To:			
From:	To:			
From:	To:			
From:	To:			
From:	To:			
From:	To:			
From:	To:			
From:	To:			
From:	To:			
From:	To:			

Consultant: _____ Day: _____ Date: _____		Interviewee Name/Title	Address Phone Number	Relationship to Institution, Directions, and Other Comments
From:	To:			
From:	To:			
From:	To:			
From:	To:			
From:	To:			
From:	To:			
From:	To:			
From:	To:			
From:	To:			
From:	To:			
From:	To:			

Letter Requesting an Interview

\<Date\>

\<Inside Address\>

Dear _____ :

    The Salvation Army of Licking County has recently completed a planning process, which has identified a number of needs to improve its facilities. The total cost of these projects is estimated at $5 million. We are seeking the opinions and perceptions of community members and friends regarding the viability of a capital campaign to support a portion of this effort.

    To assist us with this important task, we have retained the services of *Carlton & Company,* a professional consulting firm that has worked with a number of nonprofit organizations throughout the country. Bill Carlton will conduct the study for us.

    Our purpose in writing you is to request your assistance — we need your advice and counsel. We ask that you set aside 30 to 45 minutes of your time in the coming weeks to be interviewed by Mr. Carlton. He will ask your opinion on a number of issues related to the proposed plans and the feasibility of a capital campaign. Your responses will be tabulated by *Carlton & Company* and kept strictly confidential.

    THESE MEETINGS WILL NOT BE SOLICITATIONS FOR FUNDS. We are simply seeking your input and guidance. A representative from the Salvation Army of Licking County will call you in the next week or two in the hopes of scheduling a convenient time for you to be interviewed.

    Thank you for your anticipated participation in this most important effort.

                                       Sincerely,

                                       President/Board Chair

Telephone Script for Scheduling Planning Study Interviews for Capital Venture^{SM} Consultant

Calls can be made the week of September 25, 2006, following the attached scheduled for Linda Lysakowski, ACFRE.

Good morning/afternoon, this is (your name) _____ **calling on behalf of HRC.**

A few days ago we mailed a letter to you (or _____ the person on our list if you are speaking with a secretary, receptionist, or another person answering the phone) **in anticipation of HRC's proposed Capital Campaign, currently under consideration, for a new campus and requesting that you meet with Linda Lysakowski, our consultant, to discuss this project.**

On October 9 through October 12, Linda Lysakowski of CAPITAL VENTURE^{SM} will be interviewing individuals who have received this mailing and whose opinions we value. Linda will take only 30 to 40 minutes of your time to discuss the project and possible upcoming capital campaign that would provide funds toward this project.

Would you (or _____ the person on our list if you are speaking with a secretary, receptionist, or another person answering the phone) **be available for a short meeting on** _____ **date @ (time)** _____ **A.M./P.M.?**

Pause for response. If day/time is not convenient, continue with

If not, then would _____ **date @ (time)** _____ **A.M./P.M. be better for your** (or _____'s the person on our list if you are speaking with a secretary, receptionist, or another person answering the phone) **schedule?**

Close by reiterating the day, date, time being scheduled, repeating with:

Great, Linda will plan to meet with you (or _____ the person on our list if you are speaking with a secretary, receptionist, or another person answering the phone) **on (day)** _____ **, (date)** _____ @ **(time)** _____ A.M./P.M. **at** _____ **location.**

Thank you very much for taking the time to speak with me to schedule this meeting. Your (or _____'s the person on our list if you are speaking with a secretary, receptionist, or another person answering the phone) **input is very important to us and we know your** (or _____'s the person on our list if you are speaking with a secretary, receptionist, or another person answering the phone) **time is very important to you** (or _____ the person on our list if you are speaking with a secretary, receptionist, or another person answering the phone).

If you do not know the location of where we will be meeting with any individual and do not know how to tell us to get there, please ask for directions. Be sure to obtain the e-mail address of everyone with whom you confirm an interview.

After hanging up, please be sure to complete the scheduling form with name, phone number, and directions (if not at HRC).

Each potential interviewee who can be interviewed needs to receive Letter 2 and the preliminary case for support.

Letter Confirming Interview Appointment

<Date>

<Inside Address>

Dear _____ :

I would like to take a moment to thank you for agreeing to participate in the planning study process on behalf of <organization name>. Your input and guidance will greatly assist us as we continue our strategic planning.

To confirm, <Consultant name>, with Ketchum will plan to meet you on <day, date, time> at <location>. The meeting will last approximately 45 minutes.

In anticipation of your meeting, enclosed for your review is <organization name>'s case statement, which provides a summary of the organization, its present and future priorities, and its proposed plans.

Again, thank you for your participation in this important process.

<Appropriate Closing>

KETCHUM
www.ketchum.viscern.com

Planning Study Appointment Schedule

as of September 13, 2006

Date	Time	Linda Lysakowski, ACFRE
Mon., Oct. 9	7:00 A.M.	
	8:00 A.M.	
	9:00 A.M.	
	10:00 A.M.	
	11:00 A.M.	
	1:00 P.M.	
	2:00 P.M.	
	3:00 P.M.	
	4:00 P.M.	
	6:00 P.M.	
	7:00 P.M.	
	8:00 P.M.	
Tues., Oct. 10	7:00 A.M.	
	8:00 A.M.	
	9:00 A.M.	
	10:00 A.M.	
	11:00 A.M.	
	1:00 P.M.	

Date	Time	Linda Lysakowski, ACFRE
Tues., Oct. 10	2:00 P.M.	
	3:00 P.M.	
	4:00 P.M.	
	6:00 P.M.	
	7:00 P.M.	
	8:00 P.M.	
Wed., Oct. 11	7:00 A.M.	
	8:00 A.M.	
	9:00 A.M.	
	10:00 A.M.	
	11:00 A.M.	
	1:00 P.M.	
	2:00 P.M.	
	3:00 P.M.	
	4:00 P.M.	
	6:00 P.M.	
	7:00 P.M.	
	8:00 P.M.	
Thurs., Oct. 12	7:00 A.M.	
	8:00 A.M.	
	9:00 A.M.	
	10:00 A.M.	
	11:00 A.M.	
	1:00 P.M.	

Appointment and Personal Data Form

Carlton & Company
Fund-Raising Counsel

Appointment date: _____

Time: _____

Made by: _____

Name of interviewee | Title

Firm | Nature of business

( )

Business address (including city, state, and zip code) | Phone

( )

Home address (including city, state, and zip code) | Phone

Special relationships with the Salvation Army of Licking County

_____

_____

_____

Past/current support: _____

_____

_____

Other committee memberships, offices held, etc.: _____

_____

_____

General information: _____

_____

_____

Travel directions: _____

_____

_____

_____

Compiled by: _____

Interviewer Questionnaire

CAPITAL VENTURE   **Confidential**
10245 S. Maryland Parkway #1188
Las Vegas, NV 89123
(702) 892-0955, fax (702) 892-0655

Planning Study Interview

1. Client: _____ Date: _____

    City: _____ State: _____ Zip code: _____

    Interview #: _____

2. Interviewee's name: _____   Relationship to HRC:

    Title: _____   ❑ Board member

    Company: _____   ❑ Vendor

    Business address: _____   ❑ Volunteer

    _____   ❑ Donor

    Business phone: _____   ❑ Community leader

    Home address: _____   ❑ Other

    _____

    Home phone: _____

3. Interviewee's perception of the HRC:

    ❑ Excellent   ❑ Good   ❑ Average   ❑ Poor   ❑ Unaware

    Comments: _____

    _____

4. Among the following HRC services, what service do you believe is the most important?

   - HRC Child and Parent Services (CAPS)
   - HRC Calaveras Head Start/State Preschool
   - HRC Community Services Program
   - HRC Child Care Resources
   - HRC Mother Lode Women, Infants, and Children (WIC)
   - HRC Calaveras Crisis Center (CCC)

5. Are there any other services you feel the HRC should be providing?

   _____

6. Are there other organizations in the area that you see as having a similar mission or purpose? If so, which are they?

   _____

7. Interviewee's understanding of the needs of the HRC:

   ❑ Good   ❑ Poor

   Comments: _____

   _____

8. How would you prioritize the needs of the HRC?

   a. _____

   b. _____

   c. _____

9. Interviewee's acceptance of the plan:

   ❑ Right plan   ❑ Wrong plan

   Comments: _____

   _____

10. Interviewee's approval of campaign:

    ❑ Yes   ❑ No

    Comments: _____

    _____

11. Is goal attainable?

    ❑ Yes   ❑ No   If no, suggest goal _____

12. Is top gift available?

❏ Yes   ❏ No   If no, suggest amt. _____

13. Timing of campaign:

❏ Good   ❏ Not Good   If not good, suggest time _____

14. How would you rate the Calaveras county economic outlook?

❏ Excellent   ❏ Good   ❏ Average   ❏ Poor

15. How would you rate fund raising of the HRC board?

❏ Excellent   ❏ Good   ❏ Average   ❏ Poor

16. Are there other area major campaigns which you believe might conflict with a capital campaign effort by HRC and, if so, what are they?

_____

_____

17. What is the priority of this campaign in relationship to interviewee's personal philanthropic goals?

❏ High   ❏ Medium   ❏ Low   ❏ Nonexistent

18. What is the likelihood of the interviewee making a gift?

❏ Lead gift   ❏ Top 10   ❏ Next 20   ❏ Other   ❏ None

Where on the scale of gifts might the interviewee's personal gift fall?

$_____

19. What is the likelihood of the interviewee's corporate gift?

❏ Lead gift   ❏ Top 10   ❏ Next 20   ❏ Other   ❏ None

Where on the scale of gifts might the interviewee's corporate gift fall?

$_____

20. Is the interviewee the decision maker for corporate gift?

❏ Yes   ❏ No   ❏ If no, who _____

Corporate areas of interest:

_____

_____

21. What are the chances of the interviewee's involvement in the campaign?

❏ Leadership   ❏ Somewhat involved   ❏ Not involved

22. Suggestions for top 10 donors:

Name _____ Amount $_____

Name _____ Amount $_____

Name _____ Amount $_____

Name _____ Amount $_____

Name _____ Amount $_____

Name _____ Amount $_____

Name _____ Amount $_____

Name _____ Amount $_____

Name _____ Amount $_____

Name _____ Amount $_____

23. Leadership suggestions:

Accepted
Leadership Position

Name _____ Position _____ ❏ Yes   ❏ No

Name _____ Position _____ ❏ Yes   ❏ No

Name _____ Position _____ ❏ Yes   ❏ No

Name _____ Position _____ ❏ Yes   ❏ No

Name _____ Position _____ ❏ Yes   ❏ No

24. Direct quotes from interviewee:

_____

_____

_____

_____

25. Interviewer's comments:

_____

_____

_____

_____

_____

Interviewer name _____

Letter Thanking Participant(s)

Date   Letter 3

INTERVIEWEE NAME
Company Name
Address
City, State, Zip Code

Dear NAME,

Thank you, again, for meeting with me yesterday morning, to discuss HRC and its mission:

> *"With passion and dedication, HRC serves families, children, and individuals*
> *by providing exceptional community-based programs and education."*

Your time and attention are very much appreciated, and your comments and conversation very informative. It was a pleasure meeting with you.

Sincerely,

Sue Kreeger, CFRE
Senior Consulting Associate
Capital Venture

Alexis de
TOCQUEVILLE
INSTITUTE
Guiding Volunteer Leaders

Capital Campaign Feasibility Study Report

Conducted for

Mountain View Waldorf School
Loudenville, Vermont

June 2005

Martin L. Novom, CFRE
Principal

"We are, each of us angels with only one wing;
and we can only fly by embracing one another."

— Luciano de Crescenzo

Table of Contents

I. INTRODUCTION

It can be a challenging and sometimes uncomfortable time for any school contemplating a significant change in its buildings or programs. The challenge or discomfort can be greatly magnified when there is an intention to fund the changes with charitable gift support. It can seem as if the new improvements sought can't materialize until the School has cleared up unclear intentions, gathered the collective will of the participants and, perhaps most importantly, demonstrated a recognition of its strengths and weaknesses.

The Fundraising Feasibility Study documented in this report is an attempt to focus the energies of the Mountain View Waldorf School as part of its work to develop a new campus. It can be formulated in a question:

"What do we need to do to prepare ourselves for the future?"

This is not a small question; it is more like a quest. This report, including the work of volunteers and staff, and the thoughts and feelings of the interviewees, is a result of the attempt to answer that question.

While beginning the task of campaign preparation seems straightforward, finding answers to this question requires clarity and persistence. Fortunately, we have at hand decades of practice in American philanthropic support in preparing and measuring philanthropic program readiness. The unique nature of a Waldorf school, however, requires much more than an off-the-shelf method developed for traditional not-for-profit organizations. This report includes a description of the methods and philosophy necessary to find, in the mirror of self-knowledge, just how the School can prepare for such an effort.

Background of the Process

This report is, first and foremost, a summary of the reactions to the question above. Developing an answer starts with creating a draft case for giving, a copy of which is included in the appendix. At the time of the interviews it represented the best description to date of what was being proposed to prepare the Mountain View Waldorf School for the future and the financial commitment it might entail.

The School engaged the services of the Alexis de Tocqueville Institute and its Principal, Martin Novom, as professional philanthropic council and educator to work with the Capital Campaign Planning Group (hereafter the CCPG) and the Development Director, Ρου Νελλισ, to design and conduct a comprehensive fundraising feasibility study.

The testing of the case for giving began with the commissioning of a Fundraising Feasibility Study (hereafter called the "Study"), which is the subject of this report. The Capital Campaign Planning Group (CCPG) was specifically formed and mandated to be the stewards of the process to test the case.

Purpose of the Report

This report is designed to help the School prepare for a proposed campaign by measuring its readiness. Campaign readiness can be determined by a number of specific indicators. There are some simple and rather straightforward questions to be answered about the size and strength of potential donor support and the size and readiness of potential volunteer support for a campaign. Of considerable interest is the determination of the likely and collective response to the proposed campaign dollar goal.

This report helps fulfill the purposes of the Study by providing detailed findings, conclusions, and recommendations derived from a series of interviews. Embedded in the interviews are answers to the essential questions:

    a. What volume and size of gifts can realistically be expected?

    b. What is the depth and intensity of volunteer support for such a campaign?

    c. What is the perceived strength of the volunteer leadership?

    d. What unresolved organizational issues need addressing?

Feasibility Study Design

In order that the reader of this report obtain full value from the findings, conclusions, and recommendations, it is important to have some understanding of the methods used to obtain the perspectives, opinions, and observations that provided the raw data (the interviewee responses) included in this report.

With the support and involvement of the faculty and the board, a Capital Campaign Planning Group was established with the specific mandate to assist the leadership of the School in the consideration and planning for a possible capital campaign. Their work included such tasks as:

    1. Overseeing of the design of the study.

    2. Overseeing the writing of the case for giving.

    3. Gathering of information, financial and factual.

4. Recommending a schedule of study report presentations.

5. Communicating with the board, faculty, parents, and friends.

As advisor to the School, I provided:

- Criteria for the selection of prospective interviewees.
- A list of interview questions.
- Editorial assistance for the case for giving.
- A timeline for the study process.
- Monitoring of the study process to keep it focused and productive.

Criteria for Interviewee Selection

Prospective interviewees were gathered into three groups:

1. Significant donors

2. Opinion shapers

3. Cross section

The group called *significant donors* was made up of individuals or families recognized as capable of making the largest gifts within the current donor base of the School. This group made up a preponderance of the interviewee pool. This reflects the pattern of charitable gift distribution in our culture (and in Waldorf Schools), where more than 80% of the gifts come from close to 20% of the contributors. This group comprises approximately 60% of the interviewee pool.

The second group, *opinion-shapers,* are those individuals known within the School community by their actions and activities in support of the goals of the School. They are respected for their involvement regardless of their financial capacity. Ideally, they would make up about 25 to 35% of the prospective interviewee pool.

The third group, called *cross section,* represents a sampling of those from across a variety of community members. This group, while it makes up the smallest number, ensures that the list of interviewees includes a wide range of perspectives.

The Interviews

The three groups make up the interviewee pool. The original design called for about 30 interviews. We did in fact end up with 30 interview sessions and, including couples, 43 individuals were interviewed.

Virtually all the interviews were conducted in one of two places, a room at the school or a conference room at the law office of Χοοπερ, Δεανσ & Χαργιλλ. The law office was used during the week and the School on weekends. Most of the interviews were conducted during the week at the law office. Martin Novom conducted 24 of the interviews, and Γεοργε Χλεωελανδ conducted six interviews. Only one interview was conducted over the phone with an out of state interviewee. Two interviews were started in person and then completed over the telephone. Only one interview was not completed.

Once the list of prospective interviewees was finalized by the CCPG, the following process was generally used. Personal letters describing the study and the interview sequence were mailed, inviting each prospective interviewee (or interviewee couple) to participate. These were followed by phone calls to gauge interest and, hopefully, to schedule an interview.

Once an interview had been arranged, a letter confirming the time and date was sent. Accompanying that letter was the draft case for giving. The interviewee or interviewee couple was requested to read the case before the time of the scheduled interview.

Each interview was a generous 60 to 75 minutes, a few took longer. Each was assured of confidentiality and told that, while they might see their words in a quote, no one would know the source of the quote. Their name would appear only in the appendix of the Study Report.

The questions were designed with this specific case for giving in mind. They were ordered in such a manner that the responses provided the maximum opportunity for gaining clarity and insight about the issues, feelings, and perceptions concerning the School and such a project.

The raw data was collected in the interviews long hand, by the interviewer. They were, at the end, typed into a single word-processed document, totaling 92 pages.

The majority of the interviews had the entire written record for the session read back for verification. Where this was not the case, sections where the interviewer felt there might be transcription errors were read back immediately.

Additional Data

Quite intentionally, the results of several questions are not reported here. There are at least three reasons:

1. Sometimes a question was used to make a comfortable transition.
2. A question resulted in negligible data.
3. It provided information only useful should the School decide to launch a campaign.

Any useful information that doesn't break confidentiality will be turned over to the development director.

What Is the Alexis de Tocqueville Institute?

While I have been a consultant in philanthropy since 1992, I have long felt the need for an organizational framework focused on the key questions of volunteerism, charitable giving, and governance. As of January 1, 2001, all of my educational and advisory work is performed under the banner of this Institute. The tagline for the Institute is "Growing Volunteer Leaders."

The Alexis de Tocqueville Institute takes its name from the French diplomat and traveler who extensively toured the United States in the 1820s and published his findings in *Democracy in America*. Tocqueville is still studied widely by historians, social critics, and students of the nonprofit sector. I chose to name the Institute after him because of his vivid descriptions of philanthropic (volunteering, giving, and governance) activity and his insights as to the importance of philanthropy for the United States as a culture and as a political entity.

Cautionary Note

It is quite easy for the reader, in the rush of anticipation or depth of concern, to draw quick conclusions, particularly if they seem to support preconceived perspectives.

It cannot be stressed highly enough how important it is to read the finding and conclusions more than once. It may be prudent to read them, put the Report down, and read them again at a later time, before coming to any conclusions or taking any action. The pursuit of highly sought goals for a Waldorf school can be highly charged emotionally. Thoughtful consideration can be priceless.

Note of Thanks

This work would not have possible without the help of the Capital Campaign Planning Committee. A special thanks go to its members: Αλεχ Βεηρ, Μιχηεαλ Ολιχκ, Ροτη Ηαμιλτον, Ρου Νελλεσ, Ειργινια Νοσσιoo, and Βενδυ Ταλμ. I also want to thank the attorneys and staff of the law office of Χοοπερ, Δεανσ & Χαργιλλ for their gracious hospitality in providing a room for interviews.

Looking Ahead

I have enjoyed working with the School and I have also greatly appreciated the spirit of collaboration I have experienced. This is an exciting time for the Mountain View Waldorf School, and I am grateful to have been part of it.

Sincerely,

Martin Novom, CFRE
Principal
Alexis de Tocqueville Institute
June 6, 2005

II. Interview Findings

Reporting Methodology

The findings from the interviews are covered first. They are grouped as:

A. Experience of the School

B. Strengths of the School

C. Areas Needing Improvement

D. Response to the Case for Giving

E. Financial Support for this Project

The responses from the interviewees were collected in two forms:

1. Multiple-choice responses (excellent, good, fair, poor, etc.)

2. Narrative responses

A copy of the complete questionnaire, without the white spaces used for writing in answers, can be found at the end of this appendix. Both types of responses are summarized here, question by question. Both the multiple-choice and the narrative responses are reported as percentages. In addition, whenever there are sufficient numbers of requested or spontaneous responses, selected quotes are included.

For some of the questions, up to nine (9) of the interviewees did not provide answers. In the case of the multiple-choice questions these are noted as "n/a," not applicable. Of these only one (1) was the result of not being able to complete the interview. In the remaining eight (8), these interviewees were not sufficiently familiar with the School to respond.

In each of the multiple-choice questions, several interviewees choose to answer by choosing more than one category. These multicategory responses were recorded and are reported separately.

About the Language

The quotes are as close as possible to the actual statements made. This provides for greater authenticity but sometimes for awkwardness of language.

About the Percentages

The percentages are rounded up or down to whole numbers (14%, not 14.2%; 19%, not 18.7%). For that reason, some of percentage totals may not add up to exactly 100 percent. Many of the narrative questions resulted in most interviewees making comments that fell into more than one answer category. Comments are clustered by topic, and the frequency of each comment is the basis for the percentages in the open-ended questions. The base number for each question varies according to the number of interviewees who responded to that question.

A. EXPERIENCE OF THE SCHOOL

Q: "Would you describe for me your experience of the School?"

The responses to this question generated 7 pages of single-spaced transcript. There were 43 respondents (in 30 interviews) and their answers are clustered and reported here, in order of frequency, within the following categories:

1. This is a wonderful place

2. The Waldorf philosophy

3. The level of creativity

4. A high amount of acceptance

5. The quality of the education

6. How nuturing it is

7. Needs more organization

1. **This is a wonderful place, 59%:**

   I think it is fantastic.

   We are excited to have the School here.

   The School has been very good for the children.

   We were delighted when our grandchildren started at the Mountain View Waldorf School.

   Mountain View Waldorf School is a vital part of the community.

2. **The Waldorf philosophy, 49%:**

   I've been interested in Waldorf schools since my child was born.

   My wife and I have been very attracted to the Waldorf philosophy.

   I really enjoyed the philosophy, the educational emphasis.

   It has bought a calm tranquility in my life. I have learned so much from the teachers and now from the children.

3. **The level of creativity, 47%:**

   My child's public school teachers say that he has great creativity due to Waldorf skills.

   I like the focus on the spirit of the child versus loading them up with data.

   I have a sense of freedom and creativity.

4. **A high amount of acceptance, 28%:**

   It's an accepting environment.

   I do like how people treat each other here.

5. **The quality of the education, 26%:**

   It was an unquestionably good experience.

   The public school teachers were impressed with my child's group skills and conflict resolution.

6. **How nuturing it is, 23%:**

   It was a really good environment for my child to start out in.

7. **Needs more organization, 15%:**

   There is a lack of administrative expertise. The board does not always like to take advice when it's offered.

Q: *"How would you rank your experience?"*

Interviewees indicated a category that best described their experience. Couples were counted individually. The chart below lists only the single category responses. All of the four (4) multicategory responses are listed separately. The base for percentages is 39 responses. Remember, percentages are reported as whole numbers and this can sometimes add up to higher than 100%.

Positive	Conflicted	Neutral	Negative	n/a
80%	5%	15%	0%	0%

There were 43 total responses to this question. The results of the multicategory responses were:

- Three (3) "positive to conflicted"
- One (1) "positive to negative"

B. STRENGTHS OF THE SCHOOL

Q: *"What do you think the School does best?"*

This question brought out six (6) major strengths:

1. Curriculum and child development
2. Brings out the best
3. Part of the world
4. Creativity

5. Cares for children

6. An alternative education

1. **Curriculum and child development, 28%:**

   They gently assist in the child's development as it naturally progresses.

   An environment for our children to flourish.

   Because of the developmental approach, they didn't force them to do things they weren't ready for.

   When they educate our children, they do it with a reason behind it.

2. **Brings out the best, 21%:**

   Each interaction, positive or negative, is an honoring of the moment.

   It provides an opportunity for kids to reach their full potential.

   Fills their emotional, cognitive/intellectual, and social needs.

3. **Part of the world, 21%:**

   Makes kids aware of being part of a larger community.

   The way they use the natural world for a frame of reference for lessons.

4. **Creativity, 9%:**

   I think there is a creative spirit.

   What it did best in my opinion was feed the children's imagination.

5. **Cares for children, 21%:**

   The School does a really good job of caring for the children.

   Cares for children.

6. **Alternative education, 7%:**

   I'm all for having an alternative for the children in the valley.

C. AREAS OF IMPROVEMENT

Q: "What would you like to see improved?"

The answers were grouped in these categories:

1. I don't know enough to say.

2. The building and the grounds.

3. Organization of the School.

4. Communicating just what the School is.

5. It's not clean enough.

6. The budget is too sparse.

1. **I don't know enough to say, 30%:**

   I don't have enough hands-on experience to say.

   I am too removed to comment.

   It's hard to say when you really don't know.

2. **The building and the grounds, 28%:**

   They need space that includes outdoors and involvement with animals and gardens.

   A nice space, a nice school.

   The building needs improvements. The floors are concrete, and it tires out the teachers. The play space is next to Route 16. It's noisy and has diesel fumes from the road.

   I've worked on the building and I've found areas that are structurally poor.

3. **Organization of the School, 14%:**

   It is no longer a small community of friends who can take on any job we need to have done.

   We are still at the stage of everybody doing everything. We need to start valuing people's time and expertise in terms of money.

   On the Parent Association we don't know where our part ends and the School part starts.

   The board needs to embrace differing opinions. The board only wants like-minded people. They tend to micromanage. Won't accept input from committees.

4. **Communicating just what the School is, 12%:**

   The professionalism of our interfacing with the community.

   Communication of general Waldorf education principle to the parents, to the public schools, to the community at large.

5. **It's not clean enough, 9%:**

   The place looks worn out and isn't inviting.

   It's filthy, especially the bathrooms. Parents have organized, with faculty permission, the cleaning of the bathrooms. Cleaning them once a week is not enough.

6. **The budget is too sparse, 5%:**

   When the issue about the greater school community taking responsibility for the teachers comes up, which would be reflected in tuition, they refuse.

   They could use more students. That way you'd have the ability to pay the teachers more money and would ensure the continued survival of the School.

D. RESPONSE TO THE CASE FOR GIVING

In order for the School to plan a course of action for a proposed capital campaign, it is important to be able to distinguish between general support for an organization and the financial commitment for such a proposed plan. At this point in the interview, reactions to the case for giving were sought. Each person interviewed was sent the draft case, asked to read it in advance before the interview and come prepared to comment on it.

Q: "What was your reaction to the case for giving?"

Positive	Conflicted	Neutral	Negative	n/a
63%	16%	16%	5%	0%

There were 43 responses to this question. Of those, none were multicategory:

Q: The question *"What do you like about the case?"* brought out six main clusters:

1. It was nicely presented.
2. View of the past, view of the future.
3. I love the cover photos.
4. The portrait of Waldorf education.
5. Working with Τιν Μουνταιν.
6. I like the quotes.

The base for percentage computation for this question is 43.

1. **It was nicely presented, 49%:**

   I liked its appearance.

   It was well written.

   It impressed me that it was very organically put together.

   It was beautifully written.

   Professionally done.

2. **View of the past, view of the future, 23%:**

   The history of the School is interesting. I know it but it is nice to review it.

   It is a nice synopsis of what has happened up to this point in the valley with a view toward the future.

   They went into where they are now and what they see for the future with this project.

   The history of the School and the principles they adhere to.

3. **I love the cover photos, 16%:**

   I like the back cover because of the kids. The picture makes me experience the responsibility that the School has toward these children.

   Especially the one in the back. It shows the image of "we are coming from here going to there."

   The vision that the front and back covers brought was beautiful.

4. **The portrait of Waldorf education, 9%:**

   The ability to serve children with diverse strengths and weaknesses and develop each child to his or her fullest potential.

   I like the way Waldorf education is described.

   It does really convey what the School is all about.

5. **Working with Τιν Μουνταιν, 7%:**

   I liked the location, side by side with Τιν Μουνταιν.

   I like that they are going to coordinate with Τιν Μουνταιν.

6. **I like the quotes, 7%:**

   I like the quotes that focus my attention.

   I like the quotes, they were very useful.

Q: "What would you like to see improved or changed with the case?"

The three groups of comments were:

1. It's not professional enough.
2. It doesn't explain the value of the School to the community.
3. This project seems extravagant.

The base for computing percentages for this question is 41.

1. **It's not professional enough, 29%:**

   It felt as though we had to squeeze in a whole lot of information. There were four different headings on one page and three different columns. My eye went crazy.

   It's not up to the caliber of the School.

   The cover doesn't say it's for the campaign. It looks like something that is a generic brochure for the School.

   I might hand it to a graphic designer to make it easier to read.

2. **It doesn't explain the value of the School to the community, 17%:**

   A missed opportunity to educate people about the School.

   I don't think the real message is being conveyed.

I realize this is not a community that accepts private education, and we need to demonstrate its value.

3. **This project seems extravagant, 7%:**

   I didn't like the cost. It seems like a lot of money.

   I feel it is overly ambitious.

Q: "If you could rank the parts of the project, in what order of preference would you put them?"

The interviewees were asked to the rank the spaces as their first, second, or third preference. The base for all percentages was 43 responses.

Space	First	Second	Third	
Administrative space	6.9%	20.9%	72.1%	100%
Early childhood center	44.2%	46.5%	9.3%	100%
Elementary school	65.1%	23.3%	11.6%	100%

Q: "Will the School community support this project?"

Yes	Probably	Possibly	No	Don't Know	n/a
61%	31%	6%	0%	3%	0%

There were 43 responses and, of those, seven (7) were multicategory:

- Four (4) "yes to probably"
- One (1) "yes to no"
- Two (2) "probably to possibly"

The leaders of the School need to have some insights about why supporters and friends feel the way they do. To assist them, this follow-up question was asked:

Q: "What makes you say that?"

The four groupings of comments were:

1. Because they love the School.
2. Is the money there?
3. I don't know everyone at the School.
4. This is very big.

1. **Because they love the School, 50%:**

   My experience of being here is that both the faculty and parents are standing on the front line waiting for the race to begin.

   Because the School is parent driven and that parent drive is strong.

   Can't imagine anyone involved who wouldn't.

   Families who committed to get their children a Waldorf education and will do whatever it takes.

2. **Is the money there?, 16%:**

   Everybody would want to help but not everyone can.

   Strong conceptual support, limited ability for financial support.

   I have reservations. Generally, this is a low-income community. Can they afford a multimillion-dollar school?

3. **I don't know everyone, 8%:**

   I didn't say yes because I don't know most of the people that are here now.

   I do not know how large the community is.

4. **This is very big, 5%:**

   The magnitude of it. It feels so huge.

   This would be the biggest undertaking from a fundraising perspective in the 6ηιτε Μουνταιν ςαλλευ to my knowledge.

Q: "Would you be likely to support it?"

Yes	Probably	Possibly	No	Don't Know	n/a
74%	16%	0%	2%	7%	0%

Here we find 43 responses and no multicategory responses.

Q: "Among other organizations that you are interested in and support, what level of priority would this project have for you?"

Top	High	Middle	Low	Don't Know	n/a
26%	34%	13%	8%	16%	3%

This question got 43 responses. Of those, six (6) were multicategory ones:

- Three (3) "the top to top 3"
- One (1) "top 3 to middle"
- One (1) "middle to low"

E. FINANCIAL SUPPORT FOR THIS PROJECT

Here we are looking for the contrast and similarities between general interest in the proposed project and specific answers regarding the possibility of financial investment in the project.

Q: *"Is the need of $2,900,000 in cash and pledges to pay for this project a realistic amount for the School to expect to raise?"*

Yes	Probably	Possibly	No	Don't Know	n/a
21%	21%	18%	12%	30%	0%

The total number of responses was 43. Of those, nine (9) were multicategory responses:

- One (1) "yes to possibly"
- Two (2) "probably to possibly
- Three (3) "possibly to no"
- Three (3) "no to don't know"

Q: *"What would the School be facing to raise that amount of money?"*

There were four (4) topic clusters in the responses:

1. A lot of work, a lot of time.
2. What's wrong with public school?
3. Lots of capital campaign competition.
4. The public high school efforts.

1. **A lot of work, a lot of time, 26%:**

   Hours and hours of work, unrelenting work.

   Doing a project like this is not easy, it's complicated.

   Getting it done in as short an amount of time as possible may be their biggest obstacle.

   There has to be a resolve or a personal commitment. You have to push through when it becomes impossible. As a mother giving birth you reach that point when you know you would give anything to be done but you have to keep going until you are holding your baby in your arms.

2. **What's wrong with public school?, 17%:**

   The perception that the School serves such a limited population.

   I give because my child goes there. Why should someone whose child doesn't go give?

   Some people I know outside the school have commented, "These Waldorf people are snotty."

3. **Lots of capital campaign competition, 17%:**

   The community is tired of people looking for money.

   They are up against other committed fundraising.

   Huge fundraising competition in the area.

4. **The public high school efforts, 14%:**

   The new high school project is in direct competition.

   We are building a new high school and renovating the middle school, and that will be in the forefront of people's minds.

Q: "What conditions or activities outside the School community might affect the School's ability to reach this goal?"

The comments were focused on six (6) major areas:

1. The economy
2. The high school and middle school
3. Fundraising competition
4. Unhappiness with public schools
5. Building awareness
6. Taxes being paid for public schools

1. **The economy, 16%:**

   The stock market situation is not like it was before.

   I can only project the economy as being one.

2. **The high school and middle school, 14%:**

   The new high school is placing a tremendous strain on the community's financial status. This may inhibit local sources of money.

   They are putting up a $40 million high school.

3. **Fundraising competition, 14%:**

   A lot of competition for a relatively small but generous pool of philanthropically inclined people.

   A lot of people have been out knocking on doors.

4. **Unhappiness with public schools, 14%:**

   In the current political climate, schools with creative curriculum are an endangered species.

   A positive thing might be the fact that more parents are unhappy with public education.

5. **Building awareness, 11%:**

   People who could afford to send their kids here don't know about it.

   There are large numbers of people searching for natural products and foods. Those who support this might be Waldorf supporters.

6. **Taxes being paid for public schools, 8%:**

   A major, major item has to do with the tax support for education as it's being approached in New Hampshire.

Q: "Do you think that this is a good time for the School to begin a major campaign?"

Yes	Probably	Possibly	No	Don't Know	n/a
40%	11%	16%	8%	21%	5%

These had a total of 43 responses. There were five (5) multicategories:

- One (1) "yes to probably"
- One (1) "yes to no"
- One (1) "yes to don't know"
- Two (2) "possibly to no"

At this point in the interview, each interviewee was handed a sheet of paper labeled "Table of Gifts" (a copy of which is in Appendix C). The design and layout of the table is explained. It was the subject of the next few questions.

Q: "Does this proposed table of gifts look attainable to you?"

Yes	Probably	Possibly	No	Don't Know	n/a
8%	19%	22%	22%	24%	5%

The percentages were based on 43 responses, of which six (6) were multicategory:

- Two (2) "yes to don't know"
- Two (2) "probably to possibly"
- Two (2) "possibly to no"

Before the next question, reported on the following page, each interviewee heard the following: "This next question is in no way intended to be a request for a commitment. However, your response will help the School to be able to project giving levels in a proposed campaign. Your response will only be disclosed anonymously."

Q: *"If you were likely to contribute, please indicate at at what level might you consider contributing."*

Response	Lower Number	Higher Number
1	$25,000*	$75,000
2	**1,000**	**75,000**
3	50,000	50,000
4	50,000	50,000
5	**25,000**	**50,000**
6	25,000	25,000
7	**10,000**	**25,000**
8	**10,000**	**25,000**
9	15,000	15,000
10	5,000	10,000
11	**1,000**	**10,000**
12	**2,500**	**5,000**
13	**2,500**	**5,000**
14	2,500	2,500
15	2,500	2,500
16	2,500	2,500
17	2,500	2,500
18	2,500	2,500
19	2,500	2,500
20	**1,000**	**2,500**
21	**1,000**	**2,500**
22	1,000	1,000
23	1,000	1,000
24	1,000	1,000
25	1,000	1,000
26	1,000	1,000
27	1,000	1,000
28	Declined comment	
29	"No answer at this time"	
30	"I'd rather not say"	
Total	$245,000	$446,000

*Bold numbers indicate that the response was in a range.

Q: *"Could your gift be matched by your employer?"*

Yes	Probably	Possibly	No	Don't Know	n/a
7%	0%	0%	60%	12%	21%

Each interviewee was then shown a list of the board of trustees (see Appendix D) and asked:

Q: "Here is a list of the board members of the Mountain View Waldorf School. What is your perception of the board's potential to mount a successful capital campaign?"

Excellent	Good	Fair	Poor	Don't Know	n/a
13%	48%	5%	5%	25%	5%

There were 43 responses, and of those, three (3) were multicategory:

- One (1) "good to fair"
- Two (2) "good to don't know"

Q: "Would you accept a volunteer leadership position in this campaign if you were asked?"

Yes	Probably	Possibly	No	Don't Know	n/a
5%	5%	17%	74%	0%	0%

There were 42 responses and, of those, one (1) was multicategory:

- One (1) "no to don't know"

Q: "Are there ways you would be willing to be of help (as a volunteer)?"

Yes	Probably	Possibly	No	Don't Know	n/a
34%	16%	12%	42%	2%	0%

There were 43 responses, including two (2) multicategory:

- Two (2) "yes to probably"

Q: "Can you think of someone you feel would be a good volunteer campaign leader?"

The list, ranked by number of times they are mentioned, reports only those names with two or more mentions. In all, 18 names were reported.

Γιννυ Νοσσιφφ	6
Σανδυ Βροων	4
Δαωιδ Βροοκσ	3
Χηαρλεσ Γρεενηαυγη	2

Q: "What are the important points about this project that you would emphasize to potential donors?"

These open-ended responses were in three (3) clusters:

1. Choice in education.
2. The School as a community asset.
3. We have no choice.

1. **Choice in education, 23%:**

   It broadens the appeal of the community by offering an educational choice.

   Schools are the first thing people look at who are planning to move here. There is general dissatisfaction with public education..

   Mt. Washington Valley needs an excellent alternative to public school education. This is it.

2. **The School as a community asset, 18%:**

   The new location will be good for the community because of the programs that can be offered in the meeting space.

   It is hard to keep workers in the area, and one of the reasons is the child care issues.

   The education and growth of kids affects everybody.

3. **We have no choice, 8%:**

   This is now or never.

III. CONCLUSIONS

Developing Conclusions

This section was derived from analysis based on the findings of the 30 interviews, and up to 43 responses, much of which was reported above. While the primary source for the conclusions are the comments of the interviewees, these findings were analyzed and weighed in the light of several sources of knowledge and experience. These include the professional philanthropic experience of Martin Novom and that of his consulting colleagues throughout North America. This is supplemented by personal experience as a trustee and a volunteer in the nonprofit sector and guidelines from the fields of American volunteerism, charitable giving, and trusteeship.

An attempt has also been made to incorporate insights on organizational life, human relationships, and money drawn from study and practice stemming from the work of Rudolf Steiner.

Reader's Perspective

It is important to recall the sequence of the questions and how they were reported. The format for the content of this section relies on an *overview* of the responses, not on an analysis of each element of the questionnaire. We will be reviewing the findings by focusing on three areas of interest:

1. The School and the plan
2. Leadership and volunteer support
3. Financial support

It is hoped that by making the process by which conclusions have been reached as *transparent* as possible, readers can make their own determination as to whether they can arrive at the same or similar conclusions.

Cautionary Note

Just as a reminder, it is far too easy for the reader in the flush of excitement or depth of concern to draw quick conclusions, particularly if they seem to support preconceived views. As stressed earlier in this report, it is important to *read the conclusions more than once.*

A. THE SCHOOL AND THE PLAN

In their pursuit of the School's campus development, the pedagogical and volunteer leaders of the Mountain View Waldorf School understand that the purpose of the study is to help them determine whether a capital campaign, if launched, can be successful. While the attention of this section is directed to the conclusions about interviewees' perceptions of the case for giving, we must start with the thoughts and feelings of interviewees about the School itself.

Interviewee Participation and Follow-through

One must take note of the level of participation, follow-through, and completion of interviews as a whole. While nearly 40 names were on the list of potential interviewees, only a few declined to be interviewed. The biggest difficulty in setting up interviews was the timing of them, falling as it did in and around spring break.

Twenty-nine (29) of the thirty (30) interviews scheduled were completed. We had one or two interviews where the interviewees did not show up, but those were rescheduled and can be attributed to busy lives and frail memories. An observation one can make from this is that there was a *strong level of participation.*

Another indicator of the feelings about the School is the degree of follow-up shown by the extent to which interviewees *actually read* the draft case for giving before coming to the interview. All interviewees received a letter confirming the appointment time and place *and* a specific request to read the Case. *Two* copies of the case were provided to couples to help ensure they would be able to read it.

Of the 43 interviewees who participated, about 80% reported they had read the case in advance of the interview; 17% "skimmed" it. In those couple of instances where the interviewees did not read the case, a follow-up phone call was arranged allowing them time to do so. In these instances the remainder of the interview was conducted on the telephone. This is a typical response rate. Given the awkwardness of the timing of the interviews (around a school break), I would say that the numbers are an indicator that the interviewees took this responsibility seriously. That, in effect, says that they hold this planning process and the School in high regard.

Feelings about the School

While it is sometimes difficult for parents and other friends of the School to separate their feelings about a plan for growth from their feelings about the School in general, we are fortunate here to have such an opportunity. The nature of the questions asked during the interviews helped make that somewhat possible.

Experience of the School

The interviews began with an open-ended question, "What has been your experience of the Mountain View Waldorf School?" The answers are very instructive.

Only one of the seven clusters, "Needs more organization," was critical in nature, gathering 15% of the total volume of comments. On the other hand, "This is a wonderful place," "The Waldorf philosophy," and "The level of creativity" gathered 59%, 49%, and 47%, respectively. These are high numbers for such a question. It is hard to review the entire section, all seven clusters, and not feel the very high level of value and appreciation the interviewees have for the School.

This is reflected again when we review the data from the question, "How would you rank your experience?" "Positive" was the answer for 80% of the interviewees. The level of conflicted responses was only 5%. Even if you figure in the three (3) multiresponse answers, which included "conflicted" in their range, the total potential "conflicted" number ranks very low. Consider, too, the fact that in the 39 single-answer responses no one gave a "negative." The one multiresponse of "positive to negative" can be seen as one more "conflicted."

What do we draw from this? The objective observer should be able to report that virtually all of the interviewees pretty uniformly rank their overall experience of the School as overwhelmingly positive. We gain a significant degree of understanding when we look into the open-ended questions.

What the School Does Best

The second open-ended question of the interviews, "What do you think the School does best?" offers some greater specifics. In a way, trying to separate out the various good qualities of the School is artificial. Schools, like people, are complex. We are not just one thing, we are many things at once. Schools are no different. However, in order to gain a clearer picture, we need to engage in this somewhat artificial examination.

Five of the six clusters focus on the attitudes, behaviors, and conduct of the School for and toward the children. The objective reader can see a collective praise for the curriculum and how it reaches the child at just the right place for the child's development. How the children are allowed to unfold and how they are cared for, lovingly is clearly described. Some 86% of the comments, adding together the totals of the first five (5) clusters, speak of a place dedicated to the unfolding of children, alive and alert to the world. Only the sixth cluster, alternative education, contains any sense of the School as an abstract entity.

Areas Needing Improvement

In reviewing this part of the report it is important to remember that interviewees were specifically *asked* to give comments. This is not the natural tendency of people unless they have some burning issue or problem on their minds. Once they have been asked to focus on it, we can, of course, expect them to attempt to be as articulate as they can. After all, we have noted that the respondents hold the process and the School in high regard. They are attempting to assist the School in being clear about what the School has asked for—comments on becoming a better Waldorf School.

Having said this, it is instructive that the largest cluster, 30%, is "I don't know enough to say." Three out of ten people couldn't think of anything that the School needed to do to improve. This sounds like a group of happy *or* only mildly informed people. Anyone knowledgeable about the names of the families in the School can see names of nonparents (relatives and local friends) in the list of interviewees in Appendix B. One can deduce, then, that some of these are the source of the mildly informed responses.

Fortunately, the second largest cluster, "the building and the grounds," with 28%, are commenting on the things that the new building and land plans are attempting to solve. Perhaps for this reason, those types of comments are given somewhat tentatively, even gently.

This is not the case with the next four (4) clusters. Taken separately, one could easily lose sight of them. However, taken together, they are a collective statement that much more is being expected of the School.

At 14%, "Organization of the School" is the one most notable of the four. Here, interviewees are pointing out some of the areas of the School that are no longer performing up to expectations. Given the age and maturity of the School, such statements are understandable. The practice of everyone doing everything in an "around the kitchen table" style is no longer appropriate.

Specific comments were made about the role of the Parent Association and the working style of the board. Such items come up again in the section on leadership.

Some of the strongest comments in the entire interview data come up in regard to School building cleanliness. It appears that several interviewees are acquainted with the efforts of parents to help clean and maintain the School. While expressing appreciation that volunteers are helping, it doesn't blunt the fact that some interviewees, notably parents, think the School building is shabby and dirty.

The two other clusters, "Communicating just what the School is" and "The budget is too sparse," are expressions with a little less energy behind them. Unlike the cleanliness question, these appear to be motivated by an effort for the School to capture missed opportunities. About 12% of the responses to the improvement question seemed to be aimed at wanting the School to be all that it can be so it can attract all the families that *should* be enrolled. If, the thinking seems to go, we did a better job of communicating what the School is, *all of these additional families* would be here. And, finally, the smallest cluster, 5%, "The budget is too sparse," speaks to the hopes interviewees have that if the operating budget was bigger, more support and health benefits for teachers and staff would be possible. This, while a criticism, has as its aim the support of the much beloved faculty and staff.

Reaction and Support

Members of the volunteer and pedagogical leadership of the School should take heart at the general response to the case. The question, "What is your reaction to the case for giving?" resulted in a 63% "positive." That is almost two thirds of the interviewees giving their approval to the case for giving. If you also consider the low figure of 5% for "negative," one can easily draw the inference that the case gets a generally high acceptance.

We have to pause, though, and consider the responses that were "conflicted" and "neutral," each 16%. Taken separately, they are not overly difficult. However, when you consider their combined effect is 32%, you have just about a third of the interviewees who are either ambivalent or unmoved by the case.

"What do you like about the case?" contains a road map for the writers and editors of the case. The design, format, and quality of writing were praised. Several of the design elements got specific mentions of appreciation. For example, even those familiar with the history appreciated reviewing the key points of the past. Several notable comments about the front and rear photographs were made, with at least two interviewees waxing eloquent over them. Several people commented on the use of quotes. Here, as elsewhere, the connection with Tin Mountain was mentioned favorably by 7% of the respondents.

The responses to the question, "What would you like to see improved or changed with the case?," presented three varied views. One cluster expressed the need for a more professionally produced document, some 29% of the comments. The second cluster again pointed to what the interviewees saw as a missed opportunity, that of using the case as a vehicle to improve the understanding of the School's value. The third cluster, with 7%, voiced a concern over the total cost and size of the project. This concern is repeated elsewhere in the report.

Summary—The School

The 43 interviewees' responses to questions about the School and the case for giving are sending us strong and clear messages. Given the platform to speak about the School, they express deep appreciation and a view of a hopeful future.

Any school on the verge of great change usually has ragged edges. Parents and friends want the School to be all that it can be. Where there is great love, there are also great expectations. Some of us only need think back to our own youth and how our parents might have expressed their love for us by placing more weight on what we needed to do to be a better person. Expectations can sometimes be felt as burdens.

The good news about these expectations is that they are not unreasonable. There is the hope that the Mountain View Waldorf School can grow to a place where the tasks of a more mature school can be accomplished with the support of an expanded budget.

This can be a school where there is a focus on external communication, health benefits for faculty and staff, and a staff member or professional service taking care of cleaning. At the same time, the organizational issues and how they are tied up with decision making are a function of the School's moving from one level of operating complexity to the next level. Some members of the School community are more patient than others in waiting for this organizational growth to take place.

Summary—The Case

The School has a case for giving that can form the basis of planning and preparing for growth. The notion of change, planned change, has been put on paper and made real.

There is much in the case that speaks to the needs of the present interviewees as prospective donors.

There is, however, an assumption among some that a wider audience is necessary, one that doesn't yet know enough about the School, in order for the School to reach the dollar goal described. It appears that many of the comments about the need for changes in the case are based on this assumption. I will have more to say about this assumption later.

B. LEADERSHIP AND VOLUNTEER SUPPORT

Leadership in Nonprofits and Waldorf Schools

In order for those of us gathered around the Mountain View Waldorf School to take up a serious discussion of volunteer leadership, we need to start from a general overview of the nonprofit sector and the question of leadership.

Nonprofit organizations, be they Waldorf schools or some other type, rely on volunteer leadership on the board and in other authorized positions. Without competent and committed volunteer leadership, the nonprofit sector would not function as forcefully or as effectively. Some of us have had less-than-ideal experiences with volunteer committees or even with a board of trustees. While not the exception, these are also not the rule.

While this is not the place for a treatise on the benefits of volunteer leadership, based on my work with more than 50 Waldorf schools, it is my opinion that Waldorf schools cannot function effectively without a cadre of striving volunteer leaders. It is not enough to have a board of trustees. A Waldorf school needs—I might even say requires—a growing, changing, and evolving pool of volunteers and volunteer leaders. In addition to a wide variety of life experience and skills, they provide a linkage to parents and to the community at large and build and maintain an envelop of warmth surrounding the School. This zone of warmth can be seen as one of the organs of the body of the School.

Leadership in the Context of a Campaign

Fortunately, the consideration of a capital campaign has its own opportunities for the School to contemplate the quality and quantity of volunteer leadership it needs. Perhaps the three most important elements of a successful capital campaign are:

1. Strong and capable volunteer leadership.
2. A well-planned campaign strategy.
3. Sufficient volume of leading gifts.

Those, of course, do not guarantee success. Their absence will, however, make success *very* difficult to attain. Often, it is the quality of volunteer leadership of a campaign that will develop, or not, an adequately planned campaign strategy. Also, the quality of the volunteer leadership can mean the difference between attracting, or not, the vital element of enough leading gifts.

Perceived Leadership at the School

When asked, "Would you accept a volunteer leadership position in this campaign if asked?," 74% declined. While this is a high number, it alone should not be an immediate cause for concern. It is often the case that volunteers do not immediately put their own name forward. Worth noting are the low percentages of "yes," 5%, and "probably," 5%. Combined these show that only 10% would consider putting themselves forward as possible leadership for a capital campaign. A more hopeful sign would have been to have a significant number in the "possibly" or "don't know" categories. Seventeen percent is not a low number for "possibly," but it is not a number big enough to count on. The objective observer could say perceived volunteer leadership is weak.

We should at this point also consider the impact of the number of volunteer names that came from the question, "Can you think of someone you feel would be a good volunteer campaign leader?" Eighteen names is quite good. Four names had at least two mentions, which helps demonstrate that a group of individuals are believed to be worthy of an assignment of volunteer leadership.

Volunteering in Nonprofits

Volunteering for philanthropic support work is measured differently than leadership. Here, the absence or presence of a certain number of volunteers is not the only useful indicator. Rather, it is the quality of volunteering that matters in a capital campaign. Will they take the assignment seriously? Will they take the time to become adequately informed? Will they follow through on what they say they will do? Will they be committed in soliciting contributions?

Volunteering for a Possible Campaign

In response to "Are there ways you would be willing to be of help (as a volunteer)?," 42% said "no," 34% said "yes." Combining these with the 16% "probably" brings a generally positive count to at least 40%. In trying to measure volunteer readiness, the multicategory responses also need to be factored in. Both them were "yes to probably." If the School is especially effective at informing and uniting *all* types of volunteer interests, including those who would never want to ask for money, it might see as many as 45 to 50% of its total volunteers participate, perhaps even more.

Trustees in Nonprofits

Up to this point in the discussion, little has been said about the perception of the role of the board or its role in a potential campaign. Generally, in the conventional nonprofit sector, volunteer campaign leadership may or may not come solely from the board. Whether from within or without their ranks, it is widely accepted in the nonprofit world that it is *the task of the board* to find suitable campaign leadership, empower and entrust them and their team, equip them with adequate resources, monitor their progress, and highlight their successes.

Trustees at the School

With this as a background, we can review the responses to "What is your perception of the board's potential to mount a successful capital campaign?" "Excellent" drew 13% and a much higher "good" of 48%. That is a combined number of 61% positive. If you include the two multicategory responses with "good" as part of the range, we are looking at a positive percentage in the low to middle 60s.

The workings of a Waldorf school board are never completely painless. When big changes are being considered, the board, regardless of its effectiveness, can often feel like the target of pointed questioning, even strong disagreement. Given a couple of the comments of interviewees, the board of the School is no stranger to this.

Summary—Volunteers, Leadership, and Trustees

Because these three topics of volunteers, leadership, and trustees are intimately linked, what one can say about anyone of them, one can say about all. Let's start with the obvious and work to the not so obvious.

It appears from the interview data that more people are willing to volunteer for a possible capital campaign than are willing to volunteer to be a leader for one. This is not surprising. First, more people generally are willing to follow than to lead. Second, the School is contemplating a large goal that clearly has some people nervous. The issue may have as much to do with the fact that the level of understanding of what a campaign volunteer leader is supposed to do is still incomplete. When you don't know what someone is asking you to do, the common response is to decline to do it. One way to look at this reluctance of potential leaders to step forward is to determine what level of support these prospective volunteer leaders need in order to feel comfortable taking on leadership assignments.

We also need to see this reluctance in the context of all volunteerism, including the trustees, who are, after all, volunteers. Some of the longer-term participants in the School have expressed, some directly and some indirectly, that it is perhaps time for a new look at what is needed in the assortment of volunteer and staff positions.

When we look at all the human beings who take on the wide variety of tasks at the School (outside the curriculum), we have an entire range of ongoing and intermittent volunteer, part-time staff, and full-time staff positions. It is clear to the outsider, and, certainly to those with a long-range perspective, that the School is operating more or less with a set of volunteer and staff positions that have grown from one year to the next apparently without long-range planning. What the interviews are telling us is that it is time to revisit the current array and assignment of staff and volunteer positions. By this I mean a review is in order of all nonteaching activities with an eye to looking at them afresh based on *what the School needs in the short and medium term.*

The message of the interviews for the trustees is not so sharp and distinct. The generally positive response toward the board as capable to mount a campaign may be more a statement of people's feeling comfortable knowing the board has the right heart. Woven in and around other statements and issues seems to be a concern regarding the level of preparedness for a really big project. The unstated question could be voiced as, "Are we set up to handle this?" I take this to mean not just the campaign organization, but also the readiness of the board.

Like the volunteers and other volunteer leadership, it appears that the board has grown from year to year, facing its challenges as they come. The not-so-obvious message is that the operations of the board, like other volunteer activities, are due for an overview based on *what the School needs for the short and medium term.* Let's be clear here. No one is claiming that the board is falling down on the job. Rather, there is some vague uneasiness that the board operations and effectiveness of the past may not be enough to ensure success in the coming months and years.

C. FINANCIAL SUPPORT

The temptation to immediately turn to this section is strong. After all, the big question on people's mind is "Can we raise enough money?"

In order to pinpoint financial goals with acceptable accuracy, it is prudent to pay sufficient attention to data, the ambient atmosphere, and incidental information arising during the study.

Perceptions of Support

The question, "Is the need of $2,900,000 in cash and pledges for this project a realistic amount for the School to expect to raise?," registered a 21% "yes" response. If we combine the "yes" with the "probably" of 21%, we get a total of 42%. Note, however, the "no" responses are 12%. This shows a group who clearly thinks the chances are not good to raise $2.9 million. What is more notable is the largest group in the range of responses is "don't know," with 30%. We can't ignore the nine (9) multicategory responses, and adding the three (3) with "yes" or "probably" does strengthen the believability of the dollar goal, but only marginally.

The question, "What would the School be facing to raise that amount of money?," raised four (4) issues:

- A lot of work, a lot of time.   (26%)
- What's wrong with public school?   (17%)
- Lots of capital campaign competition.   (17%)
- The public high school efforts.   (14%)

These responses need to be seen in the light of the fact that almost everyone likes the idea of a new home for the School. The largest cluster relates to the effort itself, that of raising the money. Slightly more than a quarter of the respondents are concerned about how hard it is to raise money and how long it takes. They are telling us they are nervous, that it may take so much work or so much time that the campaign might not be successful.

As mentioned earlier, some interviewees are assuming that a successful capital campaign will require significant gifts outside the current circle of devoted supporters. With that in mind, it is understandable that the comments about the choice of public education play so strongly. Seventeen percent are pointing out that advocates of public school are not likely to fall over themselves in an effort to give money to such a project. And then, another 14% are reminding us that the public high school and its $40 million bond is taking up a lot of the larger community's consciousness. If you combine them, you have 31% of the interviewees telling us that public school issues may be a serious obstacle.

While the notion of hard work and public school are concerns, the fear of competition from other fundraising efforts weighs heavily on our interviewees. We see that 17% are worried about the availability of gifts from the philanthropically inclined outside the School parent body.

What can we draw as conclusions from this information?

We have a group of mostly enthusiastic parents, family, and friends who want the School to fund a new home. They feel the number might be too large, and they are worried that funds they think will be needed from outside the School community may not necessarily be forthcoming.

Individual Support for a Campaign

If we go back to the general question, "Would you be likely to support it?," we note that 74% responded "yes." Rolling in the 16% "probably" gives a total positive response of 90%. That is weighed against only 2% saying "no." This is a *very* positive indication.

When we take a look at the more specific indications for personal support, with the question, "Among other organizations that you are interested in and support, what level of priority would this project have for you?" 26% said "top" and 34% "high," giving us a combined "top to high" number of 60%. This is saying that just under two thirds of the respondents rank this proposed project as their high to most important philanthropic interest. Conversely, only 8% rank it as "low."

The interview process then zeroed in on specific dollar amounts using the proposed table of gifts (Appendix C). Each person interviewed was given a copy of the proposed table of gifts to review. When a couple was interviewed, both were handed a table of gifts sheet to look over.

"Does this proposed table of gifts look attainable to you?" resulted in a shift in responses. For this question, the "yes" was 8%, and the "probably" was 19%. Even a liberal interpretation of the combination of "yes" and "probably" is only 27%. This compares to the combined "42%" for the question about whether the $2.9 million goal is realistic. At the same time, "no" response increases from 12% with "Does the $2.9 million . . . seem attainable?" to 22 % with "Does this table look attainable?" The number of interviewees who are doubtful after seeing the table of gifts almost doubles. What this seems to indicate is that seeing the table of gifts makes the need for larger gifts more real. You don't raise $1 million by getting 1 million people to give you a dollar each. You need a handful of contributors who meet 40 to 50% of the goal.

Goal Attainment

The likelihood of reaching $2.9 million requires that we first look at the list of reported numbers listed in two columns, lower and higher. When an interview resulted in a lower *and* higher number, both numbers are printed in bold.

The 30 responses include 27 interviews when numbers were given and three (3) interviews when none where given. The total ranged from a total of $245,000 on the low side to $446,000 on the high.

The following pages use three different analyses of this range of numbers, all aimed at helping us determine what is a realistic goal for such a project.

Leading Gift Analysis

First, the largest gift indication is examined.

It is widely known in the nonprofit world that successful capital campaigns usually have at least one gift of no less than 10% of the proposed goal.

In recent years the size of this so-called "leading gift" has played a larger and larger role in campaign momentum and success. Today, it would be prudent to have a leading gift closer to 20%.

The size of the largest gift, of course, does not guarantee success. Without it, however, a successful campaign is highly unlikely.

From the list of personal responses to the proposed table of gifts, the largest gift indication is $75,000. From Table A, below, this amount is multiplied by a factor of 5 and 10. A factor of 10 would reflect the ideal of 10% of the goal. A factor of 5 would reflect 20% of the goal.

Table A
Leading Gift Analysis

	$75,000	$75,000
× factor (20% gift)	× 5	
× factor (10% gift)		× 10
Campaign Potential	$375,000	$750,000

Top 10 Gift Analysis

Another useful and common standard of measure is the total of the top 10 gift indications. Capital campaigns have historically demonstrated that the successful attainment of the total dollar goal is often dependent on whether or not the 10 largest gifts total a minimum of 33 to 40%.

Whether the lower percentage of 33% or higher percentage of 40% is relied upon for projections is mostly a function of the size of the institution. A smaller institution with a sizeable goal should probably look to 40% rather than 33%.

Table B below lists the 10 highest gifts, including range amounts. These are totaled and multiplied by 2.5, which would make the gift indications 40% of the likely goal.

Table B
Top 10 Gifts Analysis

Rank	Low	High
1.	$25,000	$75,000
2.	1,000	75,000
3.	50,000	50,000
4.	50,000	50,000

(continues)

Table B (Continued)
Top 10 Gifts Analysis

Rank	Low	High
5.	25,000	50,000
6.	25,000	25,000
7.	10,000	25,000
8.	10,000	25,000
9.	15,000	15,000
10.	5,000	10,000
Total	$216,000	$400,000
× factor	2.5	2.5
Campaign Potential	$540,000	$1,000,000

Total Gifts Analysis

The third indicator of campaign potential is that the total of the interviewees' gift indications should, under ideal circumstances, represent 33 or 40% of the campaign goal. Again, as in the last analysis, the informed approach is that the size of the goal relative to the size of the institution should be the guide, 40% for a smaller institution. Therefore, the analysis is based on the idea of the total indications being 40% of what is potentially capable of being raised.

As seen in Table C below, all the gift indications are presented with both high and low figures. These totals are multiplied by 2.5 (to measure its being 40% of the goal) to provide an indication of the campaign potential.

The 27 indications show a range of $245,000 to $446,000.

Table C
Total Gifts Analysis

	Low	High
Gift indication	$245,000	$446,000
Factor	× 2.5	× 2.5
Campaign Potential	$612,500	$1,115,000

IV. RECOMMENDATIONS

The following section is purposely composed and designed, as much as possible, to be a template for action. The opportunity exists for the Mountain View Waldorf School to direct concerted, intentional change; this section is written to hopefully assist the current and future leaders of the School.

I have divided the recommendation into two parts: those dealing with operational needs and those of the specific project. The operational issues are those things that are needed generally, whether or not the School attempts to conduct a capital campaign. The specific project is, of course, the capital campaign.

Taking Stock

Even putting aside the question of a capital campaign, the School has at least three significant sets of tasks in front of it. They include:

1. Which structures to build.
2. How and when to build structures.
3. Who should build the structures.
4. How the building process should be overseen.
5. Getting all the town approvals.

The purpose of listing these is not to frighten anyone, but instead to encourage a *hygienic* approach to growing the School. Anyone who has built a commercial or residential structure while still trying to keep a home, office, or business functioning normally knows of what I speak. It is far too easy to work to a state of exhaustion.

It will be essential for the health of the volunteers, the faculty, the children, and the School as a whole that careful planning include not only the bricks and funds, but *also care for the people*. The easiest way to keep from overworking volunteers and staff is to obtain clear and written agreements in advance of the scope of each job. Obviously, some jobs are so small they don't need to be in writing. However, such tasks as the clerk of the works, the chair of the capital campaign, and the chair of the building supervision committee need to be in writing and approved in advance.

A. OPERATIONAL RECOMMENDATIONS

Recommendation One—Building Enrollment

The School is suffering from under enrollment. What is called for is a systematic, continuous, and integrated enrollment action plan aimed at significant improvements in:

a. Outreach—making the School better known.
b. Follow-through—making every visitor and every inquiry count.
c. Retention—reenrolling the highest percentage of families possible.

This work needs a dedicated staff position. It will be more difficult to get the full results in the early stages without a full-time person, but until the operating budget of the

School is larger, it may not be financially feasible for the School to afford anything but a part time enrollment coordinator. The rationale for this investment is that it will take only a small number of new enrollments to pay for this person's part-time salary. Once the position is in place, plans should be made to invest in a full-time position, again justifying the expenditure with the revenue from new enrollments. Looking to other Waldorf schools, you will see the wisdom of such an approach.

Just as Waldorf schools around the country have been focusing efforts on building a professional enrollment position, they have also seen the merits of an active, vital enrollment committee. Even a full-time enrollment coordinator cannot do the job alone. Marketing, outreach, and community connections are all needed, as well as the oversight, advocacy, and general good-heartedness of a robust and effective enrollment committee.

In the meantime, the board can authorize and, together with the faculty, approve a written and detailed mandate of a standing board committee, the enrollment committee. This committee's job will be to develop and recommend to the board, and to the faculty, an annual enrollment action plan. The plan will be tied to the annual operating income and expense projections. The enrollment revenue sought each year will be mirrored in the goals of the action plan. The plan will include such measurable outcomes as:

1. Number of attendees at open house events.
2. Number of visitors.
3. Number of inquiries.
4. Percentage of visitors requesting further information.
5. Percentage of inquires requesting enrollment packets, etc.
6. Percentage of packets resulting in enrollments.

The plan will include an enrollment expense budget targeted to support the efforts of outreach, follow-through, and reenrollment. The purpose of the annual enrollment action plan is to provide the enrollment committee, the board, and the finance committee, as well as the faculty, with a reasonable methodology for creating, tracking, and predicting intentional enrollment growth.

The action plan should contain not only a calendar of activities, but also a determination of which members of the enrollment committee are responsible for which activities. In the early stages of the committee, before there is a full-time enrollment coordinator, great care must be taken that the outcomes in the action plan are reasonable and attainable. The first two years of such a plan will set the stage for further investment and an ongoing successful track record of enrollment efforts. In other words, build slowly, build surely.

The board and the faculty should, according to a long-range plan, be setting enrollment growth goals. The enrollment committee becomes, then, the vehicle by which the growth can happen.

Recommendation Two—Strengthening the Board

It is time for the board to take a couple of giant steps forward in improving and expanding its acquaintance with what has come to be known in the nonprofit world as the best practices of nonprofit boards. This is not offered because the board is being seen as dysfunctional or operating inappropriately. Rather, the School wants to be taken seriously in the wider community in terms of a multimillion-dollar campus plan. With such aspirations comes the requirement for the board to function with greater precision, higher levels of self-knowledge, and even greater clarity.

I recommend the forming of a governance committee. At one time it was adequate to have a nominating committee, functioning on an annual basis, whose job was to find, recruit, and help install new trustees. We have now come to realize that the issues of board performance and recruitment are part of the same continuum of activity. For this reason, I recommend that a standing board committee, the governance committee, be established by the board. Its written mandate (or job description) would include:

1. Finding and recruiting members for board committees.
2. Tracking and selecting potential trustees from such committees.
3. Selecting and recommending prospective trustees to the board.
4. Orienting and mentoring new trustees.
5. Assisting the board in developing an annual board action plan.
6. Scheduling an annual trustee self-assessment.
7. Coordinating with the officers a succession planning process.
8. Any and all efforts to foster a striving, diverse, and collaborative set of trustees.

It would be important that the establishment of the governance committee not happen all at once in the first year. In order to assure a successful outcome, it might be wise to take a couple of years to achieve this level in slow but measured steps.

However, make no mistake. The care the School takes creating and grooming an effective board of trustees will be a major signpost to the local community as to how serious the School is concerning philanthropy.

One should not assume that a serious and thoughtful effort to build a superior-quality board of trustees means that you are seeking only members with deep pockets. Quite the contrary. In a Waldorf setting, what is more important than deep pockets is deep commitment and a belief in the value of giving. As I have said before, the point in philanthropic programs, Waldorf style, is not to give until it hurts, but to give until it feels good. The depth of one person's giving, while being a private matter, can be read on their countenance. So seek not only the wealthy and influential. Seek the passionate, the thoughtful, and the energetic. The money will follow.

Recommendation Three—Balancing Volunteers and Staff

I have already mentioned the need for a reassessment of the arrangement of staff and volunteer positions of the School. You might call this zero-based planning for human resources. Let's be clear that I am speaking only of the nonteaching activities.

While there are several methodologies or approaches that can be used, I am going to recommend a joint task force on volunteers and staffing. This does not need to be a lengthy or enormously involved effort. What is important is that:

    a. The task force have a clear, written mandate approved the board, faculty, and Parent Association.

    b. The effort have a predetermined timeline.

    c. The task force have a finite life.

    d. The outcomes sought be determined early and with clear delineation.

    e. The membership be across School community lines.

    f. There be an interface with the finance committee.

The purpose of such a task force on volunteers and staffing is to help the School develop an assortment of staffing and volunteer positions that:

1. Maximize the opportunities for volunteer skills.
2. Foster the growth of volunteer leadership.
3. Where appropriate, replace volunteer intention with staff professionalism.
4. Utilize the synergy between day-to-day staff and volunteer passion.
5. Create a tiered approach to adding staff to match the budget size.

B. PROJECT RECOMMENDATION—CAPITAL CAMPAIGN

Campaign Potential

The Mountain View Waldorf School should consider launching a capital campaign based on a new case for giving, in the range of $700,000 to $800,000.

If the School is able, in the quiet phase of its campaign, to attract a gift of $100,000 to $150,000, it might be possible to stretch the goal to $900,000.

Campaign Planning

Before launching a capital campaign the following should take place:

• Settle with the architect the building sequence and configuration.

• Determine the specific building costs based on builder's estimates.

- Create and approve a new case for giving.
- Create and approve a campaign budget.
- Establish a campaign plan and timeline.
- Assemble the key positions in the campaign cabinet.
- Determine what will be campaign paid staff.
- Engage professional campaign counsel.

In addition, before launching a campaign, the board and the faculty should make known to the School community and the interviewees its intentions with regard to the operational recommendations given in this report.

Campaign Readiness

Here is a quick overview of the amounts of time that the key parts of the campaign are likely to take. They are not necessarily sequential.

Item	Time as Separate Units
Rewriting the case for giving, including obtaining approval from the board and faculty	60 to 90 days
Selecting and approving a chair of the capital campaign cabinet	30 to 60 days
From board approval to launch to first solicitation, usually the leading gift	90 to 120 days
From first solicitation to the end of the quiet phase (hitting a landmark percentage, including all larger gifts, all board, all faculty and staff)	6 months, 9 months, or more
Length of public phase	2 or 3 months maximum; the shorter the better

Campaign Plan

Given a dollar goal in the $700,000 to $800,000 range, I recommend a general campaign funding mix that includes the following constituencies:

1. Board
2. Faculty and staff
3. Leading gifts
4. Grandparents and other relatives
5. All School gifts (gifts of all sizes)
6. Foundation and corporation grants

7. School vendors
8. Local area businesses

It is *very important* that the board and the campaign cabinet be mindful that most of the contributions to a campaign will come from the individuals and organizations that already have strong ties to the School. It will be an exercise in disappointment and frustration to assume that large amounts of gift money, from either individuals or institutions, will come from other organizations near or far, just because they have it and give it away.

Who Gives, Who Gets

At the same time, it would be a mistake to ignore local like-minded donors and philanthropically inclined institutions just because they are not going to give to this campaign or give generously. This is a perfect opportunity for the School to become better known, to make its value and presence felt. There will certainly be surprise contributions. The real bonus for the School in all this will be the *new* relationships that will begin because of the campaign and the campaign energy.

For every new donor, especially those outside the current School community, the School will have both an opportunity and a responsibility for long-term relationship building. This will not be the only capital campaign in the School's history. Today's new modest-sized donor can become tomorrow's major contributor. It happens, though, only with long-term attention.

Anthroposophical and Waldorf Donors

More than just a few eager and first-time Waldorf school volunteers wonder about trying to make an appeal to anthroposphical donors and Waldorf schools around the region or even around the country. The same rule of relationship applies. If someone doesn't already have a strong relationship to the School, it is unlikely that they are going to give. If you got a letter, or even a phone call, from a Waldorf school you never even heard of, how likely would it be that you would give generously or even at all?

C. PROVIDING ADVISORY SERVICES

Martin Novom and the Alexis de Tocqueville Institute are available for campaign counsel and services to the Mountain View Waldorf School. These services include, but are not limited to:

- On- and off-site capital campaign management.
- Training of volunteers, including solicitors.
- Mentoring of chairs and key volunteers.

- Educational seminars for parents, staff, and friends of the School.
- Assistance with communication materials, printed and electronic.
- Review of current communications materials.
- Board development.
- Enrollment audit and enrollment planning.

INTERVIEW QUESTIONS 2005

1. What has been your experience of the Mountain View Waldorf School?

2. How would you rank your experience?

    ❏ Positive   ❏ Conflicted   ❏ Neutral   ❏ Negative   ❏ n/a

3. What do you think the School does best?

4. What would you like to see improved?

5. What was your reaction to the Case for Giving?

    ❏ Positive   ❏ Conflicted   ❏ Neutral   ❏ Negative   ❏ n/a

6. What do you like about it?

7. What would you like to see improved or changed?

8. If you could rank the parts of the project, what order of preference would you put them in?

    _____ Administrative space

    _____ Early childhood center

    _____ The elementary school

9. Will the School community support this project?

    ❏ Yes   ❏ Probably   ❏ Possibly   ❏ No   ❏ Don't Know   ❏ n/a

10. What makes you say that?

11. Would you be likely to support it?

    ❏ Yes   ❏ Probably   ❏ Possibly   ❏ No   ❏ Don't Know   ❏ n/a

12. Among other organizations that you care about and support, what level of priority might this project have for you?

    ❏ Top   ❏ Top 3   ❏ Middle Level   ❏ Low   ❏ Don't Know   ❏ n/a

13. Is the need for $2,900,000 in cash and pledges to pay for this project a realistic amount for the School to expect to raise?

    ❏ Yes   ❏ Probably   ❏ Possibly   ❏ No   ❏ Don't Know   ❏ n/a

14. Why do you think that?

15. (*For those who say no or possibly.*) What would be a more realistic amount?

16. What would the School be facing in its efforts to raise that amount of money?

17. Are there conditions or activities outside the School community that might affect the School's ability to reach such a dollar goal?

18. Do you think this is a good time for the School to begin a major campaign?

    ❏ Yes   ❏ Probably   ❏ Possibly   ❏ No   ❏ Don't Know   ❏ n/a

19. If not now, when?

20. Does this proposed table of gifts look attainable to you?

    ❏ Yes   ❏ Probably   ❏ Possibly   ❏ No   ❏ Don't Know   ❏ n/a

21. Do you know of any potential person or organization within the wider School community that has the financial ability to make a gift at any of the top three levels, A, B or C? (*If YES*) Who might that be?

22. Would you change or adjust the table of gifts below the top levels, say from Level C on through the bottom? (*If YES*) How?

23. (*This next question is in no way intended to be a request for a commitment. However, your response will help the School in its planning for a potential campaign.*)

    Could you indicate, please, if you were likely to contribute, at what level might you consider contributing?

    A.   B.   C.   D.   E.   F.

    G.   H.   I.   J.   K.   L.

24. Could your gift be matched by your employer?

    ❏ Yes   ❏ Probably   ❏ Possibly   ❏ No   ❏ Don't Know   ❏ n/a

25. Here is a list of the board of trustees of the School. What is your perception of their potential to mount a successful capital campaign?

    ❏ Excellent   ❏ Good   ❏ Fair   ❏ Poor   ❏ Don't Know   ❏ n/a

26. Would you accept a leadership position in such a campaign, if you were asked?

    ❏ Yes   ❏ Probably   ❏ Possibly   ❏ No   ❏ Don't Know   ❏ n/a

27. Are there ways that you would be willing to be of help?

❏ Yes   ❏ Probably   ❏ Possibly   ❏ No   ❏ Don't Know   ❏ n/a

28. (*If YES*) How might that be?

29. Who do you think would be a good volunteer campaign leader?

30. Can you think of any individuals, inside or outside the School community, who you think might be interested in this project?

31. What are the important points about this project that you would emphasize to potential donors?

32. Do you have any additional comments?

List of Interviewees

Δαωιδ Βροοκσ

Σανδυ ανδ Δαριν Βροων

Κειτη ανδ Μαρλενα Βνζζελλ

Λοισ Χαφφρευ

Διχιε Χολεμαν

Πεγγυ Χρομφελλ

Μαρια ανδ Μαρχ Δοναλδσον

Τομ ανδ Ρυτη Εαρλε

Δεβοραη Φαυωερ

Ηολλυ Ηορτιν

Τινα Χραιγ ανδ Χηαρλεσ Γρεενηαλγη

Δεβοραη Ηατχη

Μαρυ Σανδερσον ανδ Τονυ Ηευεσ

Ϳεννιφερ Ηιγγινσ

Εριχ Ηιρσχηηφελδ

Ανδρεω Κεαρνσ

Νανχυ ανδ Τεδ Κυρτζ

Ρυτη Ηαμιλτον ανδ ϑοσεπη Λεντινι

Βεττυ Λουνδ

Συτ ανδ Μαργαρετ Μαρσηαλλ

Ροβερτ ανδ Τραχυ Ματηιευ

ϑοσεπη "Βρυδ" ΜχΧαβε

Βαρβαρα Ροχκωελλ

Τηομασ Σηαφφνερ

Joαν Τ. Σηερμαν

Δοροτηυ ανδ Στανλευ Σολομον

Βετη ανδ Κιμ Τηομασ

Λισα Τηομπσον

Τηυρστον Τωιγγ-Σμιτη

Χυντηια Ενγερ

Proposed Table of Gifts

Mountain View Waldorf School   April 2005

Level	Number of Donors	Size of Each Gift	Pledged over 3 Years
A	1	$600,000	$200,000
B	1	300,000	100,000
C	2	150,000	50,000
D	2	100,000	33,333
E	4	75,000	25,000
F	6	50,000	16,666
G	8	25,000	8,333
H	12	15,000	5,000
I	20	10,000	3,333
J	28	5,000	1,666
K	36	2,500	833
L	48 or more	Up to 1,000	333
Total		**$2,900,000**	

Planning Study Report for a Proposed Capital and Endowment Campaign

Presented to the

Board of Trustees
of
Jersey University of Pennsylvania

Prepared by

CAPITAL VENTURE
(formerly Cornerstone Consulting, Inc.)

June 29, 2001

BACKGROUND

Jersey University, after engaging in a marketing study and strategic planning process, recognizes the need to increase endowment funds for scholarships in order to provide an appropriate source of funding to attract quality students. Additionally, Jersey has in recent years been aware of the deterioration of the historic buildings on the campus and, in an effort to preserve Jersey's rich history and provide a more "user-friendly" campus for its students, has determined that funding is needed to complete the restoration of its historic buildings and combine all student services into the "Quad." There is money available from the State System of Higher Education to fund the capital projects, but this money must be matched with money raised from private sources. To this end, Jersey engaged CAPITAL VENTURE in January 2001 to conduct a planning study to determine both Jersey's internal and external readiness to conduct a major capital and endowment campaign to fund these needs.

A preliminary case for support was developed, with a goal of $10,000,000 to $7,000,000 for scholarship endowment, $2,000,000 for unrestricted funds, and $1,000,000 to match the state money for capital projects.

METHODOLOGY

CAPITAL VENTURE principal, Linda Lysakowski, ACFRE, worked with Σηαρον Χαννον, Vice President of Advancement, to assess the internal readiness of Jersey to conduct a campaign, develop a preliminary case for support, and provide guidance for the selection of persons to be interviewed. Δρ. Χλιντον Πεττυσ also met with Linda to provide input into the case for support. Judith Snyder, CFRE, also a principal of CAPITAL VENTURE, met with the trustees to explain the methodology of the study.

A preliminary case for support was drafted and printed in booklet form to be mailed to each interviewee as their appointment was confirmed. Νανχυ βασσυμ coordinated the scheduling of all appointments. A total of 60 interviews were conducted by Linda Lysakowski, ACFRE; Judith Snyder, CFRE; and Nancy M. Stoever, senior consultant with CAPITAL VENTURE.

INTERNAL ASSESSMENT

Legal Requirements

As an institution of higher education, Jersey is not required to register with the Bureau of Charitable Organizations and there is no Capital Campaign Review Board in the Jersey community; therefore Jersey has met all the legal requirements to conduct a capital campaign.

Infrastructure

Jersey is in the process of acquiring and setting up a new donor database system. This system needs to be in place, and staff trained to use it before a campaign gets under way. The importance of a donor database that can record donor history and multiyear pledges will be crucial to the management of campaign data. The alumni office has a stand-alone software package and this program needs to be integrated with the advancement office package.

Financial Stability

Jersey is financially sound, has an experienced CFO, and a finance committee of trustees who are knowledgeable about the financial status of the University. Jersey has had a balanced budget and increased revenues in recent years.

Board Involvement

The board of trustees is small and is appointed by the State System of Higher Education. However, the board chair is well known and respected in the community and there are members with significant resources who can contribute to the campaign. This board has not been involved with other campaigns at Jersey, since the last capital campaign was held in the late 1980s; however, the individual board members may have some level of experience with other campaigns. There is potential on the board for major gifts, but the board has not been cultivated or involved in advancement activities. The board has reached consensus on this campaign and has approved the planning study. There are trustees who are willing to get involved in the campaign. The size of the board has been established by the Commonwealth and therefore is not able to be increased. However, an advisory board of community leaders has been established in order to increase the number of people involved in the advancement efforts of the University. There is a list of people who are on the advisory committee, but they have not met recently. There is also a campaign committee; however they have not been active, either. The chair of the board of trustees is a Jersey alum, as are several other trustees.

Management

The President of Jersey is very well known and highly regarded in the community. Δρ. Πεττυσ has been at Jersey for many years, and is well connected to the community. He is active in local organizations such as the chamber of commerce and is known to be a community leader. He also recognizes the importance of his involvement in the advancement program, and in particular in this campaign.

The vice president for institutional advancement has also been with the University for a number of years and is knowledgeable in the field of development. However, the department is understaffed and therefore staff is involved in a lot of activities including special events, which may prevent them from dedicating the amount of time that will be needed during a capital campaign. Current staffing includes the vice president for institutional advancement, assistant vice president, PR director (position vacant), PR assistant, career services, sports information director, health center director (this position will be moved to academic vice president), two administrative assistants, and two secretaries. There is no prospect researcher on staff. Grant writing is outsourced and some is done by faculty but coordinated through the advancement office. The assistant VP for institutional advancement is currently filling the PR director role. There is no writer on staff. The assistant VP also does some events; the VP does others.

There is also a Jersey Foundation, although the role of the foundation is unclear and may be duplicating efforts of the Office of Institutional Advancement. The purpose of the Foundation is to raise funds for the University and they also manage funds. There is also a separate Alumni Association, which does fundraising and manages its own funds.

Long-Range Planning

The University has a long-range plan in place with measurable goals and objectives. This plan is not reviewed on a consistent basis by the trustees and administration, and it may not be communicated to all levels of the University.

Annual Giving Program

Jersey has been successful in raising over $1,000,000 annually, however there is no formal, well-planned annual giving program in place. The University currently does grant writing through contracted grant writers, freeing the staff to do other fundraising. However, staff is very involved in special events, which can often be very time consuming. There is not much emphasis placed on the annual support from alumni, trustees, and the local community. There is some direct mail; however, no phonathons have been done recently. There is no corporate appeal. The alumni fundraising program is not coordinated within the advancement office. There are currently 10,000 living alumni and about 8,000 of these are in the database. There has been an alumni directory published. There is no student or parent solicitation, nor is there an alumni student council; however, there have been students involved in, and interested in, the advancement program.

Marketing and Public Relations

There is currently no marketing plan in place. There is also no marketing committee on the board of trustees or marketing staff. Jersey does serve a valuable need in the community and is well thought of by those who know the University; however, the community at large may not be aware of all Jersey has to offer and its impact on the community. There are annual reports and newsletters published, as well as frequent press releases; however, there is no video or a complete offering of brochures available to people interested in Jersey programs. Alumni have not been cultivated to become involved in Jersey, either financially or in marketing Jersey to prospective students.

Major Donor Prospects

There are numerous major gift prospects, both alumni and trustees. Donor history records are not up-to-date. The current system does not allow easy access to past donor history, nor has much time been spent in donor identification and cultivation. There is no formal donor recognition program in place. There are distinguished alumni awards as well as recognition gifts given to major donors, but there is no formal program in place to recognize major donors.

Case for Support

This campaign, focused primarily on scholarship endowment, is one that will be easily communicated to constituencies, and it is believed that the community would be supportive of this project. The state funding for capital needs, which requires a matching contribution from the private sector, is also something that should be easily marketable to Jersey constituents.

Summary of Interviews

Interviewees' relationship to Jersey included:

Alumni	36
Board member	3
Community leader	31
Donor	29
Former board member	1
Volunteer	1
Other	5

Please note: Some interviewees fall into more than one category.

Interviews were completed with the following individuals:

Αγνεω, Χηαρλεσ—Στατε Συστεμ φορ Ηιγηερ Εδυχατιον

Αλλευνε, Γλαδστονε (Τονυ)—Στ. ΕλιζαβετηϿσ Ηοσπιταλ

Αρνολδ, Ρομελλα—Στατε οφ ΠΑ

Βακ, Δον—Βαγγοτ & Βακ

Βενεσ, Πατ—Στατε Συστεμ οφ Ηιγηερ Εδυχατιον

Βερρυ-Ηολμεσ, Ελιζαβετη

Βλαχκφελλ, ϑαννιε—Πιτυ οφ Πηιλαδελπηια

Βογλε, Ροβερτ—Πηιλαδελπηια Τριβυνε

Βριττον, Πηυλλισ

Βροων, Ραλπη—ΠΕΧΟ Ενεργυ

Χλαρκ, Δρ. Δοναλδ

ΔεΒαπτιστε, Μαυορ Χλιφφορδ—ϐεστ Χηεστερ

Δεννισ, Σηιρλευ—Ιερσευ Υνιωερσιτυ

Δεωλιν, ϑοσεπη—Γιραρδ Χολλεγε

Ελβυ, Δανιελ—Αλτερνατιωε Ρεηαβιλιτατιον Χομμυνιτιεσ Ινχ.

Γορδον, Δρ. Μιλδρεδ—Περσευ Υνιωερσιτυ

Γρεενε, Χηαρλεσ—ΠΑΣΣ, Ινχ.

Ηαχκνευ, Δοναλδ

Ηαυρε, Συλωια

Ηενδερσον, Δαρρελ

Interviewee list (continued):

Ηιλλ, Γλαδυσ

Ηολεφελδερ, ϑαχκ—Δελαφαρε Χουντυ Χηαμβερ οφ Χομμερχε

Ηορσευ, Μιχηαελ—Στατε οφ ΠΑ

ϑοηνσον, ϐιλλιε—ΠΡϐΤ Σερωιχεσ, Ινχ.

ϑονεσ, Νατ

Κελλυ, Μρσ. Αλωυ—Κελλυ Σπορτσ, Λτδ.

Κιρκλανδ, Τηαδδευσ—Χομμονωεαλτη οφ ΠΑ

Κνοωλεσ, Δρ. Ματτηεω—ϑερσευ Υρβαν Χεντερ

Λογαν, Ρεω. & Μρσ. Τηομασ

Μονταγυε, Μρ. & Μρσ. ϐαλτερ

Παλμϑυιστ, Χατηερινε—ΥϐΧΑ οφ ϐεστ Χηεστερ

Παρκερ, Δολορεσ ΜχΙωερ

Παττερσον, Ραλπη—IBM

Παττερσον, Σαμ & Δειδρε—Σηεπηαρδ, Παττερσον & Ασσοχιατιον

Πελτζερ, Jαχϑυελινε

Πιττμαν, Ιρισ

Ποωελσον, Ροβερτ—Χηεστερ Χουντυ Χηαμβερ οφ Χομμερχε

Προυδφορδ, Υωοννε

Ροοσα, Σανδρα

Σχηυχκ, Ροβερτ (Σταν)—Ωεριζον

Σχοττ, Δονν—Υιρστ Υνιον Νατιοναλ Βανκ

Σεγαρσ, ϑοσεπη—ΥΣ Δεπαρτμεντ οφ Στατε

Σηαρπ, Αντονια

Σιμπκινσ, Σταν—Σιχκλε Χελλ Ανεμια Δισεασε Ασσοχιατιον

Σταλλωορτη, Λαωρενχε

Σταρρ, Μρ. & Μρσ. Ηαρρυ

Στρινε, Αλιχε—Ροχκωελλ Τηεατρεσ

Σωιννευ, Ρ. Ανδρεω—Τηε Πηιλαδελπηια Υουνδατιον

Τεαγλε, Λεοναρδ & ϑεαν

Τηομπσον, Σενατορ Ροβερτ

Τιλλερυ, Λορρεττα

ςανχε, ϑαμεσ—ΩΡΧ Τς/ΔΧ—NBX

ςαυγητερσ, Κεζιραη

Ωαλλσ, Δρ. Χαρλα—Πενν Στατε Ρεσεαρχη

Ωελβυρν, Χραιγ—6ελβυρν Ασσοχιατεσ

Ωηιτλοχκ, 6ενδελλ—ΕΒΛ&Σ Δεωελοπμεντ Χορπορατιον

Ωοοδσον, Ροβερτ—Νατэλ Χεντερ φορ Νειγηβορηοοδ Εντερ.

Ωορδ, Χυρτισ—ϑερσευ Υνιωερσιτυ

Ωροτη, Μρ. & Μρσ. Ριχηαρδ

The following areas were discussed with interviewees; their responses are as indicated:

1. **What is your perception of Jersey?**

Excellent	35	58.33%
Good	24	40.00%
Average	1	1.67%

Comments:

Positive comments regarding experience/education received at Jersey:

- Wouldn't trade my Jersey education for anything.
- When I needed a chance, Jersey gave it to me. Five siblings in our family went to Jersey. I was accepted there on probation and was an honor student when I graduated.
- We are both alum. We know Jersey to be a great school. We would not be where we are today without Jersey.
- There are few things for which I am more grateful and more proud than the years I spent at Jersey.
- I was given definition, character enhancement, a wonderful education, and most of all, was nurtured greater than I could have been anywhere else.
- There are people at Jersey who I have in my prayers regularly for whom I am eternally grateful.
- People at Jersey were determined to not let me fail despite my best efforts to do so.
- I have wonderful memories of Jersey. (3)
- My Jersey education was a wonderful experience. (2)
- The education was great and there was a real family atmosphere.
- Met good friends at Jersey, received a good education there.
- Loved it at Jersey.
- It was excellent when I was there.
- If it weren't for Jersey, I would not be where I am today; I love the school. (2)

Positive comments regarding experience/education received at Jersey (continued):

- I loved my time at Jersey, I chose Jersey because it was a historically black school.
- Jersey is very important to me. (2)
- We are proud of Jersey. It is a great school providing a good education. (2)
- Jersey helped me prepare for life.
- I made lasting friendships at Jersey.
- Jersey is close to my heart, if it weren't for Jersey, the local school system would not have the excellent teachers they have. (2)
- Could have nothing but glowing remarks about Jersey.
- Graduates will tell you they felt nurtured at Jersey.

Positive comments regarding administration/staffing at Jersey:

- They are doing the best they can with what they have. Δρ. Πεττυσ has turned the school around.
- Δρ. Πεττυσ has brought prestige to the University. He is "hands on" and is out there in the community. (18)
- Δρ. Πεττυσ has taken phenomenal steps to attract and recruit support and students.
- I served on subcommittee regarding civil rights; was impressed with Δρ. Πεττυσ and what a fine gentleman he is.
- Δρ. Πεττυσ has a vision of change and progress viewed by the public in a positive position.
- Δρ. Πεττυσ has brought stability to Jersey. (9)
- The teachers really help the students at Jersey.
- Δρ. Πεττυσ is doing a marvelous job; he is building a strong staff.
- Χλιντον Πεττυσ and Τετα Βανκσ are very good.
- Πεττυσ is doing a good job; taking Jersey where it needs to go.
- The administration is stable now and many faculty members have been here 20 years or more.
- The administration and faculty are really concerned about the quality of student life.
- δαδε διλσον was a powerful, charismatic leader who was succeeded by several who did not stay very long. Χλιντον Πεττυσ is excellent. Jersey is very fortunate to have him. He has done an outstanding job and is very committed.
- Δρ. Πεττυσ is a Godsend; he has done wonders for Jersey.
- In recent years, the administration has done a lot to help the image of Jersey; Δρ. Πεττυσ has shown a real commitment to make Jersey better.
- In the past there was no opportunity for long term planning; now we have good direction.

Positive comments in general about Jersey:

- Wonderful institution.
- They have strong alumni base that love the school.
- Feel comfortable recommending others to attend Jersey.
- When Jersey was flourishing, enrollment was 3,000, campus life was active, and there was a nurturing environment.
- Jersey received good publicity when they received recent large gifts.
- Good school, good mission!
- I'm glad there aren't co-ed dorms any more.
- The chapel is good; it is good to have a place to worship together. (2)
- Beautiful, tranquil setting.
- City commuters may not otherwise have wealth of cultural and nurturing activities available to them.
- They have always been there as an alternative to each student.
- The school is needed for targeted students and is underutilized.
- The hotel management program is a "rising star" for Jersey.
- Overall, it is a great school. The small size is good. There is a family atmosphere.
- The honors program is really putting Jersey on the map. (3)
- One of the oldest schools in the country, Jersey has a history of outstanding education.
- Jersey is a "diamond maker," they take a piece of coal and mold it into a diamond.
- Jersey provides opportunity to students not otherwise served/educated. It appeals to veterans. (It is important to Jersey to reach out to the Defense Department and people coming out of the service.)—Operation Boot Strap, GI Bill of Rights, and amount paid toward tuition. Compare tuitions and GI %.
- Jersey makes education affordable to those who cannot afford an Ivy League college. A scholarship made it possible for me to receive a college education. I used it all but my first semester.
- Jersey is like a family; a lot of alumni come back for homecoming.
- Jersey is in a great renaissance. There had been a 10-year down period, but $\Delta\rho$. $\Pi\epsilon\tau\tau\upsilon\sigma$ has a great vision of what Jersey can and should be and is in active pursuit of that goal. Times change, new thinking and actions are necessary.
- Jersey is a saving grace for our kids.
- Jersey serves not just its students, but also the community at large by providing a good education for people who enter every field of human endeavor.

Positive comments in general about Jersey (continued):

- Jersey is a remarkable part of the state system of higher education.
- Jersey is a good institution doing their job very well.
- Always known as a place where students who had low income and not the greatest SATs could have a chance for a college education.
- There is good spirit at reunions.

Negative:

Negative comments regarding administration at Jersey:

- There is a perception of mismanagement of funds that will require strong oversight of fundraising efforts, money raised and its use.
- There seems to be a lot of staff turnover. (2)
- There has been a 45-year perception of threat to Jersey regarding a possible buy-out from another university.
- The office of career support is not aggressive enough.
- There was a lot of bad management in past years.
- Πρεσιδεντ Πεττυσ has a good vision, but V.P.s around him have not helped him realize that vision. There needs to be a lot of change, some may think of their position as "just a job" or perhaps are "burned out."
- One area for improvement would be that when alumni help identify and recruit students; there needs to be better follow through from the admissions office. They need to inform students if they have been approved or rejected. The nuts and bolts of the admission process need improvement.
- Need to identify and recruit quality students.

Negative comments regarding academic standards at Jersey:

- Fundraising not well developed.
- Crisis oriented, need a plan.
- In the past 10 years, the academic standards have been lowered. They lost their better students to integration in the 1960s and 1970s.
- They need to improve academically.
- Greek societies have lowered the academic standards at Jersey.
- Many alumni do not send their children to Jersey.

Negative comments regarding public image of Jersey:

- We need to increase its student enrollment and change young people's negative perception.

- Without firsthand knowledge, one's perception of Jersey would not be good.
- Jersey is somewhat awkward in location and difficult to get to; it is off the beaten path.
- A lot of people aren't aware of Jersey as much as they could be; they need to publicize the good things that are happening.
- Morale seems to be a problem.
- Many employees and students are unhappy and complaining.

Neutral:

Neutral comments regarding facilities:

- I received an outstanding education at Jersey. My parents got more than their money's worth; however, I am saddened to see the physical plant falling apart. The buildings are really in need of repair.

Neutral comments regarding alumni relations:

- Older alumni are very committed to alumni, not sure if the younger ones are as enthused.
- We need more involvement of alumni with students.
- There is a need to get more alumni involved with Jersey (Washington, D.C., group is good).
- Young alumni to be involved and should be utilized with older alum contacts. (2)

Neutral comments regarding student life and academics:

- Jersey needs to be a fully operational campus attracting students from diverse areas and backgrounds.
- Would like to see Latin and Hispanic students receive attention and opportunities today as blacks received in Jersey's early years.
- It is good to give scholarships to those who have financial need, but make sure they are socially well-adjusted students.
- We need to get more businesses involved in recruiting at Jersey.

Neutral comments regarding financial and campaign issues:

- The state should support the physical plant needs; raised money should go toward scholarships and academic areas.
- We need a unified fundraising program; and need a strong advancement staff to run a campaign.
- State treats Jersey wrong.

Neutral comments regarding administration:

- Jersey has a rich history, but fell out of good graces for a time due to a tremendous turnover in administration.

Neutral comments regarding public relations:

- Jersey was strong in teaching. We now need to show what our strength is in other areas as well.
- Jersey is well known, but not in the business community.
- Jersey was better known nationally in earlier years, we need to publicize our academics and athletics more.
- PR and much more visibility are needed.
- Community needs to recognize Jersey as a valuable resource.
- Staff needs to write articles for the newspaper.
- Jersey should host events inviting people in.
- Jersey works hard and does not get enough recognition and publicity, which may be due largely to their location and state university as their neighbor. A community does not usually support two colleges/universities with endorsements, PR, etc.
- They had an excellent basketball team, but it was never known because it never got into the paper.
- Papers seem to support state university and down Jersey.
- Need better linkages in the community.
- We need to show how Jersey has participated in solutions in the community. $\Delta \rho$. Πεττυσ has done a lot to connect Jersey to the community, but we need to do more to show the community the value of Jersey.
- I know Jersey as a small university that is not positioned as a great university.
- Jersey needs more visibility.
- Jersey is a sleeping giant of unlimited potential or unforeseen doom.

2. **What is your understanding of Jersey's needs?**

Good	54	90.00%
Average	2	3.33%
Poor	3	5.00%
No answer	1	1.67%

Comments:

Comments regarding facilities:

- The quad was our life. It was sacred to us. I am glad to see they are restoring it. (7)
- Students complain about facilities and residence halls.
- Financial resources are needed for technology—computers, phone systems.
- Jersey needs a much larger gymnasium/auditorium and science center, new dorms, and a new computer lab.

Comments regarding academic and student life:

- What is the current enrollment at Jersey?
- Need to understand more about the endowment for scholarships—how will it be used; how many students will benefit?
- Money is needed to provide opportunities to the staff for continued education that will ultimately benefit students.
- Jersey has been considered by many to be 13th grade and this must change.
- Biggest issue is student enrollment.

Comments regarding public relations:

- They need to market their rich history and their current programs.
- The needs are well expressed in the preliminary case for support.

Comments regarding the need for a campaign:

- We need to do a campaign to match the state money for restoration.
- We don't want the quality at Jersey to deteriorate; we need to do this campaign.
- This campaign will be a good thing for Jersey.
- They need money.
- Not sure if alumni will buy into unrestricted funds. I have some concern about this. They need to be told exactly how this money will be used and parameters need to be established for unrestricted funds.
- Need to clarify how this campaign will fit into other commitments that have been made recently to Jersey. Will gifts to the scholarship fund be counted for this campaign? Should we complete those pledges and make new ones?
- I need more particulars about the technology needs: How do they plan to spend the unrestricted money?
- Annual fund is not strong.

3. How would you prioritize the needs of Jersey?

    a. **Top Priority**

Scholarship	15
Increase student enrollment	9
Facility/campus renovations	7
PR campaign to improve image, cultivate, grow	3
Consistency in administration	2
Academic standards	2
Endowment	2
Facility renovation	2
Continue building campus infrastructure and curriculum	1
Enlightened faculty	1
Creating an infrastructure	1
Clarify full mission and vision	1
Change perception. Many misunderstand Jersey	1
Build honors program	1
Additional students and enhancement	1
Curriculum design	1
PR to African-American groups	1
Preserving history of Jersey	1
Remain true to mission	1
Renovate the quad	1
Residence halls	1
Sound financial management	1
Student diversity	1
Image of a school for everyone	1

    b. **Second Priority**

Facility renovations	7
Technology	3
Scholarship	3
Increase enrollment	3
Strengthen academic program.	2
Unrestricted giving	2
Fundraising	2
Campaign plan	2
Increase scholarship money/make scholarship primary focus	2
Educational programs	1
Curriculum design	1
Creating community linkages	1
Business department	1

Faculty development	1
Build honors program	1
Broaden focus of studies	1
Better student programs	1
Attract students with diverse backgrounds/cultures	1
Aesthetics to attract students	1
Additional money for additional programs; i.e., band	1
Achievable goal	1
Buildings and maintenance	1
Money for operating expenses	1
Stabilize staff	1
Serious attempt to contact and include Jersey alum	1
Review student academic scholarship profile	1
Recruit highly academic, qualified students	1
Program development	1
High-profile recruitment effort to get better kids	1
Fully computer-literate graduates	1
Money (will be there when students are there)	1
Matching funds for renovations	1
Increase alumni involvement and contributions	1
Improve image	1
Academic standards	1

c. **Third Priority**

Scholarship	8
Facility renovations	4
Alumni development	2
Additional $ for additional programs; i.e., athletics	2
Improve image	1
Academic standards	1
Continue growing	1
Endowment to take pressure off parents and students	1
Facility renovation	1
General fund for opportunities that might arise	1
Getting the word out	1
Academic and technology programs	1
Improve facilities	1
Transportation to and from city	1
Increase government funding	1
Increase recruitment and outreach	1
Increase retention rate	1

Fundraising	1
Recruit highly academic, qualified students	1
Recruitment with more brochures and info	1
Residence halls	1
State allocations, shorten time to receive	1
Technology	1
Improve academic programs	1

Comments:

Comments regarding campaign priorities:

- Both scholarship and facilities are important; it is hard to prioritize.

- The two go hand in hand; it is hard to prioritize facility and scholarship; they are both needed.

- It is hard to prioritize; all three areas are greatly needed—renovations, scholarship, and technology go hand in hand.

- Scholarship monies are needed from an independent source. The academy is making a big difference to Jersey in the new millennium.

- Raising the $1 million match for $3 million from state for the quad could be a great asset for the obvious reasons and due to its accessibility to area tours, Αρστρονγ could be made into a museum and would be a wonderful tourist attraction.

- Jersey would definitely benefit from having start-up funds for marketing, feasibility studies, and more.

- Need to have a good plan.

Comments regarding public relations priorities:

- We need to have people think, "This is where good education is" when they think of Jersey.

- Need to have high school counselors recommend Jersey along with other schools.

- Technology is also important; marketing the school in national magazines is needed.

- Have to show people what Jersey is doing to make their graduates connected to the world. Must think globally.

- Need to link our successful past with a successful future.

- Need to show people we need funds from private sources even though Jersey is a state institution.

Comments regarding facility priorities:

- Focus on the quad. The quad *is* Jersey.

- Trees should be planted and gardens developed. (Jersey should establish a relationship with the state agricultural department to plant trees making the campus more appealing and increasing its curbside appeal. We should also pursue in-kind contributions from landscape companies or landscape architectural firms.

- Renovate the quad—it has historical value; have more lighting for greater illumination and student safety, especially young ladies on campus; have jitney for transportation around and surrounding campus.

- Jersey needs beautification; like Υνιωερσιτυ οφ ΜΔ. Garden at stone-wall entrance rather than mud would be a great start.

Comments regarding alumni priorities:

- We need to awaken the alumni; we have a debt to the University. We need to remind alumni of this debt and reenergize them.

Comments regarding academic priorities:

- Are they doing research? That is important.

- Mission and vision should state search for high-caliber, as well as low-income, students or those in need of financial assistance.

- We need to attract high honor students.

- Strengthen education department and establish Jersey as an institution putting out top teachers (public schools need teachers).

- Develop student recreation/activities with regular dramas, fashion shows, etc., that would be so enticing to students they would want to stay on campus rather than go elsewhere (even prefer it to going home on weekends).

4. **Do you think this is the right plan for Jersey?**

Right Plan	55	91.67%
Wrong Plan	0	0%
Not Sure	5	8.33%

Comments:

Comments regarding alumni:

- We need to make Jersey a place that alumni can look back to and be proud it is their school.

Comments regarding alumni (continued):

- This will really help Jersey and make students and alumni proud of their school.
- Many alumni feel they were never asked.
- We need a good case, and a way to make alumni feel good about giving.
- It is important to do this campaign before it is too late and the older guard, 50 years and more, are only fond memories.

Comments regarding public relations:

- We must be proactive, promoting Jersey in a positive light.
- Public perception is important.
- Case is somewhat unsophisticated. Needs spruce-up before going public and especially for anything going out for lead gifts and major gifts.

Comments regarding facilities:

- Quad has been in ill repair; grads want to see it restored.
- New books are needed for the library.

Comments regarding academic programs:

- We need to have active faculty writing and publishing articles.
- Quality programs are essential. We must emphasize strengthening programs rather than bricks and mortar.
- Need scholarships to get enrollment up; look at technology needs and plan for this; need to know who will get scholarships and which buildings will be renovated first.
- Need to show who will get scholarships.
- If this will add to the fullness of the Jersey experience for the student.

Comments regarding campaign plan:

- Would need to see more details and specifics on scholarship programs.
- This campaign would be a step in the right direction, establishing stability.
- We've got to do this!
- We need to look at every day functions of the University.
- Trying to raise money for a good cause such as Jersey is a good thing.
- They have to do this.
- This plan makes a lot of sense.
- Sounds very good.
- If they have the staff to lead a campaign.
- It should work if you can show who is managing the endowment.

- Make it clear that the state is not managing the funds.
- It's a good plan and it's time to do something!
- I trust the judgment of those studying and determining this campaign's realistic aspect. It makes sense to me.
- It's a good idea and it's time!
- If they can spearhead and do it successfully with other fundraising activities.
- It is needed; it is the best plan for fundraising I have seen.

5. **Do you approve of this campaign?**

Yes	59	98.33%
No	0	0%
Not Sure	1	1.67%

Comments:

Comments regarding campaign:

- Timing is key, as well as is who is approached.
- It is time to cultivate new and additional donors.
- The named giving opportunities are good; I like the use of the streets and buildings.
- Push the telecommunications piece; check with grads that are in the field and ask their companies for donations.
- We must give kids the opportunity to go to college, and then the burden is theirs to do what they will with that; but we must give them a shot!
- If can't raise $10,000,000 in this campaign, Jersey needs to increase annual giving efforts for scholarships.
- If the right people are doing it.
- I support anything that will enable the school to provide a better product.
- It is much needed. Jersey needs to improve to attract top students and help them develop into strong men and women; however, they need the infrastructure in place to do a campaign. I am not convinced that they have this in place.
- Good sequence and prioritization.
- Excellent idea.
- Jersey also needs a permanent endowment in other areas besides scholarship.
- Capital should be done by the state.
- Jersey has to do something—this is a long time coming. It has to come from somewhere.

Comments regarding campaign (continued):

- Suggested pledge period up to five years will bring in more money.
- Absolutely. It is time we go big and reach for the treetops!
- $2M unrestricted funds is poorly documented without substantiated need identified. Need to list three to four specific needs.
- It is important to support the academic program, technologies, etc.

Comments regarding administration:

- Need a unified University plan.

Comments regarding facilities:

- Idea to renovate is good; you would not want to tear down any part of the quad.

6. **Is the $10,000,000 goal attainable?**

Yes	51	85.00%
No	2	3.33%
Not Sure	7	11.67%

If not, suggested goal:

$25,000,000–50,000,000 (1)

$20,000,000 (2)

$8,000,000 (1)

$5,000,000 (1)

Comments regarding goal should be higher:

- The goal should be much higher. (2)
- $7,000,000 is "peanuts" for a scholarship endowment.
- They probably need more! $20 million is probably not too much.
- My first thoughts when I read this were: (1) they could raise a lot more, and (2) it should only be a three-year campaign; five years is too long; however, they could have five years to pay the pledge.
- More money is needed; you won't know how much you can raise until you try.
- The alumni really care about the school and will support it.
- We need to set the bar high; anything is possible if we work hard at it.

Comments regarding goal should be lower:

- It's a lot of money.
- Some financial objectives are not realistic.

- High debt prevents young alumni from giving large donations. Some have tuition and books on a credit card.
- They will be doing well to raise $5 million; this is a difficult time because of the stock market.

Comments regarding goal is just right:

- It is a lofty goal; doable with right campaign and publicity.
- Modest goal will help build in success.
- $10,000,000 is easily attainable; it is good to start with an attainable goal so $10,000,000 should be just right.
- $10,000,000 is a good first start.
- $25,000,000–$50,000,000 is probably what is needed; they should be able to raise $10,000,000 if packaged properly.
- It is reasonable if bullish and aggressive.
- Depends on how much you want it.
- Giving does not necessarily relate to how much you have. Jersey graduates may not be wealthy, but they will give because they love the school.
- If it is spread over several years.
- It should be double this, but this is a reasonable goal.
- In today's market, it is certainly doable.
- If done over five years. It will be challenging.
- It is a lot of money, but the alumni support of recent campaigns for many schools is mind-boggling, and Jersey needs to get started.
- Lower-end opportunities at $5,000 are good.
- Moderate but reachable.
- Over three to five years.
- Optimistic, but not foolishly so.
- Optimally hopeful that it will be; certainly should be, continued existence depends on it being.
- People who know Jersey will gladly give.
- There should be some wealthy alumni who are grateful for their Jersey education.
- Very ambitious, but it can be done.
- Other universities are doing $10,000,000 to $30,000,000 in Pennsylvania.
- With the right approach in the right areas.
- Alumni and corporate donations are needed.
- Good solicitation team with outline needed.

Comments regarding goal is just right (continued):

- Expand statewide and include all alumni.
- Funds for books are needed as well as music and transportation.
- Capital campaign and annual giving history are needed.
- How much have they raised from business and industry? Have they received any large contributions?
- Hopefully, if done the right way; but it will definitely take good planning, good contacts, and lots of organized work from committed individuals.
- You can't raise it all locally. We need to go to some national foundations and corporations.
- If it is packaged right and you use the right message with each constituency.
- If you can get a large donation, if it is spread over several years.
- If it is done right. Many other universities are raising a lot more.
- If each alum gives their fair share.
- Need to offer alumni something; need to communicate more with alumni.
- Need to have someone who can raise the money.
- I don't think they have enough staff.
- They need connections to big money.
- Not easily, but attainable. Jersey needs to get a marketing niche; location is ideal; they need the right volunteer structure and staff.
- Need to talk to the heart of alumni.
- Need to show that even though Jersey is a state university, we need private funding sources.
- Need a good plan to include all approaches for fundraising and need the staff to implement the campaign.
- Not with only alumni, because many became teachers and do not have the means to give what they would like to give; but there are enough of us who are not teachers and have good contacts.
- Student enrollment has to go up.
- Quality of education has to be high and quality education has to be a priority.
- The goal can be surpassed, but it will take a lot of work. It will take the right group with the right leadership.
- It would be good to have a vendor group soliciting them, giving them opportunity to participate.
- With institutions, corporations, and foundations.

7. Is a lead gift of $1,000,000 attainable?

Yes	43	71.67%
No	2	3.33%
Not Sure	15	25.00%

Comments:

Comments regarding lead gift being available:

- The right named giving opportunity with good PR should bring in $1M.
- There may be corporations out there just waiting for Jersey to ask.
- There are people who will give; it's a matter of marketing to them.
- Should be within the alumni.
- Sure, don't know the person yet, but we will.
- People would, could, and should.
- People like Εδ Βραδλευ could give the lead gift if the right approach is made.
- Possibly, with corporate giving. You need the contacts and feelers.
- It is optimistic, but not beyond our scope.
- With the right contact. (2)
- Naming opportunities are great to inspire people. We should have some alumni who could do $1,000,000.
- Many people may be looking for an opportunity to give back to Jersey.
- I would suggest a lead gift of $2M with one $1M and three $500,000. There are not enough donors at the lower levels to pull it all together. $2M over five years, unrestricted but delineated could be done.
- If pledged over several years.
- Jersey has already received gifts of $1 to $4 million, we should be able to get $1 million if we ask.
- Jersey should have made the corporate contacts to identify a $1,000,000 gift.
- There are "old families" and successful alums now at the stage where they will want to transfer their wealth.
- I believe there are some who could do this, but I don't know whom. (2)

Comments regarding lead gift not being available:

- Major gifts could be a problem; Jersey grads have not gone to work for corporate America.
- No single contributor, other than Εδ Βραδλευ, has that amount of money.

Comments regarding lead gift not being available (continued):

- I do not know anyone who could give $1M; are we getting out to anyone who can?
- Fundraising is new to the alumni; they haven't been asked for a lot before.

Comments regarding methods to get a lead a gift:

- You must use a relationship to gain that level of giving.
- Not unless you can get a planned gift for endowment.
- They need someone with the vision and the ability to give this much.
- Look at various planned giving opportunities.
- It depends on the alumni. Do we have someone that can give that top gift?
- If they have done good cultivation.
- We may have to contract this out; can't see us doing it.
- Men of BAXA could be very helpful.
- We need to get a big gift to get things started.
- Also look to private and corporate foundations.
- These will require the president's involvement. He is good; he can do it. He can be the key media to do this.

8. **How do you feel about the timing of this campaign?**

Good	55	91.67%
Not Good	3	5.00%
No Answer	2	3.33%

Comments:

Comments regarding timing being good:

- You have to do it sometime. There should be a lot of alumni who have achieved success and will support this campaign.
- We need to do this now. We can't wait for the buildings to fall apart.
- There is no time like the present.
- There is never a good time to raise money or not raise money, they need to jump in and do it!
- The YMCA just raised $5,000,000.
- The economy was stronger one to two years ago, but those with money still want to give to charity.
- Let's do it now! (2)

- It is the new millennium and it is as good a time as any for this outreach.
- If they have the internal buy-in to start it now.
- Get your program, get your leadership, and go for it!
- I have faith that Πεττυσ has explored the needs and opportunities and knows what he is doing.
- Many people may be looking for a tax benefit before they retire.

Comments about timing of campaign not being good:

- We should have done it during the bull market, but there is nothing we can do about that now.
- Would have been better earlier.
- Would have been better six months ago, or wait six months. It is a good time to plan now and start campaign when economy recovers (usually takes about 6 months).
- The big question is how much competition is out there.
- The economy is not good.
- Many are losing thousands of dollars and feeling insecure.
- Better one, two, or five years ago; hopefully things will bounce back.

Comments about timing of campaign not being a factor:

- You can say timing is never right. (18)
- There are many drives under way and always are.
- The campaign's success will depend on telling the story well.
- There is never a good time. This is just as good a time as any. Opportunities dictate outcome.
- There are always a lot of organizations/groups looking for money. You just have to do it.
- Six months ago would have been better; we are on the verge of a recession. But if 50% of the money is raised before the campaign is announced, it should be attainable.
- Perfect timing does not work unless you are running solid and growing your student enrollment.
- Not a bad time; two years ago would have been better.
- Need to be asking all the time; this may be difficult timing with the economy being bad.
- It was better before the recent stock market drop, but this is a good time because Δρ. Πεττυσ' leadership is making a difference. Let's hope he doesn't leave.
- If they have a good mailing list of alumni.

Comments about timing of campaign not being a factor (continued):

- They need to establish capital campaign and coordinate with scholarship drive.
- They need to give people an opportunity for matching gifts.
- If done over three to five years.
- Depends on the case for support.

9. **How do you feel about the area's economic outlook?**

Good	37	61.67%
Average	17	28.33%
Poor	2	3.33%
No answer	4	6.67%

Economic Outlook Comments:

Comments regarding economic outlook being good:

- Very affluent area.
- Unemployment is low.
- There will be more stability over the long term of the economy.
- There is abundance in the eight counties of the area; they are all doing well.
- Salaries are good now; recent grads should have more money.
- Comments regarding economic outlook being good, cont'd:
- Someone always benefits from a poor economy.
- Our economy is the best it has ever been. We have a very low unemployment rate in this area.
- Μαυορ Στρεετ coming out on top can effect this getting done.
- May soon bottom out; if so, it's a good time to hedge a loss with a tax write-off. Inflation is not going crazy yet.
- There is money out there for things like this.
- It's a progressive area.
- Generally good.
- Χηεστερ Χουντυ is the 14th most affluent community in the country. Even when there are poor economic conditions, this area is immune to them.
- This area has done pretty well.
- Have to look at long-term economy, not the recent downturn.
- The educated and trained are doing well.

Comments regarding economic outlook being bad:

- Regional weaker than national.

- People are becoming cautious right now; last year would have been better.

- Many people lost big money in this market crisis.

- Individuals may be concerned about stock market.

- A lot of money was lost in the recent stock market decline.

- Employee market has been good, however salaries for minimally qualified people are low.

Comments regarding economic outlook being average:

- Times may have been better; but times are not bad.

- There are changes in the economy with jobs and investments, but we cannot delay this effort if the University needs money.

- The economy may affect some people, but many will give regardless of the economy.

- The current stock market situation may not affect this campaign as much because many alumni may not be invested in the stock market. A lot of Jersey alumni are teachers and they may have more solid investments.

- The new administration in Washington has put government support for universities in a category with agencies that deal with social problems; I am concerned with government support of higher education.

- Stock market is down, but with a five-year pledge people may think it doable.

10. **What is your perception of the Trustees fundraising strength?**

Excellent	2	3.33%
Good	21	35.00%
Average	17	28.33%
Poor	10	16.67%
Unaware	10	16.67%

Comments:

- I do not see old money on the board of trustees or president's council, nor contacts to it.

- Couldn't ask for a better board chair.

- Should have more influential members on the board of trustees.

- Ροβ Ωονδερλινγ is a player in town. (2)

- Χηαρλιε Γρεεϝε is a big player in the area.

- We need heavy hitters, do not know University trustees very well but they do not seem to be in positions that would have or know money.
- One of the biggest weaknesses is the board and its government-appointed members who do not necessarily have the contacts needed to raise big money.
- Trustees' fundraising strength may be average to poor. There are some who can do a lot; it's a matter of getting them to do it.

11. **What is the priority of this campaign to your personal charitable interests?**

High	33	55.00%
Medium	14	23.33%
Low	5	8.33%
Nonexistent	4	6.67%
No answer	4	6.67%

12. **Would you make a personal and/or corporate gift to this campaign?**

	Personal	*Corporate*
Lead Gift	1	3
Top 10	0	0
Next 20	3	1
Other	44	7
None	2	4

Please note: some interviewees answered for both personal and corporate gifts.

13. **Where on the scale of gifts do you think your gift might fall?**

	Personal		*Corporate*	
$100,000 or higher	1	1%	3	5%
$50,000–$99,999	0	0%	0	0%
$30,000–$49,999	1	1%	0	0%
$15,000–$29,999	2	3%	1	2%
$10,000–$14,999	4	5%	0	0%
$5,000–$9,999	16	21%	3	5%
Under $5,000	22	29%	3	5%
None	2	3%	4	6%
Not Sure or Not Applicable	28	37%	48	77%

Areas of interest identified:

- Youth.

- Scholarships and internships for teachers.

- Named giving.

- Matching gifts. (3)

- How many employees are Jersey graduates? How many Jersey students could become employees? How does Jersey benefit the community?

- As a nonprofit, we can give to an event, which is easier to participate in. Εδ Βραδλευ or θιμ ϛανχε could speak at an event in the city or around the country.

14. **What is the likelihood that you would be involved in this campaign?**

Leadership	8	13.33%
Somewhat Involved	35	58.33%
Not Involved	14	23.33%
No Answer	3	5.00%

Those indicating some involvement in campaign:

Leadership:	*Somewhat involved:*	
θαννιε Βλαχκωελλ	Γλαδστονε Αλλευνε	Ωαλτερ Μονταγυε
Πηυλλισ Βριττον	Ρομελλα Αρνολδ	Ραλπη Παττερσον
Δοναλδ Ηαχκνευ	Ελιζαβετη Ηολμεσ	θαχθυελινε Πελτζερ
Δαρρελ Ηενδερσον	Ροβερτ Βογλε	Ιρισ Πιττμαν
Μιχηαελ Ηορσευ	Ραλπη Βροων	Ροβερτ Ποωελσον
Ρεω. & Μρσ. Τηομασ Λογαν	Δρ. Δοναλδ Χλαρκ	Χωοννε Προυδφορδ
Σαμ & Δειδρε Παττερσον	Δανιελ Ελβυ	Ροβερτ (Σταν) Σχηυχκ
Αμβασσαδορ θοσεπη Σεγαρσ	Δρ. Μιλδρεδ Γορδον	Σταν Σιμπκινσ
	Χηαρλεσ Γρεενε	Μρ. & Μρσ. Ηαρρυ Σταρρ
	Γλαδυσ Ηιλλ	Αλιχε Στρινε
	θαχκ Ηολεφελδερ	Λεοναρδ & θεαν Τεαγλε
	Νατ θονεσ	Λορρεττα Τιλλερυ
	Τηαδδευσ Κιρκλανδ	θαμεσ Ωανχε
	Ωιλβυρ Κιρκλανδ	Κεζιραη Ωαυγητερσ
	Δρ. Ματτηεω Κνοωλεσ	Δρ. Χαρλα 6αλλσ
		Χραιγ 6ελβυρν
		Ωενδελλ 6ηιτλοχκ
		Ροβερτ 6οοδσον
		Χυρτισ 6ορδ

15. Do you have any additional comments or suggestions?

Comments regarding volunteers:

- Need to train and educate volunteers.
- Need to know expectations of volunteers to serve on campaign cabinet.
- Need someone of national stature to lead campaign, need new blood.
- Use volunteers' time wisely.
- Σηιρλευ Δεννισ had a committee started; see if we can get them re-involved.
- We need a person with firsthand knowledge of contacts.
- They have the leadership; Πεττυσ knows who and what he needs and can get them involved.
- Βιλλ Χοσβυ would make an excellent honorary co-chair. Look beyond local— go national! Likewise, Βιλλ Χλιντον or Αννενβυργ would be an excellent counterpart, utilizing one black, one white.

Comments regarding staffing:

- Need staff to work on mailing lists of alumni.
- Not sure if we have the resources to do a campaign, we need a consultant and/or more staff. (2)
- Glad to see they are using a consultant.
- Do we have the staff to run a campaign?
- Jersey does not have the internal structure for raising funds; they will need ongoing campaign guidance with a consulting firm.

Comments regarding public relations:

- Reach out to local community.
- Hold open house, tours of campus.
- Need a marketing and public image campaign, need to fill the media with stories about Jersey.
- Sell the message; use good promotional material.
- Use focus groups to involve people.
- Constant newspaper articles and cultivation are important.
- Access leadership though churches: Παολι Presbyterian, δαυνε Presbyterian, Μαιν-λινε, with affluent members.
- All local newspapers, in student populous areas, should be involved for the needed PR.
- The theater is a good drawing card and could be used to get people out there.

- We need to educate the public of our needs.
- We need to bring people on to the campus.
- We need to instill in young people today the history and pride of yesteryear.

Comments regarding alumni involvement:

- I don't think we needed to do a feasibility study; we should be able to poll our alumni ourselves.
- The national alumni association matches gifts made by alumni for scholarship, see if they will match gifts to this campaign.
- We need more alumni involvement.
- Jersey does not have a consistent approach to its alumni, make sure our mailing list is up-to-date; provide better communication.
- We need to challenge our alumni; offer planned giving and other ways to contribute.
- Recruit alumni who are close to retirement age.
- Ask for class gifts. Each class could raise between $50,000 and $100,000.
- Have reunion classes do special fundraising program.
- Put the responsibility for the campaign on the National Alumni Board.
- Be sure to ask every alum; need a good organization to reach all alumni.
- Suggest to alumni that they put Jersey in their will. Ask classes to go together and make a class gift.
- Have alumni hold events in their homes with Δρ. Πεττυσ.
- Get the sororities and fraternities involved; they love competition. (4)
- Need a university-staffed alumni office. (2)
- Need more contact with alumni. (3)
- Welcome the alumni and their involvement.
- Link mentoring programs to campaign, use alumni for both.
- Alumni who graduated 10 to 20 years ago should be well established now and able to give.
- We need to promote the school through TV commercials with Εδ Βραδλευ and Βιλλ Χοσβυ-type people. Βιλλ Χοσβυ graduated from another university, but had many friends who went to Jersey and still owns a home in the area.
- Alumni are living proof and the best spokespeople for the university, they are priceless ambassadors.
- Jersey has not always been responsive to notifications/changes; i.e., mail went to mothers for years after change given numerous times.

Comments regarding campaign planning:

- Board contribution must be in first and should be 30% of the goal.

- Should give alumni jackets, caps, etc., for gifts. Bigger gifts to bigger donors, but something that has Jersey's name on so people notice it.

- Need to show strong board giving.

- Make sure the campaign is done well.

- Make sure they have what they need internally to run a campaign.

- The silent phase is important. Make sure the right people are behind it.

- Need to tailor the message for each different group you approach.

- Ask seniors to make a pledge of $500 a year for five years.

- Ask students to get involved by speaking at alumni gatherings about their experiences at Jersey.

- Students could also work at phonathons.

- Use the Jersey song to inspire alumni. Remind them "Jersey was there for you; now Jersey is calling you, don't fail Jersey."

- "Aim high and you can't fall but so short."

- We need a good plan; need more cultivation; need to "ask."

- Need a strong kick-off event to let everyone know Jersey is on the move.

- Need to get involved in business community.

- Pennsylvania has not yet given out its tobacco settlement money; can we get some of that?

- People like recognition; want to be remembered.

- Even if this campaign isn't successful, it will be easier next time because we have laid the groundwork.

- Talk about Jersey's religious roots (faith-based programs are BIG today). There is concern about the moral decline with school shootings across the nation.

- The campaign needs to be aggressive.

- Need more information on how scholarships will be awarded.

- Should focus on two aspects of campaign—alumni and the historic value of Jersey.

- Offer direct payment of pledges through payroll deductions.

- Needs to be a national campaign, not just the local area.

- Have to ask to get the money.

- People are careful about their giving because of scandals, need to show the need and that the money will be wisely used.
- Πηιλαδελπηια Foundation can manage endowment funds; it will give the campaign credibility.
- Remind people of planned giving opportunities.
- Need clear objectives for the campaign.
- Sell bricks on the quad—people like recognition.
- Need to go out of your way to thank people, invite them to campus, get them involved.
- Get a list of all the vendors of Jersey and solicit them.
- Need a good plan, need a meeting or reception for volunteers to get them enthused about the campaign, maybe bring in a motivational speaker.
- Contact the older people to make a gift before they go into a retirement home. There needs to be an organized campaign.
- Give people opportunities for planned gifts.
- It's time to go back to Κρεσγε for possibly $500,000 (we need to build Annual Giving prior to returning though).
- Try to get a challenge gift. (2)
- It is important to have 100% trustee participation.
- Look for matching gifts.
- A five-year campaign is too long; it will wear out the staff, and the donors get tired of a campaign that long.
- Make sure you see all the businesses in person.
- Named gifts should appeal to businesses.

Comments of general advice for Jersey:

- Should spend more money on recruitment efforts.
- Do fundraising events.
- Get IT companies to recruit more at Jersey.
- The administration and employees of Jersey need more visibility in the work force; need to go to chamber events, volunteer for committees.
- Unsure of why blacks want to remain segregated.
- Jersey was not visible in the community until five years ago. They need more corporate visibility.

Comments of general advice for Jersey, continued:

- Need to do more PR, especially in the local area, not just the Jersey area.
- Use an advisory council to add to the strength of the Council of Trustees.
- It is important to emphasize recent grads (past 10 yrs with 3 most recent) and their accomplishments plus Εδ Βραδλευ and ϑιμ ςανχε.
- Establish links to XYZ School and others around the country.
- Include business leaders expressing "choice in education."
- Improve image.
- Recruit students.
- Create student-friendly environment and promote school, flooding the area with info about Jersey for positive, steady growth.
- Increase money raised regularly.
- Increase business contributions.
- Increase government contributions.
- We need to show pictures of what the campus looks like today; show people the state of the buildings.
- Stress the historic aspects of the campus. People are interested in genealogy; tie this into the campaign.
- This is the time to grow the diverse Jersey.
- We need to put teams together to go into the schools regularly and tell them to think about further education and consider Jersey.
- Jersey will do well if they sell the vision of Δρ. Πεττυσ and if he gets out and talks to people about this campaign.
- Board members who are Jersey grads would most likely want to be involved in campaigning and would give.
- This campaign could be a very positive experience for Jersey.
- There is talk that the community wants Jersey's land for housing.
- There has been very little accountability through the system and often the right hand does not know what the left is doing.
- People must be held accountable, and work, not just fill a position.
- Need to invest in a good plan to make this happen.
- When I look at the annual report, I don't see the trustees and alumni leadership in the big giving categories.

- Need to have bigger contributions from University leadership.

- Need to have unified fundraising effort with University and alumni association involved in planning.

- Don't use "giving back to Jersey," use "investing in the future" instead.

- Important for people to hear from current students about how Jersey has affected them, how they would like to see Jersey improve, are their (students') needs being met?

- Need to think about long-term needs of Jersey and make this campaign enough to cover those needs.

- Should be active in all schools through career day.

- We have met the enemy and the enemy is us. (I am very disappointed with the alumni.)

- We need to increase Jersey's academic standards.

- Its mission of accessibility lends itself to poor economic standards rather than high academic standards.

- There is unspoken concern regarding management issues and whether they are competent to handle donated funds.

- There is question as to what happened with money raised in campaigns of recent years and how they relate to this.

- Professional development is needed to enhance and perfect teaching skills and assure current trends.

- Check annual giving history for alumni and general giving.

- Alumni lists need updating, many don't get regular solicitation and information.

- State needs to support more financial aid for students plus capital improvements.

- There is a problem with union mentality (faculty and administration).

- Students who go to Jersey often do not come from families/people mindful of the need for a degree.

- Dysfunctional families are sending children to college with a lot of baggage. There are diverse problems with relationships, rebellion, and anger. There are 1st and 4th graders given responsibility for their siblings.

- Would like faculty to be more involved with students.

- Jersey is a great institution; the story has to be told.

Recommendations

I. It is the recommendation of CAPITAL VENTURE (formerly Cornerstone Consulting, Inc.) that Jersey University proceed with a capital/endowment campaign for a proposed goal of $10,000,000. We believe that the alumni and community support evidenced during this study warrants a campaign of this size, providing Jersey can prepare itself internally for this endeavor. The following cautions and related recommendations must be addressed prior to conducting a campaign. We suggest that, once the commitment of the board of trustees is obtained, the planning and organization of this campaign start during the summer of 2001, the leadership recruitment phase of the campaign to start in fall, 2001 and that the campaign conclude by the fall of 2003. Following are the prerequisites for conducting a campaign, cautions that must be considered, and a recommended plan of action.

II. Justification for conducting a capital campaign:

A. The key ingredients in conducting a successful capital campaign are:

1. An involved and informed board of trustees committed to the campaign.

2. A pool of volunteers who are committed, skilled, and well connected.

3. A pool of informed major donor prospects.

4. A compelling case for support.

5. An infrastructure capable of managing a campaign.

6. Good public/constituent relations.

B. In relationship to these prerequisites, Jersey is well positioned in some areas:

1. The board of trustees is fairly well known and is respected in the community. The trustees, with some exceptions, however, are not very high profile and are not perceived as having access to potential major funding sources. The board of trustees should be strengthened with more representatives of major corporations at higher levels. There was a development council formed but it has not met regularly nor been asked to contribute significantly to Jersey. It will be vital during this campaign to reactivate and utilize the development council to its fullest capacity to identify, cultivate, and solicit donors. Full and early board commitment will be essential to the success of this campaign and the trustees should be capable of giving or getting one fourth to one third of the total goal.

2. Thirty-four of the people interviewed agreed to assume some involvement in the campaign and eight of these indicated that they would consider a leadership role in the campaign. In addition, 117 potential volunteers were identified by those interviews. Some time will need to be spent in identifying and recruiting top community leaders to serve on the campaign cabinet.

3. A list of 169 major donor prospects, with total potential gifts of $263,000– $12,820,000, emerged during the interview process and a total of $103,000 to $1,485,000 in self-identified lead gifts. Research into the families of Jersey's founders, current and former trustees, as well as the alumni base needs to be done to uncover those prospects who will have a linkage to Jersey, the ability and the interest to make a significant gift.

4. Fifty-four, or 90%, of the people interviewed were in agreement with the need to build the scholarship endowment fund and preserve Jersey's historical buildings and over 98% of the people interviewed approved of this campaign. However, a strong case for support needs to be made for the unrestricted portion of the campaign. Several people expressed concern that they needed to have more details about what this portion of the campaign would fund. The issue of state monies received from a class-action lawsuit also needs to be addressed, as well as making a clear statement of how much money is received annually from the state and how much needs to be raised by Jersey each year.

5. A database of alumni is available as well as a list of friends, businesses and organizations that have supported Jersey in the past. There is a database system capable of managing campaign gift entry and reporting; however this system needs to be integrated with the alumni office and a clerical support person will be needed to manage the day-to-day campaign work. The advancement staff of Jersey is perceived to be too small and not experienced enough to manage a campaign of this magnitude.

6. Most alumni seem to be aware of Jersey's current programs, and have an extremely high regard for Jersey. However, many people stressed the fact that Jersey does not have a high community profile and does not get good press coverage. The leadership of Δρ. Πεττυσ was notably a significant factor in the internal and external strength of Jersey, however there were comments that other faculty and staff need to get out into the community more in order to strengthen Jersey's position as a leader in the area. Most people felt that with better publicity, and more involvement of the faculty in the community, that the community would get behind this project.

C. **Cautions which must be considered:**

1. *The Lack of Public Awareness*

   Numerous people expressed the fact that Jersey often gets bad press or no press, and that many people really don't know as much as they could about Jersey. It will be very important to involve the public relations department in the planning for this capital campaign and recruit their support to increase and enhance Jersey's public image.

2. *The Lack of Major Donor Prospects*

A small number of major donor prospects were self-identified during this study. While many people mentioned various sources of major gifts, it appears that in the self-identification process the size gifts mentioned will not be available from these sources. It is our belief that without the support of a major donor, Jersey cannot raise the suggested goal of this campaign. However, there were a number of potential donors that we believe can make the difference between success and failure if these potential donors are cultivated and solicited using a sound and carefully planned strategy. Time must be spent in brainstorming with trustees, the development council, and other community leaders, to identify, cultivate and solicit these potential donors. We also believe that Jersey could qualify for grants from national and regional foundations and that research into these foundations will be an essential part of the campaign.

3. *Lack of Annual Fund History*

Jersey, like many state institutions, has not had a strong annual giving history, and many of the alumni expressed concern that they had not been cultivated or even asked for gifts in the past. The lack of coordination between the alumni office and the advancement office needs to be addressed during this campaign. There is also a lack of understanding on the part of many people about the need for and use of the unrestricted funds portion of the campaign. This area will need to be addressed in the case for support.

4. *Lack of a Large and Active Fundraising Board of Trustees*

As with many state universities, the trustees are a small, appointed group. The perception is that many of the current trustees will not be helpful in a major fundraising campaign. The board should be increased in size and strengthened in its fundraising skills prior to this campaign. Additionally, the development council needs to be reorganized and utilized in this campaign.

D. Recommendations:

1. Reorganize and strengthen the development council and bring them together as soon as possible, present the planning study report to them and ask for their help to identify and cultivate prospective donors and provide leadership for the campaign. Also continue to identify, cultivate, and recruit additional trustees who can bring more fundraising strength to the board.

2. A PR campaign, using press releases, newspaper ads, and billboards promoting the successes of Jersey and its uniqueness, should begin prior to the campaign. This campaign should also include internal communications on the importance of good PR, including frequent communications with alumni.

3   Recruit a Campaign Cabinet with a well known and respected community leader as honorary chair, preferable someone like Εδ Βραδλευ. It will be essential to build a campaign cabinet of 20 to 35 community leaders; about 5 to 7 of these should be trustees. These cabinet members must be people who are well known and respected among Jersey's constituents, and must be willing to both make a leadership gift themselves, and to identify and solicit others for leadership gifts to the campaign.

CAPITAL VENTURE is pleased to present this report to Jersey. We believe that with the commitment of the board and staff to make this project a reality, and the support of one or more major foundation grants, the community will support this campaign, particularly if we can focus on how this campaign will enhance the programs of Jersey. A preliminary schedule for precampaign planning and the campaign is included as a supplement to this report. We will be pleased to submit a proposal to provide consulting services for your capital campaign management at your request. Whatever your decision, we wish you well and look forward to being of service to Jersey University.

Sincerely,

Linda Lysakowski, ACFRE   Judith Snyder, CFRE
Principal   Principal

Preliminary Campaign Schedule

Board Approval of Capital Campaign	June 2001
Develop Campaign Cabinet Prospect List	July 2001
Campaign Plan, Schedule, and Position Descriptions Developed	July 2001
Trustee Appeal	August–December 2001
Campaign Cabinet Recruited	September–December 2001
First Cabinet Meeting	January 2002
Leadership Gift Appeal	January–September 2002
Campaign Kickoff	October 2002
General Phase	November 2002–June 2003

Appendix M1

The following slides are an example of the PowerPoint presentation used at the report meeting. Slides have been deleted that directly refer to our client.

Slide 2

Ingredients of a Successful Capital Campaign

- Involved and informed board
- Committed, skilled, and well-connected volunteers
- Major donor prospects
- Compelling case for support
- Strong infrastructure
- Good public relations

Slide 3

Volunteer Leadership

- 34 agreed to be somewhat involved in the campaign

- 8 agreed to consider leadership roles

- 107 potential volunteers identified

Slide 4

Major Donor Prospects

- 36 potential gifts self-identified

- $103,000–$1,485,400 self-identified

- 169 potential donors identified

- $263,000–$12,820,000 potential gifts identified

Slide 5

Compelling Case for Support

- All the people interviewed agreed there is a need for scholarships and restoration of the historic buildings

- Need to explain the need for and use of unrestricted funds in the case for support

Slide 6

Infrastructure

- Limited staff, perception that there is not enough qualified staff to run campaign
- Database in place, need to install and train clerical support
- Need policies and procedures
- Need stronger and larger board
- Need to coordinate and involve alumni
- Need to strengthen annual fund

Slide 8

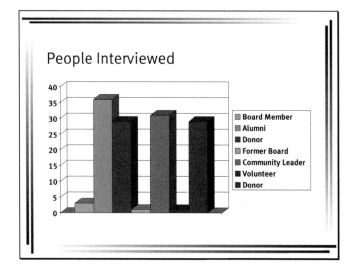

People Interviewed

- Board Member
- Alumni
- Donor
- Former Board
- Community Leader
- Volunteer
- Donor

Slide 10

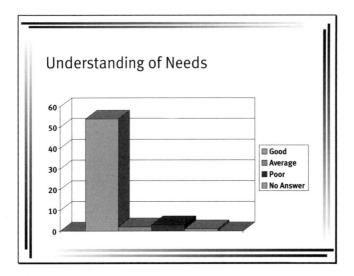

Slide 11

Top Priority

- Scholarships
- Facility/renovations
- Increased student enrollment
- Increased PR

Slide 13

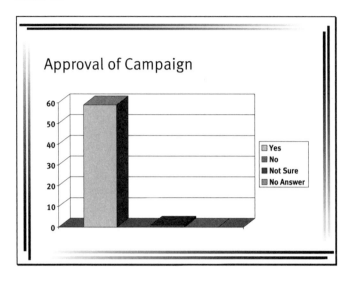

Slide 14

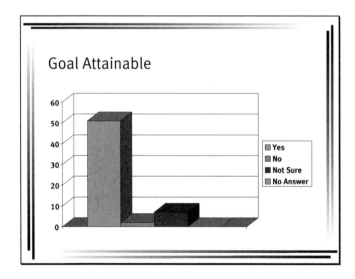

Slide 15

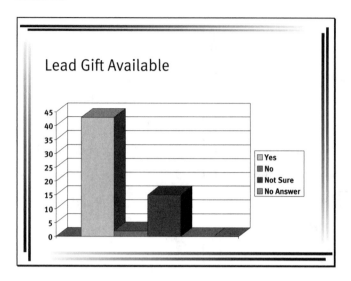

Slide 16

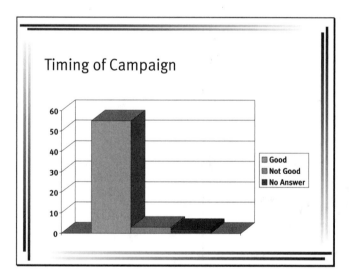

Slide 17

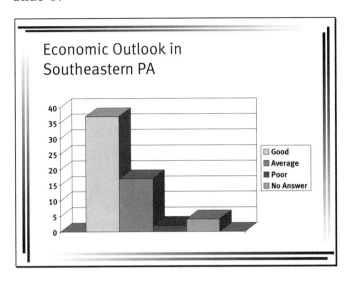

Slide 18

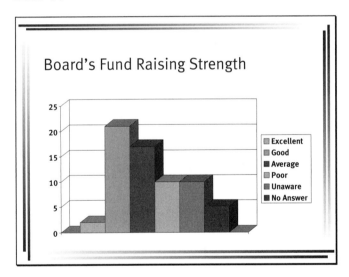

Slide 19

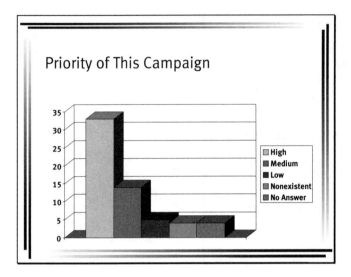

Slide 20

Personal or Corporate Gift

- Lead Gift   4
- Top 10   0
- Next 20   4
- Other   51
- None   6
- No Answer   36

Slide 21

> ## Major Donor Prospects
>
> - 36 potential gifts self-identified
>
> - $103,000–$1,485,400 self-identified
>
> - 169 potential donors identified
>
> - $263,000–$12,820,000 potential gifts identified

Slide 22

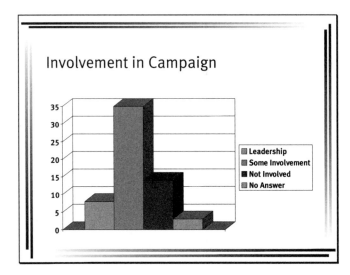

Slide 23

Concerns

- Lack of public awareness

- Lack of major donor prospects

- Lack of a strong annual fund

- Lack of fundraising strength on board

Slide 24

Recommended Goal

- $10,000,000

Slide 25

Recommendations

- Increase advancement staffing
- Strengthen case for annual fund
- Conduct a 2–3 year campaign
- Increase public relations
- Strengthen development council
- Involve alumni
- Update and integrate database

Slide 26

Proposed Precampaign Timetable

Board approves campaign	June 2001
Retain campaign counsel	July 2001
Develop campaign plan and timeline	Aug 2001
Develop position descriptions	Aug 2001
Develop list of potential cabinet	Sep 2001
Prepare final case for support	Sep 2001

Slide 27

Proposed Campaign Timeline

- Board Appeal   Sep–Dec 2001
- Cabinet Recruited   Sep–Dec 2001
- Leadership Appeal   Jan–Sep 2002
- Campaign Kickoff   Oct 2002
- General Phase   Nov 2002–June 2003

Slide 28

The L-A-I Principle

- LINKAGE—Who knows whom makes it possible to arrange an appointment to discuss the potential gift.

- ABILITY—Through research, it can be determined if a particular prospect has the capability to make a major gift.

- INTEREST—Interest dictates the size of the gift.

Slide 29

AFP Code of Ethical Principles and Standards of Professional Practice

AFP Code of Ethical Principles and Standards of Professional Practice

STATEMENT OF ETHICAL PRINCIPLES
Adopted 1964, Amended October 2004

AFP
Association of
Fundraising Professionals

The Association of Fundraising Professionals (AFP) exists to foster the development and growth of fundraising professionals and the profession, to promote high ethical standards in the fundraising profession and to preserve and enhance philanthropy and volunteerism. Members of AFP are motivated by an inner drive to improve the quality of life through the causes they serve. They serve the ideal of philanthropy; are committed to the preservation and enhancement of volunteerism; and hold stewardship of these concepts as the overriding principle of their professional life. They recognize their responsibility to ensure that needed resources are vigorously and ethically sought and that the intent of the donor is honestly fulfilled. To these ends, AFP members embrace certain values that they strive to uphold in performing their responsibilities for generating philanthropic support.

AFP members aspire to:
+ practice their profession with integrity, honesty, truthfulness and adherence to the absolute obligation to safeguard the public trust;
+ act according to the highest standards and visions of their organization, profession and conscience;
+ put philanthropic mission above personal gain;
+ inspire others through their own sense of dedication and high purpose;
+ improve their professional knowledge and skills so that their performance will better serve others;
+ demonstrate concern for the interests and well being of individuals affected by their actions;
+ value the privacy, freedom of choice and interests of all those affected by their actions;
+ foster cultural diversity and pluralistic values, and treat all people with dignity and respect;
+ affirm, through personal giving, a commitment to philanthropy and its role in society;
+ adhere to the spirit as well as the letter of all applicable laws and regulations;
+ advocate within their organizations, adherence to all applicable laws and regulations;
+ avoid even the appearance of any criminal offense or professional misconduct;
+ bring credit to the fundraising profession by their public demeanor;
+ encourage colleagues to embrace and practice these ethical principles and standards of professional practice; and
+ be aware of the codes of ethics promulgated by other professional organizations that serve philanthropy.

STANDARDS OF PROFESSIONAL PRACTICE
Furthermore, while striving to act according to the above values, AFP members agree to abide by the *AFP Standards of Professional Practice*, which are adopted and incorporated into the *AFP Code of Ethical Principles*. Violation of the *Standard* may subject the member to disciplinary sanctions, including expulsion, as provided in the AFP Ethics Enforcement Procedures.

Professional Obligations
1. Members shall not engage in activities that harm the member's organization, clients, or profession.
2. Members shall not engage in activities that conflict with their fiduciary, ethical and legal obligations to their organizations and their clients.
3. Members shall effectively disclose all potential and actual conflicts of interest; such disclosure does not preclude or imply ethical impropriety.
4. Members shall not exploit any relationship with a donor, prospect, volunteer or employee for the benefit of the member or the member's organization.
5. Members shall comply with all applicable local, state, provincial, federal, civil and criminal laws.
6. Members recognize their individual boundaries of competence and are forthcoming and truthful about their professional experience and qualifications.

Solicitation and Use of Philanthropic Funds
7. Members shall take care to ensure that all solicitation materials are accurate and correctly reflect the organization's mission and use of solicited funds.
8. Members shall take care to ensure that donors receive informed, accurate and ethical advice about the value and tax implications of contributions.
9. Members shall take care to ensure that contributions are used in accordance with donors' intentions.
10. Members shall take care to ensure proper stewardship of philanthropic contributions, including timely reports on the use and management of such funds.
11. Members shall obtain explicit consent by the donor before altering the conditions of contributions.

Presentation of Information
12. Members shall not disclose privileged or confidential information to unauthorized parties.
13. Members shall adhere to the principle that all donor and prospect information created by, or on behalf of, an organization is the property of that organization and shall not be transferred or utilized except on behalf of that organization.
14. Members shall give donors the opportunity to have their names removed from lists that are sold to, rented to, or exchanged with other organizations.
15. Members shall, when stating fundraising results, use accurate and consistent accounting methods that conform to the appropriate guidelines adopted by the American Institute of Certified Public Accountants (AICPA)* for the type of organization involved. (* In countries outside of the United States, comparable authority should be utilized.)

Compensation
16. Members shall not accept compensation that is based on a percentage of contributions; nor shall they accept finder's fees.
17. Members may accept performance-based compensation, such as bonuses, provided such bonuses are in accord with prevailing practices within the members' own organizations, and are not based on a percentage of contributions.
18. Members shall not pay finder's fees, or commissions or percentage compensation based on contributions, and shall take care to discourage their organizations from making such payments.

Amended October 2004

AFP Donor Bill of Rights

A Donor Bill of Rights

PHILANTHROPY is based on voluntary action for the common good. It is a tradition of giving and sharing that is primary to the quality of life. To assure that philanthropy merits the respect and trust of the general public, and that donors and prospective donors can have full confidence in the not-for-profit organizations and causes they are asked to support, we declare that all donors have these rights:

I.
To be informed of the organization's mission, of the way the organization intends to use donated resources, and of its capacity to use donations effectively for their intended purposes.

II.
To be informed of the identity of those serving on the organization's governing board, and to expect the board to exercise prudent judgement in its stewardship responsibilities.

III.
To have access to the organization's most recent financial statements.

IV.
To be assured their gifts will be used for the purposes for which they were given.

V.
To receive appropriate acknowledgement and recognition.

VI.
To be assured that information about their donations is handled with respect and with confidentiality to the extent provided by law.

VII.
To expect that all relationships with individuals representing organizations of interest to the donor will be professional in nature.

VIII.
To be informed whether those seeking donations are volunteers, employees of the organization or hired solicitors.

IX.
To have the opportunity for their names to be deleted from mailing lists that an organization may intend to share.

X.
To feel free to ask questions when making a donation and to receive prompt, truthful and forthright answers.

DEVELOPED BY
Association for Healthcare Philanthropy (AHP)
Association of Fundraising Professionals (AFP)
Council for Advancement and Support of Education (CASE)
Giving Institute: Leading Consultants to Non-Profits

ENDORSED BY
(in formation)
Independent Sector
National Catholic Development Conference (NCDC)
National Committee on Planned Giving (NCPG)
Council for Resource Development (CRD)
United Way of America

Bibliography

"About Capital Campaign Feasibility Studies—Third in a Series on Capital Campaigns," *National Fund Raiser,* July 1999, p. 4.

Allen, Richard Page, "Testing the Market: The Feasibility Study," in H. Gerald Quigg, ed., *The Succesful Capital Campaign: From Planning to Victory Celebration* (CASE, 1986), pp. 31–35.

Balser, Jerry, "Anatomy of a Feasibility Study," *Philanthropy Work AZ,* Vol. 2, No. 1 (Spring 2001), p. 11.

Bancel, Marilyn, CFRE, *Preparing Your Capital Campaign* (San Francisco: Jossey-Bass, 2000), pp. 79–99.

Barrett, Richard D., and Molly E. Ware, *Planned Giving Essentials* (Gaithersburg, Md.: Aspen Publishers, 2002).

"Beginning a Dialogue," *Fundraising Matters,* Vol. 9, No. 2 (Spring 2004), pp. 1–2.

Boaz, David. E, "Don't Re-Invent the Wheel," *Fund Raising Institute Monthly Portfolio,* Vol. 34, No. 9 (September 1995).

Boren, S. Alan, "Final Report Feasibility Study—Conducted for the Association for Retarded Citizens," December 21, 1982.

Caffery, Anne Napier, "Exploding the Mountain—Philanthropy as a Tool for Change," *AFP Journal,* Spring 2000, pp. 28–30, 32.

Campbell, Bruce, *Listening to Your Donors* (San Francisco: Jossey-Bass, 2000), p. 192.

Campbell, Craig, "Marketplace Only Real Way to Get True Response Results," *Fund Raising Management,* Vol. 16, No. 1 (April 1985), p. 48.

Daggett, Melinda, "The Pre-Campaign Survey: A Key to Capital Campaign Success," *Fund Raising Management,* August 1994, pp. 18–19, 63.

Dalton, Peter, "Preparing for a Major Gifts Campaign," *Fundraising Australasia,* Summer 1992, pp. 12–13.

David, Bronson C., "The Possible Dream—Base Your Campaign Formula on a Feasibility Study, *Currents,* November–December 1986, pp. 20–22, 24, 26.

Davis, Bronson C., "The Possible Dream," *Currents,* Vol. 12, No. 10 (November/December, 1986), p. 20.

Davis, Bronson C. "The Feasibility Study: First Step in the Capital Campaign," *AHP Journal,* Spring 1987, p. 31.

Development Connection, Inc., "Feasibility Study," www.developmentconnection/feasibility.

Development Management Associates, "Planning and Feasibility Study for NSFRE Foundation," Long Beach, Calif., July 1991.

DeWolfe, Janet, CFRE, "Stay Focused and on Course—No Matter What!," *AHP Journal,* Fall 2003, pp. 10–13.

Dillion, Douglas A., "Campaign Readiness Study," 2000 AHP Institute for Healthcare Philanthropy, July 9, 2000, handout notes.

Dove, Kent E., *Conducting a Successful Capital Campaign,* 2nd ed. (San Francisco: Jossey-Bass, 2000), pp. 22–29, 243–252.

Edles, Peter L., *Fundraising—Hand's-on Tactics for Nonprofit Groups* (New York: McGraw-Hill, 1993), pp. 57–65.

Essex, Inc., "Canine Companions for Independence Feasibility and Planning Study Questionnaire."

"The Feasibility Study," Columbus, Oh., Goettler Associates, Inc., 1991.

"Feasibility Study Guides Board when Funding Cuts Hit," *Board & Administrator,* Vol. 22, No.1 (September 2005), p. 3.

Frantzreb, Arthur C., "The Pros and Cons of Feasibility Studies," *Advancing Philanthropy,* Winter 1997–1998, pp. 43, 45–46.

"The Fund-Raising Survey—How to Create One that Actually Works," *FRI Monthly Portfolio,* July 1990.

Gerber, Richard J., "Consultants: the Cause of Problems," letter to the editor, *Chronicle of Philanthropy,* August 26, 1999.

"Getting the Most from Your Feasibility Study," *National Fund Raiser,* February 1997, p. 3.

Goettler, John G., CFRE, "Anatomy of a Capital Campaign," *Fund Raising Management,* June 2000, pp. 16–19.

Goodale, Toni K., "Is It Feasible?," *Fund Raising Management,* November 2001, pp. 40–41.

Graham, Christine, "Blueprint for a Capital Campaign," CPG Enterprises, 1997, pp. 5–6.

Grace, Kay Sprinkel, "Ten Things You Should Know About . . . ," *Contributions,* Vol. 11, No. 4 (July/August 1997), pp. 6, 11.

Hansler, Daniel F., CFRE, and Catherine Cooper, "Focus Groups: New Dimension in Feasibility Study," *Fund Raising Management,* July 1986, pp. 78, 80–82.

Harrison, Bill J., "Feasibility Study . . . Can We Scale This Height?," *Fund Raising Management,* May 1996, pp. 16–19.

Hartsook, Robert F., "Boards Don't Need an 800-Pound Gorilla," letter to the editor, *Chronicle of Philanthropy,* October 30, 1997.

Holliman, Barbara L., and Glenn N. Holliman, "With Generous Hearts," Ridgefield, Conn.: Morehouse Publishing, 1997.

"How to Choose Professional Counsel for Your Capital Campaign," *National Fund Raiser,* Vol. 31, No. 10 (August 2005), pp. 2–3.

"How to Conduct a Feasibility Study, *Front and Centre,* Vol. 7, No. 1 (January 2000), p. 18.

Howe, Fisher, *The Board Member's Guide to Fund Raising—What Every Trustee Needs to Know about Raising Money* (San Francisco: Jossey-Bass, 1991), pp. 61–64.

Joyaux, Simone. *Strategic Fund Development, Building Profitable Relationships That Last,* 2nd ed. (Gaithersburg, Md.: Aspen, 2001).

Keegan, P. Burke, *Fundraising for Nonprofits* (New York: Harper-Collins, 1990), pp. 92–99.

Keegan, P. Burke, "What Is a Fundraising Feasibility Study and Is It Worth It?," www-.boardcafe.org, 2001.

Kihlstedt, Andrea, and Catherine P. Schwartz, *Capital Campaign Strategies That Work* (Gaithersburg, Md.: Aspen Publishers, 1997), pp. 43–55. and 2nd edition, 2001.

Klein, Kim, "Starting an Endowment: Part 3 Feasibility Studies," *Grassroots Fundraising Journal,* August 1996, pp. 3–7.

Klein, Kim, "Testing the Feasibility of Your Capital Campaign," *Grassroots Fundraising Journal,* September/October 2001, pp. 8–10.

Klein, Kim, "Planning an Endowment Campaign," *Grassroots Fundraising Journal,* Vol. 24, No. 6 (November–December 2005), pp. 6–10.

Lamkins, Robert, FAHP, "When and Why to Commission a Feasibility Study," *AFP News,* May 1994, p. 4.

Lord, James Gregory, *The Raising of Money—Thirty-five Essentials Every Trustee Should Know* (Cleveland, Ohio: Third Sector Press, 1990), pp. 39–42.

Lysakowski, Linda, "Getting Ready for a Capital Campaign—Your Blueprint for Evaluating Internal & External Readiness," *AFP,* pp. 13–24.

McDonald, Morgan, "Pointing the Way," *Fundraising Success,* Vol. 3, No. 2 (March 2005), pp. 43–45.

Moran, William J., "An Alternative to the Campaign Feasibility Study," *Fund Raising Management,* April 2000.

Nelson, Robert E., "Ready for a Campaign?," *Fund Raising Management,* March 1979.

"New Ways to Profit from a Feasibility Study," Columbus, Ohio, Goettler Associates, Inc., 1986.

O'Shea, Catherine L., "A Stitch in Time," *Currents,* November/December 1994, pp. 24–28.

Panas, Jerold, "Right Time for a Campaign?," *Fund Raising Management,* August 1994, pp. 27–28, 30.

Phillips, Gary W., "Getting Advance Notice of Your Fund Raising Weaknesses," *NSFRE Journal,* Spring 1987, pp. 25, 27, 29–30.

"The Planning/Feasibility Study," *Fundraising Matters,* Vol. 9, No. 2 (Spring 2004), pp. 1–2.

"Precampaign Readiness," *FRI Monthly Portfolio,* Vol. 37, No. 3 (March 1998), p. 3.

"Preparing for a Capital Campaign—What to Do before You Have a Feasibility Study Completed—First in a Series," *National Fund Raiser,* Vol. 23, No. 3 (January 1997), pp. 3–4.

Quigg, H. Gerald, "The Successful Capital Campaign from Planning to Victory," *CASE,* 1986, pp. 31–35.

Robinson, Andy, "Designing Fundable Projects: The Grantwriter as Feasibility Tester," *Community Jobs,* July/August 1996, p. 7.

Russo, Henry A, *Achieving Excellence in Fund Raising* (San Francisco: Jossey-Bass, 1991), pp. 82–85.

Schumacher, Edward C., "Capital Campaigns—Conducting a Successful Fund-Raising Drive," BoardSource (formerly National Center for Nonprofit Boards), 2001, pp. 4, 6–7.

Semple, Robert F. and Associates, "The Feasibility Study."

Simon, Marion A., EdD, "The Feasibility Study," *Fund Raising Institute Monthly Portfolio,* Vol. 34, No. 7 (July 1995).

Skelton, Don, "We Doubled Our Goal—and Arrived in the Era of Modern Fund Raising," *Advancing Philanthropy,* April/May 2000, pp. 28–30.

Smith, Becky, *How to Raise The Money You Need Now!* (Norman, Okla.: University of Oklahoma Press, 1991).

Straub, Scott C., "Feasibility Study," *Philanthropy in Texas,* Vol. 12, No. 10 (March 9, 2000).

Stratton, Jeff, "Stress the Campaign Feasibility Study with Your Board," *Board and Administrator,* Vol. 19, No. 5 (January 2003), p. 3.

Thompson, David M., "The Precampaign Survey: Testing the Market," *Fund Raising Management.*

Tromble, William W., *Excellence in Advancement* (Gaithersburg, Md.: Aspen Publishers, 1998), p. 124.

"Understanding Your Market," *FRI Monthly Portfolio,* Vol. 35, No. 11 (November 1996), p. 4.

"Using Part-Time Counsel, Setting Objectives and Timing," *National Fund Raiser,* Vol. 31, No. 11 (September 2005), pp. 2–4.

Walton, Christopher R., "Rethinking Feasibility Studies," *Fundraising Management,* September 1997, pp. 14–19.

Weisman, Carol E., *Secrets of Successful Fundraising* (St. Louis: F.E. Robbins & Sons Press, 2000).

"Why Conduct a Feasibility Study," *Successful Fundraising,* Vol. 4, No. 6 (June 1996), p. 5.

"Why You Absolutely, Positively Need a Feasibility Study before Launching a Capital Campaign," *National Fund Raiser,* Vol. 28, No. 9 (July 2002), pp. 1–2.

"Why You Need a Feasibility Study Before Launching a Capital Campaign," *National Fund Raiser,* Vol. 31, No. 6 (July 2005), p. 1.

Index